BEING A
CHARACTER

Christopher Bollas

BEING A CHARACTER

Psychoanalysis and Self Experience

 HILL AND WANG

A division of Farrar, Straus and Giroux

New York

Copyright © 1992 by Christopher Bollas
All rights reserved
Published simultaneously in Canada by HarperCollinsCanadaLtd
Printed in the United States of America
First edition, 1992
First Hill and Wang paperback edition, 1994
Library of Congress Cataloging-in-Publication Data
Bollas, Christopher.
Being a character : psychoanalysis and self experience /
Christopher Bollas. — 1st ed.
p.   cm.
Includes bibliographical references and index.
1. Self psychology.   2. Personality change.   3. Psychoanalysis.
I. Title.   92-6213 CIP
RC489.S43B65   1992   616.89'17—dc20

Excerpt from "Cut" from *The Collected Poems of Sylvia Plath*, edited by Ted Hughes. Copyright © 1963 by Ted Hughes. Reprinted by permission of HarperCollins Publishers

For Mark and Blair

Acknowledgments

Ken Bruder, Edward Corrigan, Berthe Ficarra, Pearl-Ellen Gordon, and Murray Schwartz kindly read an early draft of Part I of the book, and I am grateful to them for their comments. Two of the chapters in Part I were also given a very close read by members of the Santa Barbara Summer Workshop in Psychoanalysis and I am pleased to thank the members of this group and its organizer, Laurie Ryavec.

Linda Mason, who typed the many versions of the book, and who made important editorial suggestions, has been a great help. I am also grateful to Alison Wertheimer for some deft copyediting at exactly the right moment.

I would like to thank my publisher, Arthur Rosenthal, for his unqualified enthusiasm for this book from start to finish, and for his shrewd and intelligent suggestions along the way.

And Suzanne and Sacha: thank you.

Contents

Contents • x

BEING A
CHARACTER

Introduction

We are all familiar with that arresting moment when a particular scent seems to call us from some remote village in our childhood, almost as if we can reach through the past and touch the essence of a distant self experience. Sometimes we will hear a piece of music that was popular during a very special time of our life and this too seems to elicit within us not so much a memory as an inner psychic constellation laden with images, feelings, and bodily acuities. However much we may try to tell someone about what is happening to us—"Oh, that smell, it's a flower that was in my garden when I was a child!"—we shall fail to convey the texture of our inner experience.

But we can learn something about the nature of all self experience from such intense evocative moments. For without giving it much thought at all we consecrate the world with our own subjectivity, investing people, places, things, and events with a kind of idiomatic significance. As we inhabit this world of ours, we amble about in a field of pregnant objects that contribute to the dense psychic textures that constitute self experience. Very often we select and use objects in ways unconsciously intended to bring up such imprints; indeed, we do this many times each day, sort of thinking ourself out, by evoking constellations of inner experience. At the same time, however, the people, things, and events of our world simply happen to us, and when they do, we are called into differing forms of being by chance. Thus we oscillate between thinking ourself out through the selection of objects that promote inner experience and being thought out, so to speak, by the environment which plays upon the self.

In this respect, then, the objects of our world are potential forms of transformation. When we select any series of objects—such as listening to a particular record, then telephoning a particular person, then reading from a particular book—we transform our inner experience by eliciting new psychic textures that bring us into differing areas of potential being. By studying the structural effect of an object's impact on the self, which means thinking more about the different potential transformational effects of an object, we will be able to deepen our understanding of the nature of human life. Thus I have found it rather surprising that in "object relations theory" very little thought is really given to the distinct structure of the object which is usually seen as a container of the individual's projections. Certainly objects bear us. But ironically enough, it is precisely *because* they hold our projections that the structural feature of any one object becomes even more important, because we also put ourself into a container that upon re-experiencing will process us according to its natural integrity. For example, if I put a feeling of joy derived from early adolescent skills in baseball into a piece of music—such as Schubert's C Major Symphony—and if that same week I project an erotic response to my girlfriend into Salinger's *The Catcher in the Rye*, then encountering these objects in adult life may elicit the self experiences stored in the objects; but equally, the musical experience and the literary process are different types of object, each with its own "processional potential," by which I mean that employing the one or the other will involve me in a different form of subjective transformation, deriving from the integrity of the object's structure. It is my view that psychoanalysis, among other disciplines, can be enriched if we develop a philosophy of the object's integrity which enables us to consider what forms we choose for the psychic texture of the self.

Having looked carefully at how we are brought into particular psychic states by choosing special objects of effect, I turn my attention in the first part of the book to the psychoanalytical situation, because it is where two people, occupying this most interesting space, select narrative and mental objects to bring about inner states in one another. If a patient tells me about having lunch with her mother and describes the meal in graphic detail, I am brought into the experience of eating, and if then she tells me about taking a flying lesson, I am put into a different imagining. In this book I argue that most of what transpires in a psychoanalysis—as in life itself—is unconscious. The psychoanalyst, although expert in the deconstruction of particular symptoms, transference enactments, and mental processes, is nonetheless fundamentally excluded from the patient's inner experience. This should not be news to the clinician. It was, after all, one of Freud's major points about the unconscious that it could only be known by derivative, and if we extend his theory of unconscious processes to self experience, then its essence is only fractionally knowable by the subject's own consciousness, and thus less conveyable to the other. But as they work upon preconsciously designated tasks, the analyst and the patient engage in tens of thousands of unconscious communications that each will only partially understand as crucial to the patient's use of psychoanalysis. In time the two participants create psychoanalysis together, and quite profound changes occur in both people, although we have paid more attention to the mutative shifts in the analysand than to those in the analyst. That is, no doubt, as it should be. But I devote several chapters in this book to an examination of just how analyst and analysand unconsciously work together to develop new psychic structures which the patient can then use to radically alter his or her life.

The second part of the book contains individual, free-standing chapters that echo themes established in Part I and may be read in any order. Each essay is an effort to put a very particular kind of self experience into words, whether it is the cruising homosexual's odd experience in a place of promiscuity, the tragic madness of the female cutter, the demented ferocity of the Fascist state of mind, or every person's self experience as a member of his or her historical epoch, which I call generational consciousness. The reader will note that I periodically narrate my own life history and my own nature to investigate or to argue a particular topic. I believe this is because, at certain moments, I have needed to conjure my own self experience in order to write about a topic—to be informed from within, so to speak, rather than to think about the particular self state by discussing a patient. After all, Freud suggested this form for the writing of psychoanalysis in his *Interpretation of Dreams*, a work which includes his own dreams together with those of his patients in an evolutionary dialectic that supports the construction of his theories. I think this is a unique literary form for the writing of psychoanalysis, enabling the reader to participate in that unconscious movement that contributes to a psychoanalyst's clinical practice and informs his creation of psychoanalytic theory.

Of course, Freud knew that he left himself open to a particular kind of reading which would disclose his self deceptions, but the revelation of such blindness is a crucial feature of this literary form. Naturally I am well aware that my essays leave me in a similar position, but if we are to open up the writing of psychoanalysis to bring it closer to the nature of psychoanalytic practice—and to the to-and-fro of blindness and insight—then it is a literary risk well worth taking.

Part I

1

Aspects of Self Experiencing

"I have noticed myself," writes Freud, perhaps in a double entendre, "from my own dreams how much it is a matter of chance whether one discovers the source of particular elements of a dream." Recalling a recurrent dream—a "picture of a particular unusual-looking place" which had become a "positive nuisance" to him—he wrote: "In a specific spatial relation to myself, on my left-hand side, I saw a dark space out of which there glimmered a number of grotesque sandstone figures." A faint memory suggested that they marked the entrance to a beer cellar, yet it was not until 1907, after publishing his dream book and while revisiting Padua (last seen in 1895), that he *saw* his dream! He wrote:

My first visit to that lovely university town had been a disappointment, as I had not been able to see Giotto's frescoes in the Madonna dell'Arena. I had turned back half-way along the street leading there, on being told the chapel was closed on that particular day. On my second visit, twelve years later, I decided to make up for this and the first thing I did was to set off towards the Arena chapel. In the street leading to it, on my left-hand side as I walked along and in all probability at the point at which I had been turned back in 1895, I came upon the place I had seen so often in my dreams, with the sandstone figures that formed part of it. It was in fact the entrance to the garden of a restaurant. (15)

Inserting this passage in the 1909 edition of *The Interpretation of Dreams*, Freud did not interpret it, perhaps because the sandstone dream captured a dilemma he faced while writing the book. In 1895 he had only just begun to work on what would be his greatest fresco (*The Interpretation of Dreams*), but unlike Giotto's his work was not complete. In Padua he was turned back halfway along the street. Who announced the bad news? He does not tell us. Whoever forestalled the completion of his wish may have become a dark space containing a "number of grotesque sandstone figures" sig-nifying the place of nourishment. Does this dream, which must wait until the completion of *The Interpretation of Dreams* for its place, illustrate a problem for the man who is trying, but not yet succeeding, in making his Oedipal Complex conscious? The pestering space that contains the Oedipal drama may metaphorize Freud's self experience as it artic-ulates the unconscious—that dark space of the dream world that holds the mysteries of inner life.

Interestingly enough, Freud recovered his dream by chance. Had he not revisited the scene of the day residue he might never have understood this troublesome dream. As it is, he does not interpret it. But the "meaning" of the dream (and of many dreams, no doubt) still resides in the environment, among objects now differing from all others because they have been "in" a dream.

Freud's chance discovery of the furniture of a dream typifies a compelling feature of our life. As we constantly endow objects with psychic meaning, we therefore walk amidst our own significance, and, sometimes long after we have invested a thing, we encounter it again, releasing its meaning, although, as I shall maintain, such signifieds do not often reach consciousness. Freud's exclusion of this pestering dream is interesting, then, in another respect. He would not include in psychoanalytical theory this important part of everyday life: our travel in a rendered world of psychic signifiers that light up in the subject clusters of feeling, imagery, somatic states, and memories, and reawaken the sexual states that partly drove the initial investiture.

Just how do we endow things with our psychic states? For this is not a conscious intention but a profoundly unconscious instantiation of the self into the object world. By examining how we use actual objects to initially place and then later to evoke the self, I hope to set the stage for an understanding of how the human subject *becomes the dream work of his own life*, a theme I explore in greater depth in later chapters. Let us begin, then, with an aspect of the dream itself.

Falling to Sleep

Dream life mirrors an important feature of self experience, particularly that essential split between two subjective locations: the place of the initiating subject who reflects upon the self, and the position of that subject who is the reflected-upon, turned in a brief moment into the object of thought. In the dream I am simultaneously an actor inside a drama and an offstage absence directing the logic of events. At the heart of self experiencing is a type of unconscious reflexivity, achieved through the psychic division of labor characterized by the dreamer's two essential positions: as absent producer and as the dramatized personage employed to stage unconscious thinking.

Deeply inside a dream, I am so absorbed in this hallucination that my experiences there are usually unchallenged, even when bizarre. At times, however, perhaps because a sound in the night nearly awakens me or perhaps because the dream content violates my ego's dispensation of negative capability, I very slightly withdraw my fully subjective participation in the dream and glimpse myself as this drama's protagonist. When this occurs I bear witness to my self (that's me there!) inside the psyche's place operated by the logic of the ego.

Entering a dream is rather like slipping through a window. Some nights I drift off to sleep, sliding into the seas of imagery. I may recall an event of the day or imagine a situation but then I fall away from the day. Occasionally I may capture a passing image, hoping to transform it into a dream event and thereby steal a glance into the order of that intriguing world, but such images and hypnagogic phenomena only herald the darkness essential to sleep and the dream.

The dream is an intelligence of form that holds, moves, stimulates, and shapes us. When I enter the world of dreams I am deconstructed, as I am transformed from the one who holds the internal world in my mind to the one who is experientially inside the dramaturgy of the other. Gathered and processed by the dream space and dream events, I live in a place where I seem to have been held before: inside the magical and erotic embrace of a forming intelligence that bears me. To be in a dream is thus a continuous reminiscence of being inside the maternal world when one was partly a receptive figure within a comprehending environment. Indeed, the productive intentionality that determines the dream we are in and that never reveals itself (i.e., "where is the dreamer that dreams the dream?") uncannily re-creates, in my view, the infant's relation to the mother's unconscious, which although it does not "show itself," nonetheless produces the process of maternal care. In this respect the dream seems to be a structural memory of the infant's unconscious, an object relation of person inside the other's unconscious processing, revived in the continuous representation of the infantile moment every night.

Winnicott believed that each of us begins life unintegrated, scattered islands of organized potentials coming into being. Perhaps we return to unintegration when we dream, loosening this self into an archipelago of many beings, acting various roles scripted by the ego in the theater of the night. Waking, we rise from these regressed states, both from the fetal place to the ambulatory posture and from the plenitude of selves to the discerning "I" who reflects on his odd subjects.

Freud tells us that the course of dream experience—the people, places, and events represented—renders the sleeper's unconscious wishes and memories in dramatic form, yet the self inside the dream, unbeknownst to himself (as the simple self), is alive in a theater of his represented parts. But his ignorance allows for the very intriguing rendezvous that takes place as the simple self literally inhabits his unconscious. So loss of consciousness and the presence of a simple self, unaware of where he is, is essential to the realization of self experience within the dream space.

The simple experiencing self and the complex reflecting self enable the person to process life according to different yet interdependent modes of engagement: one immersive, the other reflective. When I am "in" the dream, although as a simple self I perceive dream objects, even more importantly I endure deep experiences there. Recollection and interpretation of the dream's meaning do not necessarily address the essence of self experience gained by the simple self's movement through the events of the dream, but the complex self possesses a different psychic agenda: the aim of this position is to objectify as best as possible where one has been or what is meant by one's actions.

It is not only in the dream that one can find this oscillation; there are other fallings into simple self experiencing.

Falling in Love

Imagine I am single and in search of a partner. One day at a party (the intermediate space for instinct and object?) I see X across the room. Stunned by her beauty, eros claiming consciousness, I fall in love. No longer objective, I plunge into a powerful state of affairs, devolved into that lessened awareness necessary to deep play in the ambient fields of love.

Sadly enough, two people cannot sustain such free-falling into blissful simplicity, and couples gradually find their own natural balance between complex mental states and fallings into one another. In some respects, lovemaking is the encapsulated place of mental simplification as lovers submit to the deconstruction of erotics: the body of the other ceases simply to be an object of perception or internal representation and becomes the means of transformation—from the subject who seeks the erotic object to the subject who becomes an object "inside" the place of desire. It is a moment when the complex self (who reflectively objectifies the parts of himself within his mind) gives way to the simple self, caught up in the instincts of erotic knowledge.

Lost in Conversation

A party. Moving about the room, I meet several people and we talk about different topics. Aware of not finding the points of discourse very interesting, I do not enter into conversation: "rising mortgages," "A-level exams," "Margaret Thatcher," are not windows to the transformation of my experience into a participant subject. But then Y tells me that he is writing a book on gypsies (about whom I know little), sponsoring questions, associations, ideas, and immediately I am into conversation. I forget myself.

Certain objects, like psychic "keys," open doors to unconsciously intense—and rich—experience in which we articulate the self that we are through the elaborating character of our response. This selection constitutes the *jouissance* of the true self, a bliss released through the finding of specific objects that free idiom to its articulation. As I see it, such releasings are the erotics of being: these objects both serve the instinctual need for representation and provide the subject with the pleasures of the object's actuality.

Life is a cycle of reciprocal transformations from complex to simple self, from intrapsychic dialogues and thoughtfulness (complex states) to a seeming suspension of such internal density as we yield to an occasion in which we become a particle participant. I read a book with difficulty but finally I get into it and am lost inside its "texture." I try unsuccessfully to write a paper, but one day I sit down and instantly I am into it and lost in my own thoughts.

Those objects and experiences, keys to the releasing of our idiom, free us to experience the depth of our being and to re-experience the private logic of that culture created out of the interplay between the movement of our idiom, driven by the force of our instincts, and the unconscious system of care provided by our mother and father. We are forever finding objects that disperse the objectifying self into elaborating subjectivities, where the many "parts of the self" momentarily express discrete sexual urges, ideas, memories, and feelings in unconscious actions, before condensing into a transcendental dialectic, occasioned by a force of dissemination that moves us to places beyond thinking.

The Third Area

When Freud returned to Padua and glanced at the sandstone figures in front of the restaurant, he saw a thing which had special meaning for him, as he had unconsciously put it into a recurrent dream. Initially an object of perception, it became a mysterious figure in his dream world, and then it differed from everything else on that Paduan street because it was an objective correlative of a prior experience.

We each live amidst thousands of such objects that enlighten our world—things that are not hallucinations (they do exist), but whose essence is not intrinsic to what Lacan calls the real. Their meaning resides in what Winnicott termed "intermediate space" or "the third area": the place where subject meets thing, to confer significance in the very moment that being is transformed by the object. The objects of intermediate space are compromise formations between the subject's state of mind and the thing's character.

In the Australian wilderness the aborigine's "walkabout" is called "the dreaming." Before the gods dreamed the world it was a featureless plane, but now the landscape is a materialized metaphysic, and each tree, or rock, or hill is part of the dreamed. Wandering amidst this world, the aborigine encounters geophysical objects through which he thinks himself, as he is inspired by them to imagine his theology, culture, people, and of course himself. As Cowan claims, it is an "imaginal perception" (31).

Is this investiture of the world the work of what in "The Prelude" Wordsworth called "the first Poetic spirit of our human life" (69) when the child's imagination "did make the surface of the universal earth / With meanings of delight, of hope and fear, / Work like a sea"? Ambling through the hills and dales of the Lake District, or recollecting them in tranquillity, didn't Wordsworth conjure dense textures of self experience that brought some known, but only marginally thinkable, recollection into being? It is exceptionally difficult to capture the sense of place each of us feels within our world. As Seamus Heaney wanders across his Ireland, legend and nature blend into a particular sort of "midworld."[1] "All of these places now live in the imagination, all of them stir us to responses other than the merely visual," he says, adding that "our imaginations assent to the stimulus of names, our sense of the place is enhanced, our sense of ourselves as inhabitants not just of a geographical country but of a country of the mind is cemented." He concludes that "it is this marriage that constitutes the sense of place in the richest possible manifestation" (132).

We all walk about in a metaphysical concrescence of our private idioms, our culture, society, and language, and our era in history. Moving through our object world, whether by choice, obligation, or invitational surprise, evokes self states sponsored by the specific objects we encounter. In a very particular sense, we live our life in our own private dreaming.

Mnemic Objects

I have written of conservative objects as preserved self states that prevailed in a child's life when he could not comprehend a nonetheless self-defining experience within the family atmosphere (1987, 99). Stored unaltered because it is not understood enough to be symbolically elaborated or re-pressed, this experience of self is sustained as a recurring mood available for understanding in the future.

A child may associate a conserved self state with certain actual objects that were part of his early experiences. When I was about two years old, my father returned from the Second World War; soon thereafter my brother was born, and I attended nursery school a few hours a day for some six months while my mother nursed my brother. Very much in love before the war, my parents found themselves bewil-

1. "Midworld" is a term used by the philosopher John William Miller in his interesting book *The Midworld of Symbols and Functioning Objects*.

deringly distanced after their reuniting and a mood of sad vexation pervaded the house for some time. As part of this scene I am sure that I knew something, but I did not have the means of thinking what I knew. I term such knowledge the unthought known (1987, 277). However, at my school I think I nominated an object—a swing—to conserve some aspects of this self state. I don't know why exactly, but I imagine that this thing which had been so much fun (it is an object for a joyful two-person relation), now empty and unoccupied, signified the absence of such pleasure. Perhaps I located my slight depression in the object. I know that to this day if I see a certain type of child's swing in a playground something of the self experience prevailing at that time is revived.

These "subjective objects," to use and yet extend Winnicott's term, are a vital part of our investment in the world. Through this particular type of projective identification we psychically signify objects, but as they retain their own intrinsic value they can be said to occupy an intermediate area between the conventional use or understanding and our private one. Indeed, their appearance in our thoughts often crops up by chance, not evoked by our omniscience but entirely a matter of circumstance. The red trolley, a part of Southern California life until the late 1940s, is a subjective object for me, and when it appeared in a recent film it brought with it parts of myself. For the first four years of my life I lived in a small town in the foothills of the Sierra Nevada mountains at the end of the red trolley line that went to Los Angeles. Suddenly this streetcar appeared on the screen, evoking in me a precise self experience—specific to this trolley thing—characterized by my child self's experience, and linked to my grandfather, who enjoyed traveling on it with me, as it clicked its way through the orange groves and down the main streets of small-town America. I had not expected to see this object; it appeared by chance. When this happens to us it is as if we are inside a dream: things play us, our state of mind the outcome of events.

Is it possible that dream experience *represents this feature* of wakeful life, that as we nominate objects with our psychic states we therefore walk about in a world that elicits us through the presence of such things, an act then echoed by the dream that puts us through an experience of objects that prove exceptionally evocative?

In a sense, we are intermediates, engaged in an interplay between our idiom and its subjective objects. Some self experience arises out of the thing's play on the subject as much as from the subject's use of the object, because as we move through space and time many things pop up by chance (as aleatory objects) and sponsor a unit of experience in us that has, as it were, been contained within the real.

The Lexicon of Objects

Objects can be said to have a lexical function when we employ them to "speak" our idiom through the "syntax of self experience." The mnemic object is a particular form of subjective object that contains a projectively identified self experience, and when we use it, something of that self state stored in it will arise. As we shall see in the next chapter, however, objects process us in differing ways, and we often employ them to conjure a discrete experience in order to give expression to and gain particular notions of our idiom. The object world is, therefore, an extraordinary lexicon for the individual who speaks the self's aesthetic through his precise choices and particular uses of its constituents. If, for example, I choose to listen to a record rather than to read a book, I select a thing that will elicit inner experiencings specific to the selection of a musical object, whereas if I had selected a book I would have fancied a thing that would have sponsored another type of internal experience. Each thing in the lexicon of objects has a potentially different evocative effect by virtue of its specific form which partly structures the subject's inner experience and constitutes the eros of form in being.

We can think about this further if we consider what it is like for us to live in a day.

The Day Space

We frequently indicate how projective identification usually results in the unfortunate loss of those parts of the self projected into an object, but the intriguing mental processes involved in subjectification of an object world invite us to emphasize its positive aspects. Freud's theory of the dream's day residue, however, strongly suggests that during the day we nominate persons, objects, and events as psychically significant, so they will be residual to the day, already forming part of the potential dream furniture. In my view, to create a day's residue, the person projects a part of himself into the object, thus psychically signifying it. This gives the object meaning, converting it into a tool for possible thought: the thinking that is special to the dream state.[2] To do this, however, the subject must "lose himself" in moments of experience when he projects meaning into objects, a type of erotic action that must be unconscious and one in which the person is not being, as it were, thoughtful.[3] Indeed, he must be a rather simplified consciousness, even out of touch with himself for a moment, in order to invest the object world with psychic potential. Viewed this way, this type of projective identification is ultimately self enhancing, transforming ma-

2. In Bion's theory this is equivalent to converting a Beta element into an Alpha element. See "Learning from Experience," in *Seven Servants* (1–111).

3. Ehrenzweig writes of an unconscious "scattering" of the self. See his extraordinary book *The Hidden Order of Art*.

terial things into psychic objects, and thus furnishing an unconscious matrix for dreams, fantasies, and deeper reflective knowings.[4] The person who cannot do this will have less psychic vocabulary, fewer props for the dreaming of lived experience, and so a diminished internal world when he returns to being the complex self.

In the dream we dwell within a world apparently ordered by an intelligence quite beyond our knowledge. What then of our day? Are we inside anything at all during our day? Perhaps we are. Doesn't the theory of subjective objects suggest that we live in fields of intermediate experience, psychically furnished by objects that contain projected contents and have an independent existence? Although our waking life obviously differs from dream life, our movements within it constitute a form of "day dreaming." Is there a day space much as there is a dream space? Does it not possess its own intrinsic temporal structure (morning, afternoon, night) while containing objects that signify us and objects that will in turn be signified? Do we not choose what to do with our day? How to be in it? To use it? To have it affect us? Afterwards, is it not an object of reflection?

Sometimes we plan our day: "Tomorrow I will see my morning patients, then take a light lunch so as to work on my paper." Tomorrow, defined by my agenda, narrows the day's psychic potential to facilitate my requirements for work. If I take no phone calls, skip the newspaper, don't listen to music and don't go for a walk, etc., I am likely to have a good working day. Let's say, however, that I do not have such a precise and rigorous agenda. I read the paper, my eye catching the story of California gray whales caught in the Arctic. I wander off, the whale taking me with it to memories of my childhood along the California coast. A phone call from a friend, a letter from a colleague, a passage

4. Meltzer explores some of these issues in his own original way. For his work on dreams, see *Dream-Life*, and his theory of aesthetics may be found in *The Apprehension of Beauty*. See also Milner (1987), Stokes (1973), and André Green (1986).

from a book, evoke psychic textures, and my day, always something of a container, gradually assumes a psychic density that gives it its particular character.

A day is a space for the potential articulation of my idiom. Do I select objects that disseminate my idiom or not? For example, do I pick up a novel which I don't like but think I should read—but through which I shall not come into my being—or do I select a novel which I like, into which I can fall, losing myself to multiple experiences of self and other?[5] Do I have a sense of this difference of choice? What if I don't? What if I do not intuitively know which object serves me? If I don't know, then my day is likely to be a fraught or empty occasion. Neurotic conflict eradicates, at least for a time, potential objects. For years I refused to visit the National Portrait Gallery (always full of one excuse or another), but gradually I became aware of an Oedipally rebellious portion of myself, reluctant to pay homage to these distinguished fathers. When I resolved this conflict I was then able to go and use this object. Or I may choose an object because it is meant to resolve a state of anxiety or to recontact a split-off part of myself housed there. In other words, pathology of mind biases the subject toward the selection of objects that are congruent with unconscious illness.

Some people seem to have no sense of the day being a potential space. For the melancholic it is an unpunctuated temporality, one day no different from the next. The overly anxious person, perhaps feeling safe while in bed, views the day with trepidation: a hurdle to be leapt over before the next bedtime.

Most people have favorite times of day. I am particularly fond of the mornings. Midafternoon I am often a bit sleepy,

---

5. We may resist a novel, however, which nonetheless compels us into a dialectical conflict that elaborates the subject's idiom. So it is not a question of picking an object which one likes, but of choosing an object to which one is not indifferent, so that one is "called," so to say, into an elaborating engagement with the object.

but by early evening I recover. Each time of day may be a distinct potential space which a person employs differently. For example, if I am free to do so, I like to listen to music in the late afternoon. I think this is because in these hours I am liable to a sort of day-defining mood. If I have learned something (usually from a patient), or worked well, I am in good spirits; if not, I am inclined to be at a potential point of irritation or despair. But if I catch a few minutes of music I am usually transformed and sometimes the choice of object (what to play) is crucial. Late afternoon is sometimes problematic for me: a time of day when I may hover between contentment and discontent. I know that if I select a musical object on such occasions it is likely to transform my mood (if I so wish), but if I am depressed, I cannot usually achieve this transformation by listening to, say, Prokofiev, although Bach's sonatas for violin and piano rarely fail to lift me into another frame of mind. This choice of object (and its precise use) is the erotic of my idiom, which articulates itself in the form of self experiencing within the potential space of the day. I do not usually want to go for a walk at this time of day, as I like to walk at midday. I do not like telephone conversations in the morning, but I enjoy chatting on the phone in midafternoon.

Each provision of an object is a transformational act: for better or worse. Our successes and failures in this respect have a direct bearing on our ability to set up objects that evoke particular self states and those that do not.

Whether my choice of object is auditory for late afternoons, or gustatory for mealtimes, or conversational for evenings, I constantly engage objects crucial to my own self experiencing. Such management is part of a complex relation each of us has to ourself, and in some ways, through self care, we inherit the tasks of our mothers and fathers. The quality of any person's self experiencing will reflect the individual's skill in meeting idiom needs by securing evocatively nourishing objects.

The Day's Dream

I have frequently found that when an analysand has reported the events of the previous day, the narrative content is strikingly similar to the structure of a dream. Indeed, when I am immersed in associating to the analysand's account, and I ask for clarifications or make a comment, I will sometimes commit a parapraxis by referring to the narrative as a dream. I now think my unconscious interpretation of the psychic status of such a report is close to a certain truth—a person's account of the events of the prior day may be dreamlike.

Because a day is a potential space which we characterize by choosing certain objects and releasing varied self states, it is not necessarily an act of unconscious willfulness, as much of the time we are responding to the arrival of events sponsored by other subjects or the aleatory movements of objects. Nonetheless, each of our days begins to achieve its symbolic status as the dialectic between our unconscious wishes, needs, defenses, anxieties, and elaboratory self states engages with chance as the environment telephones us, writes to us, weathers us, offers us new books, displays wonderful-looking people, and so on.

Perhaps we may refer to the psychic contents of a day's narrative as the day's dream. A patient who breeds dogs told me of a young bitch whom she had been keeping in the house. The stud could be ordered any day in the owner's view, but the bitch was too nervous to mate. She also thought that her favorite cat would be disturbed if the young bitch mated at this point. She concluded that it was best to wait until the bitch was ready. As my patient narrated the events of the previous day, I thought about how she wished to have sexual relations with men but did not yet feel ready. I also thought about how she could not do so until the male and female (dog and cat) parts of her self were securely in place, as, in the past, intercourse had unconsciously meant the eradication of the male parts of the self, leaving her feeling a "useless woman." Unknowingly, I was responding to this narrative as if it were a dream, and from this event and others like it I think we can say that sometimes an individual lives a day in a particularly meaningful way, and that the lived experiences form a psychic tapestry that is dreamlike, to the extent that we may call it the day's dream.

The Ironic Position

The concept of self experiencing is ironic, as its referential ambiguity (does it mean the self that experiences or the experiencing of our self?) is strangely true to the complexity of being human. All self experiencing involves this split, which can be described as a division between ourself as simple selves (when we are immersed in desired or evoked experience) and ourself as complex selves (when we think about experience). Naturally such distinctive states may overlie one another, so that I may be reflecting upon an experience in the immediate past while another part of me is already deep within a disseminating experience.

I have discussed self experiencing in terms of the subject's use of an object, serving either as a mnemic object that contains a precise self experience or as a structural object to create a particular self experience by virtue of its intrinsic character. But no one can completely determine the arrival of objects in one's field, so we only provide subjective objects for self experience to a limited extent: many phenomena arrive by chance or are presented to us by others.

Interestingly enough, this duality of object arrival—by desire or by chance—mirrors the ambiguity of being that constitutes the human, who experiences himself both as the arranger of his life and as the arranged. The double experiencing of objects as vehicles of wish and spontaneous eliciters of inner experience echoes the nature of self experiencing when we are the initiators of our existence as well as the initiated.

I may appear to focus on the individual's selection of actual objects, neglecting the endogenously determined (imagined) objects and emphasizing self experiencing constituted out of the choice and use of things. But the distinction between a material object and a mental one (such as an idea, a thought about a friend, consideration of a piece of literature) need not compel us to oversimplify: obviously each person conjures internal mental objects through which he processes (i.e., articulates or elaborates) his idiom.

Choice of object is thus specific to a potential articulation of a self experience; naturally, when we select the other, the human object, as the medium for the releasing of our desire, we automatically choose the precise type of dialectical field in which mutual use is inevitable, and the play of subjectivities is given its character. Imagine that I am free during a weekend to drop in on a friend or a colleague. Whom do I choose? An important feature of such a choice depends on the idiomatic character of self experience that will be solicited by that particular person and what we create together to form our play. Such a choice of object is, of course, far more complex and evocative than the selection of a nonhuman object for releasing our idiom to its elaboration: to be with the other is to be played by them (through the other's projective identifications) as much as it is to evoke parts of themselves by virtue of the actions of our own character. It is a remarkable part of our life that this interplay takes place at such a deep level of both unconscious ego-to-ego negotiation and dynamically unconscious plays of mental content that the subject is indeed very much a simple self, inside this field, this intermediate space, where two very complex creatures are at play: idiom-to-idiom. In the best of times it is a wonderful difference, and it is knowledge of this difference in our separate subjectivities that makes our private selection of a human other as an object for self experiencing particularly significant.

The Liftings of Self

In these postmodernist days, much is written about the self as an illusion, as writers challenge its phenomenological integrity. What is it? And how, if at all, does it differ from the "I"? These are important questions, though I do not propose to examine them here. But viewed from a certain perspective, this is less of a problem than one might think. When we live according to our desire, we *naturally* choose objects in the ordinary process of selection. Some objects (a book, a friend, a concert, a walk) release us into intense inner experiencings which somehow emphasize us. I think of this as a form of *lifting*, as encounters with objects lift us into some utterance of self available for deep knowing. We shall have sensed in each such unit of experience an idiom of the self we are by virtue of the character of the evoked. As each encounter solicits us, lifts us up from our unconscious nuclearity, it shows an aspect of our self to the I and thus reveals some feature of our sensibility. Although such episodes illuminate something about us, what we know from these moments is only ever partly thinkable: the experience is more a dense condensation of instinctual urges, somatic states, body positions, proprioceptive organizings, images, part sentences, abstract thoughts, sensed memories, recollections, and felt affinities, all of a piece. It is impossible to put this complexity into words, but there is an other who is partly there and that other is the I. I have hundreds, thousands, by my death millions, of sequential self states arising from the dialectical meetings between my self and the object world, which release me to some conscious knowing of my life. Like my postmodernist cousins, however, I do not think of the self as phenomenologically unified. It cannot be, because, in the first place, the true self is not an integrated phenomenon but only dynamic sets of idiomatic dispositions that come into being through problematic encounters with the object world. But these experiencings and the I's relation to them obviously yield senses of familiarity which allow us an illusion that the self is a unity. This sense derives, in my view, from the continuous, reliable, and unconscious rapport between the I and the self's experiencings, or between the complex self position and the multitudinous simple self states. In fact, however, although these senses do not add up to a sum of the many parts, they may yield a kind of "spirit" of place, unique to the strange aesthetic of an idiom, leaving psychoanalysis in the challenging position, it seems to me, of honoring such a human spirit with a place in its theory.

The Stages of Self Experiencing

I have argued that the object world is, in many respects, a lexicon for self experience, to the extent that the selection of objects is often a type of self utterance. This idiom of self expression is a potential means not only of representing unconscious phantasies but of conjuring dense psychic textures that constitute a form of thinking by experiencing.

I have also said that we are not free to only use objects in this manner; sometimes they use us. Much of life is chance. And certainly the aleatory object has its own integrity and capacity to play upon us. Even when we determine to conjure a self experience through the lexical object, unanticipated chance phenomena contribute to the texture of being.

Let us now consider the steps common to object-derived self experiencings, whether the person is elaborating idiom through that desire that chooses the lexical object, or whether he is rendered into experience by a signifying object's aleatory jest. From the preceding discussion four stages can be identified in what we might consider the dialectics of self experiencing.

1. *I use the object.* When I pick up a book, go to a concert, telephone a friend, I select the object of my choice.
2. *I am played by the object.* At the moment of my use, the particularity specific to the object—its integrity— transforms me, whether it is Bruckner's Eighth Symphony moving me, a novel evoking associations, or a friend persuading me.
3. *I am lost in self experiencing.* The distinction between the subject who uses the object to fulfill his desire and the subject who is played upon by the action of the object is no longer possible. The subject is inside the third area of self-experiencing. His prior self state and the object's simple integrity are both "destroyed" in the experiential synthesis of mutual effect.
4. *I observe the self as an object.* Emerging from self experiencing proper, the subject considers where he has been. This is the place of the complex self.

Variations in the Capacity to Experience the Self

Self experiencing cannot be assumed. Some individuals are reluctant to live in the third area (the intermediate area of experience), insisting that the invitational feature of the object be declined. They impose their view on the object world and blunt the evocative—transformational—facet of objects in the field. They may narrow the choice of objects, eliminating those with a high evocative potential. If I read property advertisements to pass the time of day, I am less likely to be moved by this object than if I read novels or newspapers. Persons rich in self experiencing, who take pleasure in the dialectics of the human paradox, seek objects with evocative integrity that challenge and stretch the self.

We can learn much about any person's self experiencing by observing his selection of objects, not only because object choice is lexical and therefore features in the speech of character syntax, but also because it may suggest a variation in the intensity of psychic experience that each person chooses. If we live an active life, then we will create a subjectified material world of psychic significance that both contains evocative units of prior work and offers us new objects that bring our idiom into being by playing us into our reality.

2

The Evocative Object

Living our life inevitably involves us in the use of objects that vary in their individual capacities to evoke self experience. In the previous chapter I stressed how some objects are endowed with our states of self during the course of our life, mnemic objects that sometimes elicit prior states of being. They possess, in addition, a use-structure, as the employment of any particular thing brings about an inner profile of psychic experience specific to its character. Objects are also conceptually evocative as they bring to mind latent concepts.[1] If I play with my son Sacha, I am engaged with

---

1. The examination of how objects serve as conceptual signifiers is a vast and difficult area. Lacan's work is in this area, particularly in his theory of the symbolic. But if we wish to think of how an object—a bank, for example—sponsors a complex conceptual matrix, we would have to give priority to the signified, which Lacan refuses to do. Lacan, however, is interested in an entirely different order of unconsciousness from the one I am studying here; it has to do with the subject's use of an object to employ the concept latent to the thing. For the time being at least, psychoanalysts are likely to find certain philosophers of cognitive science more useful in exploring this area of unconscious thinking—particularly the work of George Lakoff, such as *Women, Fire, and Dangerous Things*. Although my use of the word "concept" and Lakoff's exploration of "categories" of the mind are by no means identical, I think psychoanalysts would benefit from his analysis of the function of mental categories in what for us would be unconscious thought.

an other—my child—who evokes a set of psychical notions sponsored by the concept "child." If I visit the National Portrait Gallery, this involves me with a different object, which for discussion's sake I refer to as a set of notions, feelings, internal relations, and use-potentials evoked by the concept "museum."

Yielding a latent concept, objects suggest psychologically distinct types of self experience, so that when a person employs an object it is of interest to note what is conceptually solicited. Mountain climbing, chamber music playing, snorkeling, and partygoing are different experiences involving different objects and therefore different concepts of one's being that ideationalize psychologically different forms for being, use, and relating. So as we think of engaging with each of these objects, a different psychic notion of what we shall be doing comes to mind, which operates on conscious, preconscious, and unconscious levels.

Objects can stimulate us in at least six ways:

1. sensationally
2. structurally
3. conceptually
4. symbolically
5. mnemically
6. projectively

They possess a sensational print that will be apprehended by the forms of sensational knowing which we employ: taste, touch, sight, sound, smell. The sensational base of an object testifies to its materiality and to the body ego's relation to it as a sensational phenomenon.

The structural integrity of an object is partly derived from

Additionally, Greimas, in *On Meaning*, provides a semiotic model of conceptual representation which is most intriguing, and Walter Ong in *Interfaces of the Word* discusses the differing types of imaginative thought.

its atomic specificity and a specific use-potential so that when it is employed it affects us in a manner true to its character. A bicycle is structurally different from a basketball, and using each promotes a unique inner experience.

Objects may also be selectively endowed with prior self experiences and some partly signify episodes in our past, becoming mnemic objects.

Other objects, however, serve as containers of the dynamically projective, helping us think the different parts of our self and others by using them (i.e., reading a book on Thatcher to process a harsh part of our personality). Mnemic objects form through a kind of associative projection, as a self state is stored in an object present at the time and part of the person's experience, such as the sandstone figures on the Paduan street. But projective objects are ephemeral and serve to think the self (and its internal objects) by the projection of parts of the self in the here and now of everyday life.

Finally, as Lacan stresses, objects have names and are part of a symbolic order, so at any one time when we use the object, it joins and evokes other signifiers.

A swing can be apprehended sensationally, using one's bottom (to sit on it), one's hands (to hold the chain), and one's feet (to push off the ground and to move back and forth). As a sensational object it also involves a proprioceptive "grasping" of it, as inner coordinates are a part of its use. An experience-structure, it promotes an inner self episode specific to the process of "swinging." A mnemic object for me, it can signify the absence of a two-person relation and the presence of aloneness. As a concept it promotes the ideas of movement (up and down), of play, of childhood, of pleasure, and so forth. As a word in the symbolic order it links to other signifiers (swing: the music of that era, and "swing" of mood), and inevitably to any other words that emerge in association to it.

As lexical elements in the syntax of potential self experience, we may use each object to conjure a specific state of self by employing it predominantly for its evocative capability in any of the above orders. Inevitably the decision as to an object's use rests with the unconscious aims of a person, so if I take my son to a park where he can swing, I may do so because the word has occurred to me by association, or because I am in the mood for highs and lows, or because I saw a swing and its function (to be the object of a child's play) appealed to me. However, once I use the object—either watching my son or sitting on the swing myself—it will then evoke its print in me according to all six evocative orders acting in a play of inner states.[2]

Objects, like words, are there for us to express ourself. We have before us an infinite number of things, which we may use in our own unique way to meet and to express the self that we are. Object selection is expression. If on a Saturday morning I wish to play football with my son rather than visit the Science Museum with him, it is because that instinct I believe we have to elaborate ourself chooses the objects "son" and "football" rather than the objects "son" and "Science Museum." Such a choice not only articulates the self (as its expression); it also encounters the self with its own integrity and forces the self to further psychic elaboration.

For example, to play football with my son is to engage with a child other in a physical activity that sponsors a complex play of evocative orders. The sensations of football

2. Perhaps the first systematic effort to rethink Freud's theory of the unconscious, aiming to separate out the different forms of unconsciousness (many of which Freud lumped into the concept of the "primary process") has been undertaken by Ignacio Matte-Blanco in *The Unconscious as Infinite Sets* and more recently in the more readable *Thinking, Feeling, and Being*. I believe there are more systems of unconscious thinking than does Matte-Blanco (for example, musical thought and visual thinking follow entirely different unconscious logics), but Matte-Blanco's work is of truly profound significance. In addition, Didier Anzieu's investigation of different "psychic envelopes" also suggests, from my point of view, a reconsideration of the differentiated complexity of unconsciousness, and his works are of considerable value: see *The Skin Ego* and *Psychic Envelopes*.

are different from the sensations of visiting a museum: one is to be played with aggressively and actively; the other is to be the place of reflective viewing. Child and football evoke different concepts (of competition and physical skill) than the Science Museum (learning about technology). The words "football" and "science" elicit associative chains of signifiers moving in very different hermeneutic spaces. Subjectively, "football" sponsors memories and assumptions in me that are very different from those parts of me lodged in the objects "science" and "museum." These different evocative orders conjure up different "me's."

Objects, as I have said in the previous chapter, often arrive by chance, and these aleatory objects evoke psychic textures which do not reflect the valorizations of desire. We have not, as it were, selected the aleatory object to express an idiom of self. Instead, we are played upon by the inspiring arrival of the unselected, which often yields a very special type of pleasure—that of surprise. It opens us up, liberating an area like a key fitting a lock. In such moments we can say that objects use us, in respect of that inevitable two-way interplay between self and object world and between desire and surprise.

If we were to study further the intermediate (or third) area, I think we should find that one important characteristic of the third area is that the individual uses things while knowing that the aleatory vector is so prominent that he will also be played upon by the object. If I go to a concert to hear a favorite symphony, led by an inventive conductor, then I shall use the symphonic object as a known structure to fall into, for processing of my idiom. Frequently, though, my particular unconscious use of the auditory object will be surprisingly displaced by the conductor's imaginative re-shaping of the object—an occasion that, unanticipated, throws me into previously unfelt areas in the prior processing of self through that particular symphonic object.

We know where to find, as it were, third areas which

maximize the interplays of life. A concert, a park, a beach, a sporting event, a party with friends, will serve our need to conjure ourself through the use of objects to be found there, just as they will delight us with the unexpected.

Forms of Self Experience

As the use of an object conjures self experience, objects "play" upon the many different somatic senses and mental faculties that constitute psychic structure. To simplify this complex issue, let us add that objects play upon different forms of self experiencing, if we are clear by this that a form of self experience is a psychosomatically distinct means of processing self states, each form fundamentally different from other forms, each constituting a capacity for the person's experiencing of his idiom evoked by the object.

Thus far I have looked at how an object is part of a psychosomatic lexicon, so that it can be used sensationally, structurally, conceptually, symbolically, mnemically, and projectively to provide a syntax for self experience. Now I shall examine the process from a different perspective. As objects have this lexical potential, are there not different forms of inner experience for differentiated use of this evocative lexicon? Some of the categories of such experience are already suggested by the nature of each evocative process, as the sensational effect depends initially, for example, on the senses.

I do not intend to examine the distinct forms for self experience in detail, but some discussion is necessary to make my point clear. For as we process our units of experience in different ways, we may represent an episode visually, linguistically, somatically, sonically, gesturally, or interpersonally. Each of these basic forms for self experience obeys its own peculiar laws of unconscious representation.

Each form gives rise to many types of communication

homologous with it: visualizing lends itself to painting, wording to writing, gesture to dance, and so forth.

We might say that specific modes of representation (e.g., writing, speaking, dancing, painting) are the expression of form potentials. Painting is only a potential forming of experience. So too are dancing, writing, and musical composition. Each form potential is neurologically, cognitively, and psychically distinct, with a profile composed of its many unique features. To paint, dance, poeticize, or compose an experience is to select a mode of representation with its own unique aesthetic. Which mode one chooses not only results in a different type of representation; it also suggests an entirely different experience in self expression.

Artists are gifted only in their exceptional use of otherwise ordinary human capacities, usually because they know more about the intelligence of form.[3] Note how Barbara Hepworth, the English sculptor, credits her forming ability to her sense of the landscape which characterized her childhood.

> All my early memories are of forms and shapes and textures. Moving through and over the West Riding landscape with my father in his car, the hills were sculptures; the roads defined the form. Above all, there was the sensation of moving physically over the contours of fulnesses and concavities, through hollows and over peaks—feeling, touching, seeing, through mind and hand and eye. The sensation has never left me. I, the sculptor, am the landscape. (1)

Hepworth links the sculptor's representational medium with her physical movements over the contours of her childhood landscape. The roads apparently defined the form. The traveling car provided her with a sensation of

3. In *Frames of Mind*, Howard Gardner argues that there are multiple intelligences; he examines in convincing detail the separate intelligences that go into linguistic, musical, logical-mathematical, spatial, bodily kinesthetic, and personal intelligence. In my view it is only a short step from this argument to the notion that there are distinct types of unconscious thinking.

moving over and through the land contours, and that sensation (a combination of several senses) became a psychic structure that now generates its own form. As Hepworth runs her hands over a piece of stone, giving it contour with her chisel and mallet, and opening up apertures for the play of light, she reshapes the object world so that external reality now bears the mark of psychic structure, the object a token of the work of two realities.

Alexander Calder believes his sense of form derives from another object: "I think that . . . the underlying sense of form in my work has been the system of the universe, or part thereof . . . The idea of detached bodies floating in space, of different sizes and densities, perhaps of different colors and temperatures, and surrounded and interlarded with wisps of gaseous condition, and some at rest, while others move in peculiar manners, seem to me the ideal source of form" (561). This is not to say that Calder's works represent the universe—or that Hepworth's sculptures represent West Riding or Cornwall. But both artists do say that certain features of the object world have had profoundly evocative effects and have in a way constituted transformative self experiencings, such that by the time of artistic maturity (or capability) they are presenting the subjective effect of this evocative object.

Remarks such as those by Hepworth and Calder are often taken to mean that art imitates the natural world. But clearly Hepworth and Calder find metaphors of their own body and sensibility "in" the natural world, landscapes that are always partly dreamscapes, that objectify their personal idiom and in turn serve as a continuous point of reference with an evocative potential to it. In other words, Hepworth's idiom finds a metaphor of its form intelligence in the landscape, while for Calder the universe objectifies his own forming intelligence.

Choosing a form is like taking a journey. Do I travel

through experience in the form of dialogue, of poetry, of dance, of painting, or of music? A form potential is a collecting structure for the representation of inner experience. To my mind, the choice of form is a kind of psychic route, as each subject, possessing many different forms for the collecting of experience, renders himself in a different medium, so that playing with the forms means simultaneously being played by them. The choice of representational form is an important unconscious decision about the structuring of lived experience, and is part of the differential erotics of everyday life.

The Sense of Mind

It is now possible to maintain that each of these unconscious means of thinking (in the initial experiencing and in the acts of representation) is a form for rendering all experiences available to the self. Further, as these different systems are coterminus with one another, the subject is an opera of unconscious forms, experiencing and representing life in dense inner textures of psychic apprehension. It is of interest that when Freud considered the different unconscious statuses of visual images, words, and feelings in *The Ego and the Id*, he addressed something of the issue we now face— namely, the nature of a deeply unconscious internal place for the intermodal registrations and representations of reality.

He believed that we have *internal perceptions* which "yield sensations of processes arising in the most diverse and certainly also in the deepest strata of the mental apparatus." I think such *sensations of processes* are inner senses of the workings of the different parts of the mind, a sense of their coterminus thinkings of reality—arguably a Freudian basis for a concept of the sense of self. "Very little is known about these sensings and feelings," he continues, ". . . they are more primordial, more elementary, than perceptions arising externally and they can come about even when consciousness is clouded." While Freud is aiming to identify what elsewhere he terms endogenous perception, I think he defines our inner sense of the aesthetic work of the mind. He concludes: "These sensations are multi-locular, like external perceptions; they may come from different places simultaneously and may thus have different or even opposite qualities" (21–22). Very close to arguing that we possess a "multi-locular" sense, derived from a psychic reality constituted from the many different forms of experience, in the *Ego and the Id*, Freud later emphasizes the work accomplished by the unconscious ego in the construction of psychic reality, and to my way of thinking, this process—the work of the unconscious ego—suggests a theory which addresses the synthetic arrangements of the multi-locular sense.

The great mass of such psychosomatic ego work will never reach consciousness. When it does, it will appear in psychic life through the modes we use to represent the dense texture of our inner experiencings. The representational unconscious is hermeneutically dynamic: it is a making meaningful of the world. But the work that characterizes the unconscious ego is the nonrepresentational unconscious that selects and uses objects in order to disseminate the self into experiencings that articulate and enrich it. The aim here is not to create meanings or to interpret reality as such, but to negotiate with reality in order to gain experience of objects that release the self into being.

The unconscious ego possesses the logic that chooses the subject's forms of experience, which I have called the eros of form. It determines what form will contain and process specific mental contents. If an analysand dramatically enacts a fear of castration by compulsively checking that all the doors in his house are shut, then the ego chooses the dramatic form to represent this mental content. However, this specific mental content could also have been represented (alternatively) in the verbal form (with a patient frequently altering the word "door"), in the visual category (by dreaming of doors), in the somatic register (by flushing red in the face and having an anxiety attack when opening doors for his business partner, for example), etc. The intelligence particular to this unconscious process is that skill in choosing the forms by which to live particular units of experience. Sensing which combination of forms to assemble to process an episode or which forms of representation to utilize for subsequent renderings is the most important task accomplished by this intelligence and is its pleasure. Clearly, pathology in the ego will reflect itself in the repetitive selection of certain forms for such self experiencing, just as psychic well-being is reflected in an ego skill that facilitates the diverse experiencing and expression of the subject's idiom.

In this chapter I have outlined a differentiation of the evocative potential of any object, in order to consider more carefully the processive effect of an object when solicited in any one moment of use. Naturally an object may be subjected to any combination of formal uses in the effort to express the self through the finding of experience. I have also considered some of the ways in which the subject uses the object, guided by a conviction that the radical difference of forms of representation suggests equally distinct means of psychic apprehension and process. If I have been successful in sketching these two places in the dialectic—the ego's range of unconscious forms for selected self experience and the object's intrinsic range of human use functions—then I may have added to our appreciation of what I mean by psychic text(ure): how the ego chooses not only what aspect of an object to use but also what subjective mode to employ in the use. Add to this the aleatory arrival of objects and the urgent demands of the instincts then I believe we gain an even greater realization of the density of the ego's aesthetic accomplishment in the setting up of self experience, just as we have previously admired its skill in constructing the dream.

The Play Work of Psychoanalysis

The analyst and his patient are engaged in a highly complex process of bringing what is unconscious into consciousness. Taking for granted these models of the mind and of technique that aim to conceptualize the differing valorizations of that movement from unconsciousness to consciousness, I now wish to add a different perspective—one that would be meaningless were it not attached to the other views of the movement toward meaning, but one which may enhance our appreciation of certain types of work within an analysis.

I refer to a special type of mutually unconscious work conducted by both participants in a psychoanalysis. Although I shall discuss this further in the following chapters, in considering how objects evoke differing states of self in the subject who uses the object, it is pertinent to stress that both analyst and patient are constantly evoking differing elements in each other. When an analyst speaks to a patient, he may have a clear idea in his mind exactly what he wishes to say to the patient, and it may make perfect analytical sense. But we know only too well that the analysand will be affected by virtually every interpretation in quite unique ways (and how could it be otherwise?). Each interpretation evokes associations, categories of thinking, and self states just as it promotes a subjective movement in the analysand that will ultimately deliver more of the analysand's idiom of thinking than the analyst's originating contribution.

At the moment of commenting on a dream image, or asking a question, or forming an interpretation, when the analyst quite rightly may assume he is objectifying the analysand's disseminated subjectivity, he is immediately launching the patient, and the analysis, into a new vector of associative play and work, as his comments evoke complex affective, ideational, memorial, somatic, and cognitive workings in the analysand.

So although, as I have argued, each ego possesses its own aesthetic intelligence, when engaged in human interaction it recognizes a place of intercommunicating that it knows quite well, where the effect of the other's evocations of one's self, rather than being placed into an evolving meaning, is open to the diverse effect of such an action. The ego knows, as it were, that units of meaning are always dispersed and scattered through the mental actions we term displacement, substitution, and symbolization. This is its habitat. Its language. And in the interactions of two subjects both possess egos that work upon each other in exactly this way; specifically, any subject who receives the other's word and presence is open to evocations of self that cohere and then scatter in the disseminations ordered by the ego that processes the meanings of life. As such, any two egos know that to communicate with one another is to evoke each other, and in that moment, to be distorted by the laws of unconscious work. To be touched by the other's unconscious is to be scattered by the winds of the primary process to faraway associations and elaborations, reached through the private links of one's own subjectivity. To know the other and to be known is as much an act of unconscious evocation that parts the subjects and announces the solitude of the self as it is an act of intelligent comprehension in which one can put one's knowing of the self and the other into coherent thought and structure of language.

In Chapter 4 I shall discuss how certain lasting psychic structures are formed in a psychoanalysis. To understand my emphasis on the unconscious factors contributing to such structures, it is important to bear in mind the means by which two subjects evoke one another, inaugurating a reciprocal engagement in simple and complex self experiencing, in which both participants engage in moments of deep experiencing and episodes of reflective objectification. This is what I term *play work*, to honor the to-and-fro of work and play, of reflecting and experiencing, that takes place between the two participants in a psychoanalysis.

But now an interlude, as I consider just how our idiom informs the other and leaves a trace of its character.

3

Being a Character

"Something—which we could call ruminativeness, speculation, a humming commentary—is going on unnoticed in us
always, and is the seed-bed of creation," writes Helen Vendler: "Keats called it a state of 'dim dreams,' full of 'stirring
shades, and baffled beams.'" She quotes Wordsworth:

> Those obstinate questionings
> Of sense and outward things
> Falling from us, vanishings,
> Blank misgivings of a creature
> Moving about in worlds not realised (226)

In moments of consciousness we are partly aware of these
dim dreams that stir within us, even though such inner
senses lack the memorable precision of the dream content.
Our inner world, the place of psychic reality, is inevitably
less coherent than our representations of it; a moving medley
of part thoughts, incomplete visualizations, fragments of
dialogue, recollections, unremembered active presences, sexual states, anticipations, urges, unknown yet present needs,
vague intentions, ephemeral mental lucidities, unlived partial
actions: one could go on and on trying to characterize the
complexity of subjectivity, and yet the adumbration of its

qualities does poor service to its reality. So too with self representation. How do we express the self? We speak, but only ever partly, and the unspoken is as intrinsic a part of our utterance as the enunciated. The symbolic, its rules of engagement known to the unconscious, links signifiers in infinite chains of meaning, just as the individual's diction texture and sonic imagery speak another tongue. "The image functions within the poem like the nerve of a thinking brain," writes Seamus Heaney (78) of a poem by Yeats, to which we may echo a larger assent—that images constitute another mode of self expression, each an intense condensation of many ideas thought simultaneously. We also gaze upon a dumb show of the other's gestural masque. "What is the life value of a gesture?" asks Lukács: it is "a movement which clearly expresses something unambiguous . . . the only thing which is perfect within itself." "The gesture alone expresses life," he concludes (28), a view Winnicott would arrive at many years later when he coined the term "true self" to designate the sign of life in the individual. We could go on —to somatic expression as another order of representation; indeed, to the hidden work of thinking proper revealed in the unconscious logic of sequence. Our listing of the many avenues of self expression could never truly honor the nature of human expression.

We are on different terrain as psychoanalysts, however, when faced with deciphering a sample of mental illness; psychological disturbance seems to organize the individual's self expression in such a way as to foreclose contact with the baffling complexity of mental life. In *Studies on Hysteria* Freud recounted a summer day in the 1890s when he climbed a mountain in the eastern Alps and, "feeling refreshed and rested, was sitting deep in contemplation of the charm of the distant prospect." He was quite elsewhere: "I was so lost in thought that at first I did not connect it with myself when these words reached my ears: 'Are you a doctor, sir?'" A rather depressed, but, we might add, determined adolescent of eighteen had followed the famous doctor to the top of the mountain, where she spoke her symptom. "It comes over me all at once. First of all it's like something pressing on my eyes. My head gets so heavy, there's a dreadful buzzing, and I feel so giddy that I almost fall over," and Katherina goes on. As she lists her physical symptoms Freud somewhat impatiently asks for news from the world of thought. "When you have an attack do you think of something? And always the same thing? Or do you see something in front of you?" "Yes," she replies, "I always see an awful face that looks at me in a dreadful way, so that I am frightened," and Freud, true to his Poirot self, investigates the story, unravels clues, and at six thousand feet helps his analysand of the moment to unravel her mystery (125–26).

Of course we know the rest of the story. Psychoanalysis preoccupied itself with a symptom that caused an expressed mental suffering; it named types of cases—hysteric, obsessional, etc.—to identify groups of common ailments and has led in our era to classifications of humanity according to broad psychic characters: borderline, neurotic, schizophrenic, and so forth. One may wonder, though, if we have not unwittingly shadowed the restrictions imposed by illness with our own corresponding restrictions in theory. Freud's lost-in-thought self was interrupted by his attending to a young girl's symptom, just as later absorption in the great depths of his self analysis was abandoned in order to treat the other. Has psychoanalysis discarded an early effort to be lost in thoughts, to be inside the complexity of subjectivity by concentrating attention on the identifiable samples of psychic life: the symptom, the obvious character trait, the narrated history?

I am not suggesting that we have erred in attending to the symptom or the mental structure of a character pathology; surely a narrowing of focus is necessary to think about the nature of mental illness. But if we think of these objectivities of self experience as fundamentally characteristic of that inner life, then symptoms, defense constellations, and dream contents mislead us. Like all of us, Freud lost in thought is participant in his own destiny just as the dream which collects us into units of narrative experience is also typical of life.

Being the Dream Work

I would like to use the individual's construction of the dream as a model of the articulation of a person's character, and in so doing to suggest a different fate—or at least a more complex fate—for the human subject than is suggested by the ego-psychological ideal of a progressive adaptation to reality. For although it is true that as we develop we acquire more sophisticated mental structures enabling the self to achieve greater psychic integration and increased ego skill in adapting to reality, it seems to me equally valid that as we grow we become more complex, more mysterious to our self, and less adapted to reality. How can one account for this rather troubling contradiction?

There is, as Freud has taught us, a psychopathology of everyday life characterized by the utterance of latent unconscious thoughts through the parapraxal skills of the ego: words are distorted or forgotten, actions are bungled in ways that spell out other hidden ideas. Each night, with luck, we dream, and this event is so instrumental to mental health that dream deprivation can lead eventually to a clinical psychosis. In human relations individuals regularly project parts of themselves into their others, shaping their relational world according to the idiom of their internal world, creating a village of friends who constitute a secret culture of the subject's desire.

Parapraxal utterance, symptomatic expression, screen memories, erotic fantasies, dreams, transferences, somatic states, ordinary relational projections, moods, and so on are all features of subjectivity that enable the person to express himself unconsciously. The self does not evolve unconsciously; rather, the self *is* unconsciousness, a particular inner presence, reliably vectored by the forms "it" uses to find expression. If this sounds mysterious, as if one is assigning to subjectivity a movement beyond our consciousness, then so be it: we *are* that mystifying to consciousness. In some respects we are originally so; I believe each of us at birth is equipped with a unique idiom of psychic organization that constitutes the core of our self, and then in the subsequent first years of our life we become our parents' child, instructed by the implicate logic of their unconscious relational intelligence in the family's way of being: we become a complex theory for being a self that the toddler does not think about but acquires operationally.

Our private idiom and its operational matriculation into processes of care that are theories of being leave each of us as adults with a substantial part of our self somehow deeply known (profoundly us) yet unthought. The theory of the id was a crucial first step in conceptualizing an important "itness" to us, something at our core, something that drives consciousness: a figuration of personality that conjures specific objects to unravel its code by such objectifications. Above all, our itness, or our idiom, is our mystery. We imagine, dream, abstract, select objects before we know why and even then knowing so little.

As a child develops he or she chooses friends, forms of play, objects of intellectual interest, and aspects of the mother and father, to give expression to the self. Such choices are, at the best of times, spontaneous and unconsciously determinate, as is the *jouissance* of the true self as "it" finds bliss in the grasping of very particular objects to yield specific experience. This joy reflects the inner sense of the self's release to its being, and the pleasures of a child who is choosing objects of desire is unmistakable to those of us who witness it. But we also see all children held up by a mood which Freud and Breuer argued, as early as 1897, was evidence of the presence of unconscious conflict at work. Child psychotherapists observe children struggling with internal objects constituted from the conflicts of intrapsychic life, just as they may feel through their countertransference the child's representation of a part of the mother or father deposited in them through parental projective identification. Of course, each child has his own particular life history, composed of the essential mixtures of life: the first day of school, the first physical injury, a death in the family, a move.

However are we to describe the character of the internal world, given its dense complexity? We do not have separate or overlapping lines of development, we have mazes of evolving devolutions. Although our internal world registers the multivalent factors of units of experience, rendered into textured condensations of percepts, introjects, objects of desire, memories, somatic registrations, and so forth, in fact *we become a kind of dreaming*: overdetermined, condensed, displaced, symbolic. Instinctual, ego-characteristic, receptive, and accident-prone, we "work" our days into their notional status as vague forms of thinking. Our weeks, months, and years pass by as we continuously work experience into psychic material, most of it beyond consciousness but certainly preconsciously familiar as "our" inner texture.

Of course, themes emerge. We do have identifiable patterns to our being. We can rightly claim to have identities and speak of ourself with some sense of what is being addressed. But these "contents" are not the stuff of life any more than the dream content is the dream work. Most of the time we are simple selves engaged in the life equivalent of the dream work, and although we do have a sense of being in this place of self dissemination, it is rather like living an essential chaos.

How else can we describe the state of being a simple self, immersed in the projective subjectification of reality, as anything other than a chaos of forms, as we dissolve consciousness, disseminate parts of the self in units of experience, are evoked by objects that arrive by chance, and in turn use objects as lexical elements in the elaboration of idiom? To be the simple experiencing self the individual must abandon self objectification and surrender to experience, a dissolution essential to the subjectification of reality. The schizophrenic's continuous unrelenting self observing is in some respects testimony to his difficulty in yielding to generative projection. The fear of being trapped inside the object world or of losing the self to such abandonment prevents some psychotic individuals from giving themselves to the dreaming of life.

Indeed the capacity to be the dream work of one's life, to devolve consciousness to the creative fragmentations of unconscious work, is evidence of a basic trust in the reliable relation between such dreaming and the consciousness that results in our reflections. Knowing that we will awaken from our dreaming, that we shall endure episodes of self observation and analysis, helps the individual to trust in the wisdom of surrender to subjectifications. Indeed this trust owes much to the nature of the first years of life, when we were a simple experiencing self participant in a thinking or dreaming world of the mother's unconscious. If a child feels that his subjectivity is held by some container, composed of the actual holding environment of parental care and subsequently the evolving structure of his own mind, then the subjectifying of the world feels licensed, underwritten, and guaranteed. But if this right is not secure, then a child will feel hesitant to release the elements of self to their experiencings: such abandonments feel life-threatening.

We dream ourself into being by using objects to stimulate our idiom, to release it into lived expression. We do not think about it at all while doing it. We are just inside something—our dream work—that is itself a pleasure. It is subjectivities' *jouissance* to find the means of being dreamed into reality; there is true joy in finding an object that bears

its experience which we find transformational, as it metamorphoses a latent deep structure into a surface expression.

Winnicott stressed how in play the child's excitement
expressed the sense of risk involved in committing oneself
to the imaginary. What would turn up? Abandoning oneself
to play, what would happen? Or perhaps more accurately,
exactly whom do we become as we express our idiom in
play? To be a character, to release one's idiom into lived
experience, requires a certain risk, as the subject will not
know his outcome; indeed, to be a character is to be released
into being, not as a knowable entity per se, but as an idiom
of expression explicating a human form. Even in these
moments of self expression the individual will not know his
own meaning, his reflections will always lag behind himself,
more often than not puzzled by his itness, yet relieved by
the *jouissance* of its choosings.

Personal Effects

Do I know the other's character, who the other truly is?
Have I the means of transcribing the other's subjectivity to
some collectable place? Only to a limited, if useful, extent,
as we shall see. But we can observe an individual's personal
effects and to some extent witness the idiom's lexical expressions implied by object choice even if what we see is more
like a jumbled collection of manifest texts. I may visit a
friend's house and find that he has selected sky blue for the
walls of his living room, white for the kitchen, rust for the
study. I may see that he collects records, particularly Mahler,
and I may note that the recordings are by Simon Rattle and
Klaus Tennstedt. I may see that his book collection is largely
fiction, especially thrillers, but that he has a substantial
literature on oriental rugs, which marries up logically with
the many such rugs scattered about the house. Photos of
fishing expeditions tell me he likes to fish, plenty of *haute*

cuisine pots and pans inform me he likes to cook, a messy desk that he is not so well organized, a jug full of sharpened pencils and no pens that he prefers to erase error and anticipates its reliable arrival, the absence of TV that he may seek to be unaffected by it and one could endlessly describe what else is missing. But what have I learned? Well, I have some evidence of his personal effects, don't I, but unfortunately I do not know what these objects mean to him. Neither can I assume that all I see is actually his personal choice. After all, the specific Mahler recordings could have been gifts from a friend and the shining pots evidence of a wish never actualized. But I think it is fair to say that many of the objects I see do reflect the friend's dreaming; like dream props they are overdetermined, possible condensations of wishes and needs (the pots could reflect conflicts) or they may be substitutions (blue wall instead of red) or displacements (thrillers instead of pornography). What I believe we see, then, is something of the dream work, although the latent dream thoughts are not for us to know.

We are, however, imagining the room without its inhabitant. What if we could watch this person move about his room, picking up objects, moving them about, giving form, as it were, to his person? To make this imagining sharper, throwing into relief the point I wish to make, let us think of this person's idiom by conceiving him to be a ghost. We are in the room, then, with a ghost, whom we can see only as objects are stirred or moved around the room. By seeing the objects move, rather like observing the wind by watching the moving trees, we would, in effect, be watching his personal effect as he passed through his life, and theoretically, we could film subjectivities' enacted dissemination by catching the movement of objects over time.

This metaphor enables me to get closer to what I want to say about the nature of human character. It allows us to consider the *forms of existence* selected by any human life, sculpted through the choice and use of objects, but unencumbered by the imposing physical presence of the subject who seems to be self defining in and through his own presence. The ghost moving about the room does not, however, indicate the most important place of the moving object, as we are not witness to those internal objects conjured in the mind. But we do know something of this movement when our internal world is characterized by the other's effect upon us, something that the theory of projective identification and other theories of unconscious communication now address. In other words, we are internally shaped by the presence and actions of the other. Although it is difficult to witness how one person "moves through" the other, like a ghost moving through the internal objects in the room of the other's mind, we know it is of profound significance, even though exceptionally difficult to describe.

Let us think of someone in particular—our father, for example—to see what we register within ourselves; what we think of. Perhaps some image of the father's expression will cross our mind, but this hardly adds up to the experience that is taking place within us. Indeed it is important to stress that at the moment of thinking of the father we are undergoing an experience, as inner constellations of feelings, unthought ideas, deeply condensed memories, somatic registrations, body positionings, and so forth are gathering into an inner sense. But what is this? The total experience is, in fact, the effect upon ourself (naturally reflecting the self we are as well as the other whom we represent) of the father. And if we think of anyone else, our mother, our spouse, one of our children, a close friend, a neighbor, a shopkeeper, then we feel an inner forming inside ourself, a restructuring of our inner world that is evoked by the name of the person we are then considering.

I think that this inner form within us, this outline or shape of the other, dynamic yet seemingly consistent, is indeed rather like a *revenant* within, as we have been affected by the other's movement through us, one that leaves its ghost inhabiting our mind, conjured when we evoke the name of the object.

Gathering Our Self

But what, then, of our self? To begin with the simple, and misleading again, what happens as we look about our room, our house, what do we see of this very particular self that we are? Well, certainly here or there we can identify objects that serve to bring us into a dreaming episode, when we imagine our self into its being. I have several copies of *Moby Dick* on my shelf, a faint trace of my Ph.D. thesis on Melville. I know that by choosing Melville's book I selected an object that allowed me to be dreamed by it, to elaborate myself through the many experiences of reading it. In some ways its mental spaces, its plot, its characters, allowed me to move elements of my idiom into collaboration with the text and hence into being. Selecting it as the object of such personal concentration was an intuitive choice, in my view, based on my knowing (yet not knowing why) that this book—rather than, say, Hawthorne's *The Scarlet Letter*—would bring something of me into expression. I did not think, at the time, that it connected to an episode at the age of eleven when I was swimming some hundred yards off the shore of my favorite cove in my hometown when I saw what initially looked to me like a large reef moving in my direction. In fact, it was a whale and it passed by me so closely that although it did not touch me I could still feel it. It was a profoundly upsetting moment and linked in the unconscious, I believe, to an experience at the age of nine of riding up over a wave to collide with the bloated body of a woman who must have been dead at sea for some time—an experience whose memory I repressed, but which "resurfaced" some years after writing the dissertation when I incorrectly assumed that it was pure fantasy. Although I subsequently discovered its authenticity, it nonetheless collected to it, like a screen memory, many factors in my psyche which had then organized into a repression. Thus in choosing to work on *Moby Dick* (embarked on in 1969, the nine perhaps designating the task of elaborating a prior experience at the age of nine) I selected an object that I could use to engage in deep unconscious work, an effort that enabled me to experience and articulate something of my self.

I can retrace some of my psychic footsteps, and a favorite novel allows me to detect some of its unconscious meaning. Interesting though this may be, it is the exception: so much of what we choose to process the self is ahermeneutic. For example, why at twenty did I develop a passionate interest in Beethoven's Third Symphony? This interest was circumstantially elicited as I happened to hear it in concert, but I felt very drawn to it. Like a holding environment, a musical work puts the listening subject through a complex nonverbal inner process. I also heard Bach's Mass in B Minor, and Mozart's *Don Giovanni* that year and went to a James Brown and a Janis Joplin concert, all of which I enjoyed, but the Third Symphony became a musical object that I listened to again and again. In my twenties I sought many musical objects, works of passionate investment succeeding one another, yet is it possible to discover the meaning, the unconscious message of such works, as it is possible in part to specify with *Moby Dick*?

These two works of art, used by me, are intended to shadow an earlier example of trying to see what we can know about a person by noting the very particular objects he selects in the course of a life. Although in considering what I can know of myself by listing such important actual objects, I obviously operate in a different field than in the example of visiting a friend's house to see his personal effects. But when I think of *Moby Dick* or when I recall the period of my youth when I listened to the Third Symphony, memory becomes a kind of gathering of internal objects, developing an inner constellation of feelings, ideas, part images, body positions, somatic registrations, and so forth that nucleate into a sustained inner form.

Inhabited by the Object World

I am inhabited, then, by inner structures that can be felt whenever their name is evoked; and in turn, I am also filled with the ghosts of others who have affected me. In psychoanalysis we term these "internal objects," which clearly do not designate internal pictures, or clear inner dramas, but rather *highly condensed psychic textures*, the trace of our encounters with the object world.

This suggests, among other things, that as we encounter the object world we are substantially metamorphosed by the structure of objects; internally transformed by objects that leave their traces within us, whether it be the effect of a musical structure, a novel, or a person. In play the subject releases the idiom of himself to the field of objects, where he is then transformed by the structure of that experience, and will bear the history of that encounter in the unconscious. To be a character is to enjoy the risk of being processed by the object—indeed, to seek objects, in part, in order to be metamorphosed, as one "goes through" change by going through the processional moment provided by any object's integrity. Each entry into an experience of an object is rather like being born again, as subjectivity is newly informed by the encounter, its history altered by a radically effective present that will change its structure.

To be a character is to gain a history of internal objects, inner presences that are the trace of our encounters, but not intelligible, or even clearly knowable: just intense ghosts who do not populate the machine, but inhabit the human mind. If idiom is, then, the it with which we are born, and if its pleasure is to elaborate itself through the choice of objects, one that is an intelligence of form rather than an expression of inner content, its work collides with the structure of objects that transform it, through which it gains its precise inner contents. This collisional dialectic between the human's form and the object's structure is, in the best of times, a joy of living, as one is nourished by the encounter.

I believe we have a special knowledge of the nature of this dialectic, and the Freudian unconscious is the stuff of that knowledge. That is, the processional integrity of any object —that which is inherent to any object when brought to life by an engaging subject—is used by the individual according to the laws of the dream work. When we use an object it is as if we know the terms of engagement; we know we shall "enter into" an intermediate space, and at this point of entry we change the nature of perception, as we are now released to dream work, in which subjectivity is scattered and disseminated into the object world, transformed by that encounter, then returned to itself after the dialectic, changed in its inner contents by the history of that moment.

But are such moments the arrival of essence, the deep truth of subjectivity? In a way yes, in a way no. It is true that as we evolve we release our idiom into units of being and that in time we gain a sense of the self that we are. But that is all. We gain only a sense. Or the sense is more importantly valued than what we perceive to know about the history of the self or the character of its mental process. Only a sense partly because the fate of each of us is to be dreamed by the contexts of idiom and object and partly because the forms of experience and for expression undermine thematic serenity. So although I may rightly say that I know certain themes of my identity, although I may specify my life history and establish the narrative of myself, the truth of my life, one I believe true of all of our lives, is that to be human is to be recurrently lost in thought (and the use of object) when we are involved in the process of living and informed by the ghosts of experience. We live this process all our life, we know it deeply, yet it is exceptionally difficult to describe, even though psychoanalysis has selected samples of the process and subjected them to great scrutiny.

What we come to know as we mature into more sophisticated creatures is that we add new psychic structures that make us more complex, increase our capacity for the dream work of life, and therefore problematize the sense we have of an established reality, a world of psychically meaningful convention, available to us for our adaptation. As we age we know that our destiny is a rather paradoxical psychobiological unraveling. Wisdom is measured by increased uncertainty about the meanings of our self, or of life. Decentered by experience, radically historicized, not given integrating memories neatly unifying the nature of life, we are nonetheless inhabited by the *revenants* of the dream work of life, thousands of inner constellations of psychic realities, each conjurable by name or memory, even if few are truly intelligible. And as we mature, is it any surprise that we come to believe more and more in life's mystery and in the strangeness of being human, as we are in possession of—or is it possessed by?—these inner realities, which we know, but which we truly cannot think, however hard we try. And yet they are there. Not only there, but the inner senses we have when we think of our inner objects seem more a part of us than anything else. How do we name them?

The Spirits of Life

I shall extend the metaphor of our containment of ghosts, the feeling of being inhabited by our history and its objects, by saying that the objects we contain are spirits. We contain what for us will have been the essence of our encounters with objects, reflecting in the synthesis something that transcends our idiom and the structure of the object, but which owes its origin to each. They are the stuff of psychical reality.

They can neither be seen nor described. It is possible to inaugurate an effort of representation through free association, but what that gains is less the articulation of the content of the spirit than its elaboration through the formal effect of the free associations, particularly if we consider this from the viewpoint of the transference and the countertransference, where what is being addressed tends to be enacted in the form of the discourse. I can talk to my analyst about my father, but what happens over time is that he will know him less through the precise contents of the associations than through some intriguing effect upon himself which gathers into his inner experience something of the nature of what I hold within myself.

Being a character, then, means bringing along with one's articulating idiom those inner presences—or spirits—that we all contain, now and then transferring them to a receptive place in the other, who may knowingly or unknowingly be inhabited by them. My analyst may know, for example, when his inner experience constellates that presence I have objectified as "father," but in the ordinary to-and-fro of life, as we pass back and forth the spirits of life, we hardly know quite whom we are holding for the other, however briefly, although we will know that we are being inhabited. And perhaps we struggle to conceptualize in the vernacular philosophy of everyday life the nature of spiritual communication (of transference and countertransference), as we shall, for example, say that person X emits certain "vibes" which we may or may not like. We also say that we are or are not on someone's "frequency," just as we also claim that we are or are not "in tune" with X. Why are we using sonic images to talk about certain types of human communication? Possibly because the sheer unspecificity of the content of what is being discussed is true to the sense of the occasion; one cannot be specific, although the selection of the sonic form is clear enough and points to a belief in the shaping effect of form as the conveyer of meaning.

Being a character means that one is a spirit, that one conveys something in one's being which is barely identifiable as it moves through objects to create personal effects, but which is more deeply graspable when one's spirit moves through the mental life of the other, to leave its trace. Perhaps there is a special form within each of us for the perception of this type of communication. Maybe we have a special ear for it, as we may have for music. If so, then we are capable of a kind of spiritual communication, when we are receptive to the intelligent breeze of the other who moves through us, to affect us, shaping within us the ghost of that spirit when it is long gone. It also suggests that some people may be spiritually impoverished, with a diminished capacity for the reception of spiritual communication, meaning that they lack an intelligent inner space available to receive the other's spirit. Some individuals may be spiritual imperialists, greedily moving through others, militantly affecting people in destructive ways. Can we talk about people who are more or less spiritually good, and those who are spiritually bad, if in daring to include a morality to interpersonal life, we have in mind both the capacity to be inhabited by the other and the capacity to know the limits of any other to host us?

Spirit is, however, a word that opens itself to many ideas, lending itself, by its very polysemy, to a kind of mystification. Indeed, Derrida reminds us that the overusage of this word in the nineteenth century, its incantatory presence surrounding the interrogation of the nature of thought and being, eventually marked "a lack of interest, an indifference, a remarkable lack of need . . . for the question of the Being of the entity that we are" (19). Use of the word "spirit" indicated an indifference to the investigation of thought itself, and were this to be the fate of the entry of spirit in my discourse, it would be a sad folly indeed. Is it possible to resist the pendulum force of intellectual passions that perverts the use value of any idea? Is it possible for spirit to enter into the language of psychoanalysis without falling in love with its suggestive power? Or will it herald the movement of a neosurrealist romanticism in which the ungraspable, the seeming essence of experience, displaces the effort to dissect, to deconstruct, indeed to despiritualize?

To my way of thinking, the challenge is to find a middle ground, a "midworld," in which the vector of idiom signified by "spirit" is allowed its contribution to the mulling over of self experience as is the vector of objectivity signified, say, by the word "empirical," or "observational." These vectors create a tension in the individual if allowed to be, and clearly there is an inclination to please the self by ridding the midworld of one or another of these disquieting words or forces that attract attention and make claims upon consciousness.

This is the way it should be, however, and our concepts should sustain the "experience of questioning" (Derrida) as preliminary to the gathering of data or the supply of observations. "The more original a thought," says Derrida, quoting Heidegger, "the richer its Unthought becomes. The Unthought is the highest gift (*Geschenk*) that a thought can give." In our place and in our time the word "spirit," perhaps unsaturated with meaning and yet evocative, may call forth associations, as did the word "id" in the early half of the first century of psychoanalysis, as then did the word "ego" in the midcentury, and more recently as does the word "self." But our words often need displacing (as I may be doing with Winnicott's phrase "true self" by substituting "idiom" for it) because the overusage of a term, though transitionally essential to individual and collective efforts of objectifying the signified, eventually loses its meaningfulness through incantatory solicitation, devaluing any word's unthought potential.

To be a character, then, is to abandon the "it" of one's idiom to its precise choosings, an unraveling and dissemination of personality: a bearer of an intelligent form that seeks objects to express its structure. The idiom that gives form to any human character is not a latent content of meaning but an aesthetic in personality, seeking not to print out unconscious meaning but to discover objects that conjugate into meaning-laden experience. As we move through the object world, breathing our life into the impersonal, we gather and organize our personal effects. As we collide with other subjectivities, we exchange differing syntheses, and leave the other with his or her inner senses of our self, just as we carry the spirit of the other's idiom within our unconscious. We can conjure these spirits within us as we evoke the name of the other, although what we deeply know is only ever partly thought, and strangely defies the codes of thought we have valued so highly in Western culture. And of ourselves, I think it can be said that we are spirits, that we shall scatter our being throughout the object world, and through the winds of interforming human mutualities. A dream that defies its content, it enjoins the world through the dream work. We will have had, then, a spiritual sense, a notional grasp of the force to be what we have been, and this presence, valued yet ungraspable, is consolation amidst the human march to wisdom's end, punctuated, as always, by the question mark.

4

Psychic Genera

Although the child's first response to a severe environmental impingement is an important part of the formation of a trauma, it is with its "second" occurrence, upon a reawakening in consciousness, that its truly disturbing nature is revealed. Not only burdened by memories of the actual event, the person now feels inhabited by it from within the psyche-soma. Originally an externally sponsored shock, it becomes intrapsychically organized and incessantly reasserts itself. Intrapsychically sponsored eruptions of emotional turbulence emphasize the true helplessness, confusion, and isolation of the traumatized, echoing something of the child's original aloneness.

A victim of child molestation at the age of thirteen, however, may report this to a friend and be helped by the cohesive effect of narrative, even though this will not end the trauma. It is liable to an overwhelming reappearance later on, often "triggered" by a nonmolesting event, perhaps in the course of lovemaking. At least when the thirteen-year-old becomes an adult he is likely to have a memory of turning to someone for help, and the memory of the environment's response and the therapeutics of the talking cure will be an important part of self recovery.

If a molested child of five is unable to speak of this to someone, then his problem will be compounded in adult life when an event may evoke it; for, as the child did not speak the molestation to someone in the first place, it will not have been narratively objectified. There will be no memory of having told someone about it and thus there will be no generative side to the recollection, only the trauma.

This may be one of the reasons why some adults will be confused upon experiencing an uncanny feeling that they have been the object of some abuse. Did it actually happen or is it imagined? Psychic confusion is part of the full effect of trauma because, unable to narrate the event in the first place, the person now re-experiences isolation, this time brought on by the aloneness of mental confusion. The feeling that it might not have happened, that it could be invention, underscores this person's increased lonesomeness, particularly as he is disinclined to report such feelings. A prominent feature of the original impingement is the child's felt separation from his family and fellow kind, as he is made different by the action, isolated by it, and rendered speechless.

In this chapter I shall put forward the view that trauma has an opposite—genera[1]—which is the psychic incubation

---

1. Heretofore "genera" has been the plural form of the noun "genus," which means class or kind. But a different noun structure has always been hidden within it, based on the Latin origin of the word, "gignere," which means to give birth. The Aryan root, "gen," also means to beget. In *Creative Evolution* Henri Bergson almost transformed "genera" into a verbal noun when he linked it to reproductivity and to his concept of vital energy. In the late nineteenth century, perhaps "genera" still carried within it the notion of a dynamically moving structure, but twentieth-century thought has denuded the word of its dynamic origins, and it is now used only to refer to classes of objects, although it would be allowed that such classes do evolve. I think it is within the spirit of the original base of this word (to give birth, to reproduce) to use "genera" as both a singular and a plural noun, simply because the word "genus"—its theoretically proper singular form—now definitely refers to a a single class or species, and does not contain in English a sensible verbal noun meaning. I also find that I cannot say "a genus" when referring to the dynamic organization of an evolving psychic structure. So I suggest that we create

of libidinal cathexes of the object world. The sense of how to gather psychic investments to an inner area of work derives from the individual's experience of elaborating his own idiom, a process that involves the selection of specific objects which release idiom to its expression. As we are born with our idiom and as it is elaborated through parental provision, the individual develops a belief in psychic dissemination, which leads him to assume that he can articulate his idiom through the psychic freedom of object representation and the liberty of object choice.

Naturally, as this freedom to evolve the self is facilitated and influenced by the mother and the father, any sense a person has of the nature of personal elaboration will bear the marks of maternal and paternal provision. In fact, what we might think of as primal genera—specific nascent factors of the infant's idiom that sponsor early aesthetic cohesions of the object world—are met by another organizing intelligence: the logics of parental provision. The question is, can the idiom of the child elicit generative parenting so that the articulations of subjectivity use the materials of reality to promote elaboration?

If genera develop through the successional elaboration of idiom, trauma leads to the person's binding of the self, which sponsors a type of psychic pain and leads to a very different kind of unconscious work. Thus these two principles, of trauma and genera, begin as fundamental ego dispositions toward reality, derived from the infant's and child's experience of the mother and the father. Children whose parents

---

a contemporary, though restricted usage, in which "genera" also refers to a particular type of psychic organization of lived experience that will result in creative new envisionings of life, either in psychoanalysis or in other walks of life. In the psychoanalytic context it matches exactly with trauma. The plural noun was "traumata," but this is rarely used. Sometimes writers use "traumas" for the plural form, but increasingly "trauma" is used for both singular and plural noun forms. As the entire aim of my neologistic use of "genera" is to pair it with "trauma," in order to clarify complex issues having to do with the nature of mental development, I feel justified in this small act of linguistic violence.

are impinging or acutely traumatizing collect such trauma into an internal psychic area which is intended to bind and limit the damage to the self, even though it will nucleate into an increasingly sophisticated internal complex as resonant trauma are unconsciously "referred" to such an area for linked containment. Children who experience parents as contributing to the elaborative dissemination of their personal idiom will subsequently develop an open-mindedness to the contributing effects of the object world.

Some interpersonally derived psychic trauma are enforced mental labors in which the subject processes the other's unconscious projective identifications, which necessarily become part of oneself but which are contained and limited. If the trauma is subsequently symbolically elaborated (in discourse, painting, fiction, etc.), the aim may be to evacuate its disturbing effect through the work of repetition and displacement, while symbolically elaborated genera create intensified re-envisionings of reality which, however anguishing, are the pleasure of the ego's creativities. Psychic genera are wished-for psychic workings which reflect the subject's introjective choices as he feels free to follow the unconscious articulations of his own idiom and are part of the eros of form. The child who is binding a psychic trauma into a collection of ideas aims to minimize contact with the external world and to nullify the ideational, affective, and interpersonal effect of traumatic psychic complexes. The child who nurtures his own genera seeks novel experiences that will bring him into renewing contact with his ideational and affective states, often within an enriching interpersonal environment.

A trauma is just that, traumatic, and the subject who contains such anguishing complexes will usually not seek to symbolically elaborate them, not have them, as it were, spawn newer, more radical perspectives on life; but a trauma is represented, in actings-out, in creative works, in human relations. It is important to make clear here that the effect of trauma is to sponsor symbolic repetition, not symbolic elaboration. Nonetheless, certain writers, painters, musicians, and so forth only ever repeat themselves, and their works are valued as significant symbolizations of human life—which they no doubt are. A subject whose principle of engagement with reality is generative will seek to work unconsciously on specific issues that will enable him to re-envision his reality and in turn sponsor new ways of living and thinking. But again, it is important to qualify this: the incubation of genera can be, and usually is, the work of great personal struggle, as any change of one's status quo involves emotional turbulence.

In essence, genera are, first, the inherited proto-nucleations of any child's idiom, so that if he is free to elaborate himself, then life will be punctuated by inspired moments of self realization, deriving from the instinct to elaborate the self, which I have termed a destiny drive (Bollas, 1989). If we look upon infants as embryonic characters and early childhood as a form of germinal settlement (which includes parental unconscious contributions), then subsequently the child and adult will be elaborating different areas of the self at different times, with differing paces of articulation, under differing circumstances. The relatively successful expression of particles of personality idiom, a movement from deep structure to the surface engagements of life, gives the adult an inner knowledge of the development over time of deeply private, as yet mentally inaccessible areas of the self.

Although this chapter focuses on how genera are formed in psychoanalysis, each of us possesses unconscious knowledge of how this is accomplished; a person's idiom is itself an implicate logic of form—partly inherited, partly acquired—which generates visions of self and object. The unconscious skill involved in selecting objects that will release this form to its realizations derives from the infant's innate ability to fashion a psychic reality from lived experience. The sense of vision that most people possess is energized by the destiny drive, the very particular urge to develop the form of one's private idiom through the articulating and elaborating experiences of object usage. "Form, after all, is nothing but content-as-arranged," writes Vendler (3), and in thinking of personality as form, we can say that each person's idiom is the peculiar manner each individual possesses of shaping the contents of life. Given the urge to find objects through which to come into one's shape—and to fashion the object world at the same time—I think of personality as an erotic aesthetics, an intelligence of form that desires to come into existence. This dissemination of our personality suggests principles of creativity which we may follow, the cultivation of genera being one such outcome.

Perhaps it is possible to see how trauma-developed psychic processes will be conservative, fundamentally aiming to control the psychic damage, desensitizing the self to further toxic events. Thus, trauma can be seen as allied to the indigenous inner principle of the death instinct, which aims to preserve a constant state by ridding the subject of excitation; only in the beginning trauma is the effort to rid the self of excitation sponsored by the external object (or actual other) rather than in the more classical and Kleinian formulations which emphasize the death work's effort to rid the subject of the disturbing effects of instinctual urgency. The trauma-evolving child is already a self developing along very particular lines, such as those conceptualized by Fairbairn in his theory of the infant's internalization of the bad object, where the aim is to control the negative effect of bad parenting by taking the negating objects into oneself.

The child who internalizes fundamentally generative parents—who contribute to the evolution of his personal idiom—aims to develop such inner processes and to seek excitation and novelty as means of triggering personal growth. As such, genera link up with the life instincts which aggressively seek the procreative combinings of self with object.

The child who establishes inner psychic holding areas for the containment of disturbed parental communications or shocking events seeks to break links between the referred contents and their preconscious derivatives. To use Bion's language: he attacks the linking function that is vital to K (knowledge) and works to devitalize the pain of its meaning by transforming it into − K, thereby giving to such inner experiences an empty or vacuous feel. Pain is thereby transferred into nothingness. In the child's cultivation of internal possibilities for creative revisioning of self and reality, links between inner areas of such work and the data of life that seem related to it are sought, thereby establishing a valorization of unconscious work informed by the K function.

Genera and trauma are broad principles, and psychoanalysts will be aware of the countless exceptions to the rule. A child raised by impinging parents may partly fend them off and defiantly preserve a part of himself capable of wresting contributive factors from the parents and their substitutes. He would then have his particular sense of how to be contributed to and, in turn, how to subsequently hatch intrapsychic areas for the work of genera. Alternately, a child who has facilitative parents may, as a result of the birth of a sibling, embark on a prolonged bout of unconscious hate that will convert facilitative parental endeavors into mnemic traces of parental procreativity, which is therefore envied and so the continuous source of trauma.

We can view genera from another psychoanalytic model: the topographic point of view. Freud's theory of repression identifies a crucial pathway of mental conflict, when an individual preconsciously represses unwanted feelings, ideas, and experiences to the unconscious, where such banished contents immediately constitute a nucleus of interlocking ideas. Consciousness has been denuded of a part of its contents and repression signifies a diminution in the person's self awareness. However, as such ideas are, according to Freud, instinctually driven, there is an intrinsic energy to find expression, to return to consciousness for fuller mental realization, a procedure that can only be done by changing the nuclear ideas through displacement, substitution, etc., to achieve some derivative expression. When the repressed ideas fail to find adequate escape from banishment to the system unconscious, they tend to collect to them further ideas and affects that occur in subsequent moments of consciousness as these ideas disappear from the mind like refuge seekers in the now increasing colony of banished ideas—a group that paradoxically gains in strength as it is oppressed. Psychoanalysts accept the clinical validity of this theory. They see how patients present gaps in conscious contents that point to repressed or withdrawn ideas and feelings, and how such unwanted ideas are maintained by anticathexes, by forces or mental energies opposing their return to consciousness. They can hear in the parapraxes, or detect in the symptom, or unravel in the dream the effective ability of repressed states of mind to re-enter consciousness in disguise.

In many respects the theory of genera is inspired by the theory of repression. At the heart of the matter is my view that there is a collecting psychic gravity to unconscious clusters of ideas that are organized, dynamic, and representationally effective in consciousness. But the theory of repression points only to the banishment of the unwanted, and I am convinced that other types of ideas are invited into the unconscious. To complement the theory of repression, we need a *theory of reception*[2] which designates some ideas as the received rather than the repressed, although both the repressed and the received need the protective barrier provided by the anticathexes of preconsciousness. But if the

2. The idea of a receptively derived unconscious, as partner to a repressed unconscious, suggests the possibility of a maternal type of unconscious work that collaborates with paternal action. The metaphors I use—to conceive, to impregnate, to incubate, to give birth—consider a certain type of unconscious creativity differing from the paternal metaphors which stress repression, domination, and disguised representation.

aim of repression is to avoid the censoring or persecutory judgments of consciousness, the aim of reception is to allow unconscious development without the intrusive effect of consciousness.

Thus with reception the ego understands that unconscious work is necessary to develop a part of the personality, to elaborate a phantasy, to allow for the evolution of a nascent emotional experience, and ideas or feelings and words are sent to the system unconscious, not to be banished but to be given a mental space for development which is not possible in consciousness. Like the repressed idea, these ideas, words, images, experiences, affects, etc., constellate into mental areas and then begin to scan the world of experience for phenomena related to such inner work. Indeed, they may possibly seek precise experiences in order to nourish such unconscious constellations. The contents of the received are then the nuclei of genera which, like the repressed, will return to consciousness, but in the case of genera as acts of self enrichment rather than paroled particles of the incarcerated.

In this chapter I shall allow the work of repression to become part of a broadened view of trauma, insofar as repressed contents denude the self of representational freedom, bind unwanted ideas, and feel endangering to the self. Quite rightly, the analyst will work with shrewd tact and analytical cunning to designate affects, words, memories, etc., that will serve to release such contents into bearable consciousness just as he will analyze the resistance to such experiences. The clinician working with the analysand's receptive unconscious activity will sense that the patient is withdrawing ideas, feelings, or memories from narrative representation and selectively from consciousness in order to work upon them from within the unconscious, without the premature expression in consciousness that would foreclose deep unconscious work. In such moments the analyst may let the patient be, understanding that the receptive process needs unconsciousness to be effective.

In the rest of this chapter I discuss what I mean by the principle of genera, which is intended on the one hand to define a form of internal work that results in an important new way of seeing the world—one which would apply to people working on scientific, artistic, or vocational problems or tasks—and yet on the other hand one precise enough to enable the clinician to see how psychoanalysts and patients unconsciously collaborate to construct psychic structures that change the analysand's view of himself and his world. I shall conceptualize this phenomena, in turn, from the axis of three different psychoanalytic models of the mind: topographic, ego-psychological, object-relational. I hope thereby to indicate the value of a theory of psychic work that is distinct from the exclusively pathologic models, although genera formation is born of conflict and promotes emotional turbulence.

Combinatory Play

The unconscious play work that a subject devotes to any set of received "issues" incubates an internal organization derived from and devoted to such effort. A scientist working on a scientific task, for example, plays with many ideas; years may pass before he has an inspired idea that heralds an important discovery, one that will change his outlook on handling his future work. A composer is at work on a symphony. Perhaps, like Aaron Copland, he is asked to write on Lincoln, and, like Copland, he asks himself how Lincoln sounds.[3] It could be that an idea will come to mind immediately, but more likely the symphonic idea will derive from

3. In her lyrical and intelligent book *Notebooks of the Mind*, Vera John-Steiner explores the many types of creativity, and I have used her work to support my own clinical findings. However, were one to study the conviction in creative persons of what I term genera, then Vera John-Steiner's book would be an excellent point of departure.

intensive unconscious play work until something announces itself. A psychic nucleus derives from the many moments of distinct consideration brought to bear on the task. Such a generative structure will now sponsor many new ideas that ultimately will constitute the symphony, eventually achieving a semi-autonomous status, and in the process changing the composer's conscious intentions, and possibly altering his way of composing future works.

Ordinarily, then, genera are produced after a period of play work and, once established, transform the subject's outlook on life, generate new questions and new works, and contribute to the formation of new genera.

Einstein wrote of his "rather vague play with the . . . elements" in his mind's eye, which he also described as a form of "combinatory play" that he believed to be "the essential feature in productive thought—before there is any connection with logical construction in words or other kinds of signs which can be communicated to others" (43). This play with the elements, prior to logical construction, is the receptive process that occurs inside each of us as we form genera: a combinatory play that leads to the eventual establishment of a new perspective. It is not irrelevant that Einstein twice refers to this as play, which brings to mind Wordsworth's description of the infant's aggressive receptivity: "Hence his mind, / Even in the first trial of its powers, / Is prompt and watchful, eager to combine / In one appearance all the elements / And parts of the same object" (67).

One cannot overemphasize the long hours of effort devoted to the work of reception. Any psychoanalyst and his analysand know how many hours of analytical labor are precursor to a psychic discovery. He would sympathize with the mathematician Henri Poincaré's description of the effort that goes into discovery:

> For fifteen days I strove to prove that there could not be any functions like those I have since called Fuchsian functions. I

was then very ignorant; every day I seated myself at my work table, stayed an hour or two, tried a great number of combinations, and reached no results. One evening, contrary to my custom, I drank black coffee and could not sleep. Ideas rose in crowds; I felt them collide until parts interlocked, so to speak, making a stable combination. By the next morning I had established the existence of a class of Fuchsian functions, those which come from the hypergeometric series. I had only to write out the results, which took but a few hours. (36)

Poincaré would not have reached his discovery without many hours of labor. Nor would he have achieved this breakthrough if he had not tolerated his ignorance, which I liken in the psychoanalytic situation to the capacity to tolerate not knowing what one is doing, so that uncertainty becomes a useful feature to the private work of the receptive process.[4]

Poincaré's illustration of that internal combinatory process describes the inner *sense* that one has of the embryonic form of a generative structure, which in his case resulted in his discovery of Fuchsian functions, and which for the psychoanalyst announces itself as a particular type of interpretation that becomes a psychically seminal vision: a condensation of many trial ideas and explorations of thought now cohered into a germinal point of view that generates new perspectives.

Trauma and the Search for Negative Qualia

A psychoanalyst and his patient could cumulatively construct traumatic psychic structures if they collected material to support a perspective that only repeated itself. Analytic work may sometimes have to be this way for a while; for example, in the case of interpretive work about certain patients' grandiosity in which the analyst must repeatedly confront

4. See *The Shadow of the Object* for a discussion of the receptive process, and also the work of Peter Thomson.

the analysand. At least the psychoanalyst will be aware that such interpretations may be recurrently traumatic to the patient and relentlessly resisted, before nucleating, if ever, into genera. Certain analysands are for a long time only traumatized by psychoanalysis, a fact which must be respected and which inevitably invites us to continuously rethink technique.

Psychic genera worked on in a psychoanalysis are the outcome of the mutual contribution of analyst and patient —a reflection of the patient's life instincts such that, in spite of resistances, he can unconsciously specify a complex of work that must be accomplished in order to achieve a significant new perspective that will enhance living. Unconscious recognition of the areas of such work motivates receptive action. Memories, instinctual representations, self experiences, and dreams that relate to the inner complex gravitate toward it in unconscious and preconscious holding areas. Their diverse but specific structure gives each potential genera its feel.

"Wordsworth had to grope along the grains of the language," writes Seamus Heaney, "to find the makings of a music that would render not so much what Hopkins called the inscape as the instress of things, known physically and intuitively at such times" (47). Incubating genera creates, in my view, such an "instress" which can be felt and which guides the subject's graspings among objects as he intuitively shapes his own spirit out of receptive intelligence.

The "work" of trauma will be to collect disturbing experience into the network of a traumatic experience (now a memory and unconscious idea) while the play work of genera will be to collect units of received experience that interanimate toward a new way of perceiving things.

An individual may, however, struggle with traumatic inner constellations and, by transformations of the trauma into works of art, achieve a certain mastery over the effect of trauma. The view that the artist transforms trauma and psychic pain into an artistic object is a common psychoanalytic perspective on the nature of creativity. And an individual may indeed work on a trauma to transform its psychic status by developing from it a new psychic structure that establishes a new perspective. Thus genera can and do emerge from the play work devoted to the transformation of psychic pain and traumatic perspectives.

But in psychoanalysis we find many persons who collect negative qualia around traumatized areas of the self, just as we find patients who seek experiences that though psychically painful are nonetheless essential to the formation of genera. A trauma-evolving person, or an individual living episodes of experience from this position, will seek negative qualia in objects and experiences. He will either find unpleasant or disturbing objects and experiences or he will transform potentially positive qualia into negatives. Hence, the object relations of each action will partly reflect the nature of the unconscious work being employed. A person who unconsciously develops a first-stage impingement into a full trauma will collect negative qualia into an ever-nucleating condensation that may intensify until the point of conscious emergence, when the subject is deeply disturbed by the eruption of the accumulated disturbed contents. The full trauma may be released into experiencing by a dream, an event, or a person. An individual who cultivates genera seeks objects and experiences that yield positive qualia, although positive here does not mean optimistic, good, or conflict-free, but something that will link with and possibly elaborate the psychic material that is incubating into a new vision.

Indeed, genera have no moral value, as it were, and a person could cultivate inner psychic structures and visions that others would find aesthetically, politically, or socially repellent. To distinguish genera from trauma one must ask only if the individual is free to organize the data of life into new visions that change the meaning of existence, a continuing process of discovery, or, as in the case of trauma, whether the person is organizing the material of life in a repetitive way, one aim of which is to denude the ego of a creative play upon the stuff of existence.

A trauma-seeking patient will unconsciously sabotage the analytic work by seeking negative qualia, either by distorting the analyst's remarks, by turning the generative comments into destructive ones, or by spoiling some of the analyst's internal states. For example, a patient "abused" as a child by parents who prematurely involved him in their conflict and in their sexual life—by inappropriately disclosing things to him—was afraid of his own capacity to destroy the other's peace of mind by attacking the other's mental life, thus feeling ultimately rejected because the other would depart in hurt or horror, leaving the patient guilty and furious. This only became clear after some time in the analysis when I examined certain countertransferences I had and linked them to the patient's transferences. I found that the patient, who knew some people I also knew in the analytical world, would often—in passing—say nasty, gossipy things about these people, for a moment affecting my internal representations. Did X really do that to his wife? I wondered. Did Y really say that about Z to W? I puzzled. Such slight shocks were not lasting, but one day the patient came to the hour and mentioned a play about psychoanalysis which he knew I was interested in: he also knew that I was to review it, but that I had not yet seen it. "Well, I have seen the play and it was just awful and my friend, A, who reviews for *The Times*, thought it was an intellectual sham and bogus drama. I wonder what you will make of it when you view it." For the moment I felt as if this play had been spoiled in advance of my seeing it. I was mildly irritated. In a separate moment in the same session, the patient reported an irrational fear that I was going to peremptorily end the analysis. I said that he was unconsciously inviting me to have my internal representation of the play damaged just as his internal world was spoiled by envy and rivalry.

The patient understood the interpretation and spoke of his inclination to damage his relationships by isolating features of the other person or by remembering only unpleasant experiences, thus collecting part experiences into a traumatic gestalt. As he did this he was aware of an inner sensation, associated with such spoilings, linked to anal mental contents that found expression through certain interactional processes.

From this perspective we may argue that the inner mental sensation associated with spoiling is the emotional climate of his traumatic thinking: specifically the feeling image derived from the search for damaging experiences. The individual who contributes to genera, however, seems to have a different psychic library, generated by the mental feeling derived from the creative effort of thought. Such an internal object may be associated by the person with the search for meaning or truth or beauty, and perhaps it is simultaneously an objectification of a frame of mind and its internal presence.

Indeed, a person who is at play with a life issue is constantly contributing to the generative internal object. The scientist at work on a task contributes new data and new observations to the generative internal object each day of his life, adding to the compositional shape of such an internal structure. No contribution to solving a scientific problem, to the final product of a poem, or to the designing of a car engine is lost on the unconscious.

The "Feel" of Genera

Scientists, poets, composers, and other people involved in creative efforts of thought have mental representations of the singular effort of mind brought to bear on their tasks. Most of them "see" an abstraction of the problem and its solution, even though it has not yet arrived. I wonder if this internal abstract picture—more an endopsychic graph—is the presence of an internal object, as defined by Hinshel-wood: an internal object (rather than an internal represen-tation) is the presence of a structure that is mentally sensed. An individual who is at play work on a genera would, then, have a "sense" of an internal object's "constitutional evolu-tion," formed by the psychic gravity of multiformal process-ings of units of experience cohering into a nucleus of potential meaning movements. Heaney writes: "It is that whole creative effort of the mind's and body's resources to bring the meaning of experience into the jurisdiction of form" (47). This "coming together" of many separate factors, a condensation building around a convergence of issues in life, would naturally sponsor a sense of itself as a psychic numen. One would feel this as a kind of familiar force of psychic gravity attracting ideas, questions, and play work and constituting a place of creativity. A person who is concentrating the issues of life, or some of them, into a trauma, on the other hand, might well have an internal object that is the place of such work, to which he turns for traumatic networking, and the psychic sensation involved would be disturbed, as if one were playing a mad internal drum.

Einstein's conceptualization of creativity is perhaps the best-known description of the internal object as inner ref-erence point. "The words or the language, as they are written or spoken, do not seem to play any role in my mechanism of thought," writes Einstein. "The psychical entities which seem to serve as elements in thought are certain signs and more or less clear images which can be 'voluntarily' repro-duced and combined" (43).

Sometimes a single word or phrase may serve as a locational sign of this internal object to which one may turn. Hart Crane writes: "It is as though a poem gave the reader as he left it a single, new *word*, never before spoken and impossible to actually enunciate, but self-evident as an active principle in the reader's consciousness henceforward" (182). This is a kind of evocative psychic genera, achieved through the work of the poem (a structure) and changing the poet's vision of reality. I shall, however, not be exploring this interesting aspect of the formation of genera, when—as with Hart Crane—we encounter an evocative object that is apparently not the result of our own inner labor, but which nonetheless is inspiring and seemingly introjected as a psychic structure that sponsors important new visions. The best moments in any person's formal education are composed of just such evocative occasions when an object (a theory, another perspective) radically alters one's way of imagining reality. I think it is highly likely, however, that such introjective epiphanies are the outcome of substantial unconscious work that preceded them.

"My own experience of inspiration," writes Stephen Spender, "is certainly that of a line or a phrase or a word of sometimes something still vague, a dim cloud of an idea which I feel must be condensed into a shower of words" (118). This "dim cloud of an idea" which Spender condenses into "a shower of words" brings to mind Freud's theory of the dream work, as a condensation of all the elements relevant to psychic life (instincts, affects, memories, existential experiences) which may be the prototype of all creative discoveries. The construction of a genera is somewhat akin to dream work, as we unconsciously labor to receptively condense many phenomena into a psychic structure that will eventually disclose and disseminate itself. It is less an effort of representational thought, more an act of *operational intelligence*. Lyotard reminds us that Freud says the dream work "does not think, calculate or judge in any way at all; it restricts itself to giving things a new form" (20). To Lyotard the thoughtless movement of condensation is desire, desire in its essence, prior to any derivative representation. By collapsing words into things, condensation becomes a thing of sorts—an inner thing—that is the inchoate movement of desire. "The 'language' of the unconscious is not modeled on articulated discourse, which, as we know, finds utterance according to a language. Rather, the dream is the acme of the inarticulate deconstructed discourse from which no language, even normal, is entirely free" (33). So too with the receptive process, those inner workings, prearticulate yet gravitational, compelling yet silent, until the day when suddenly the mind is inspired to new visions.

Perhaps genera are what Wordsworth means by a "fructifying virtue." "There are in our existence spots of time / Which with distinct preeminence retain / A fructifying virtue" (51), a creative force emanating from a very particular moment in one's ontology. "There exists / A virtue which irradiates and exalts / All objects through all intercourse of sense" (67), such a virtue the disseminative spirit of a generative part of the self. If the theory of repression embraces a concept of ultimate expression, in the ideas of the return of the repressed and in sublimation, the received unconscious finds expression through the development of psychic structures that come into consciousness in a shower of disseminative energy. The ego is not working to disguise genera; it is using displacement, substitution, and symbolization as part of the *jouissance* of representation.

I think of imagist theory, which Heaney believes yields a "sense of that which presents an intellectual and emotional complex in a moment of time" (89). Baudelaire, Poe, Rimbaud, Pound (and one could go on) believed that the image concentrated life into it. Wordsworth's "spots of time," Einstein's "signs," Spender's "dim clouds," or anyone's inner image of psychic procreativity serves as a kind of internal point of reference of that highly complex protean vision waiting to be born, raised, and articulated.

Each of us will, then, refer ourselves to particular inner images that indicate the psychic gravity of work taking place at a deeply unconscious level. Note how Henry Moore describes his inner place of psychic labor:

This is what the sculptor must do. He must strive continually to think of, and use form in its full spatial completeness. He gets the solid shape, as it were, inside his head—he thinks of it, whatever its size, as if he were holding it completely enclosed in the hollow of his hand. He mentally visualizes a complex form from all round itself: he knows while he looks at one side what the other side is like; he identifies himself with its centre of gravity, its mass, its weight; he visualizes its volume, as the shape that the shape displaces in the air. (74)

Although Moore's internal object seems concrete, like a sketch of a particular piece of sculpture, it is in fact the representation of sculptural form itself. It is a way of collecting in a psychic place the individual sculptor's nascent shaping of an actual object, a process that begins with a dynamic inner form.

Moore's object for the psychic location of inner creative work is somewhat unusual; many creative people depict their inner creations as taking place in a less than lucid space. No doubt each person chooses a metonym that ultimately signifies the place of genera even though it does not depict the process itself.

The Poetics of Psychic Structure

Few writers have described the anguish of constructing a generative internal structure as well as Paul Valéry. Like many creative people, he says that chaos, or "disorder in the condition of the mind's fertility" (106), is the internal feel of this phase of work, something which may correspond in the psychoanalytical situation to the bewildering intersections of the patient's and analyst's free associations.

Valéry says that we wish for an inner experience that assembles disorder into structure. I do not think he believes it is only a wish, but a recurring fact which, perhaps because of its comparative rarity, elicits our desire: "Sometimes what we wish to see appear to our minds . . . is like some precious object we might hold and feel through a wrapping of cloth that hides it from our eyes. It is and it is not ours, and the least incident may reveal it. . . . We demand it, being faced with some peculiar combination of elements all equally immanent to the mind" (101). Are these wrappings layers of preconscious membrane that protect unconscious workings from premature consciousness, thus heightening Valéry's sense that the internal object in question is both his and not his?

Even while rooting about among pregenerational ideas, we sense which image, sound, movement, or feeling promises to become part of a generative conceptualization as we "grope along the grains" of experience. In conversation with Aaron Copland, Harold Clurman asked if composers played a measure over and over, testing out ideas. Copland replied that it might seem dull, but even if you repeat an idea "you have a different idea of where it will go. It is the process of saying, how will this first idea inspire me toward the next one." John-Steiner writes: "Composing thus emerges as a process which demands—as do other forms of creative endeavor—an ability to synthesize germinal ideas into elaborative structures" (157). This description of musical structure is a useful illustration of how genera work, involving elaborations which continue throughout a lifetime. Always "there" for use, genera, like a composer's protean visions, remain in mind for re-usings.

Germinal ideas may only make themselves felt in the process of articulation. Picasso writes: "The picture is not thought out and determined beforehand, rather while it is being made it follows the mobility of thought" (57). It is a commonplace for artists to state, quite sincerely, that the work seems to arise of its own accord. As Amy Lowell writes: "A common phrase among poets is, 'it came to me.' So hackneyed has this become that one learns to suppress the expression with care, but really it is the best description I know of the conscious arrival of a poem" (110). Perhaps this is an additional reason why the writer, musician, or painter consciously feels that the created object is its own creator.

"In the very essence of poetry there is something indecent," writes Czeslaw Milosz in *Ars Poetica*. "A thing is brought forth which we didn't know we had in us, / so we blink our eyes, as if a tiger had sprung out / and stood in the light, lashing his tail" (3). As we contain many generative structures, often conceived through long hours of labor, the moment of original impregnation unknown to us, it is little wonder that such inner resources should seem so surprising, and yet our unconscious commitment to producing them—or, more accurately, to their production of us—remains undaunted. This containment of so many semi-autonomous psychic workings may be one of the reasons why writers or philosophers are disenchanted with the notion of a unified self. This view is not simply a postmodernist position. It was well put in 1915 by the Portuguese poet Fernando Pessôa: "I feel multiple. I am like a room with innumerable fantastic mirrors that distort by false reflections one single pre-existing reality which is not there in any of them and is there in them all." We can imagine what it is like if a person does not have a sense of an integrated self, as genera then might be cultivated by split-off portions of the personality, leading toward a powerful sense of fragmented multiple personalities. Pessôa continues: "I feel myself living alien lives, in me, incompletely, as though my soul shared in all human beings, incompletely, through a sum of non-'I's' synthesized in an afterthought 'I' " (5).

But perhaps these alien lives are the seemingly independent creatures of genera, that unconscious that "lives" inside us, is part of us, but sponsors ideas, images, and feelings which "we" often find disturbing and wish we didn't have. These are the "dark embryos" of thought that T. S. Eliot described as "a something germinating in [the poet] for which he must find words" (in Heaney, 70). Why are they alien? Perhaps because psychic structures feel mysterious. More akin to what René Char termed the "increate real," genera cannot be found in the external world and possess no material actuality, although paintings, poems, musical compositions, and other forms of art express such internal processes. But such psychic gravities are profoundly real to us.

Steps in the Formation of Genera

1. The conception of an inner space devoted to the formation of a generative psychic structure is likely to be the outcome of an unconscious protean moment when lived experience evokes intense psychic interest that constellates initially around the evoked ideas, feelings, and self states and gels into a form of unconscious desire for "its" evolution.

2. The nascent unconscious ideas, feelings, or self states constitute a psychic gravity that draws to it relevant data.

3. The unconscious collection of hundreds of links to the psychic complex gives rise to inner senses of generative chaos.

4. Chaos is tolerated, indeed facilitated, as the subject knows it is essential to the process of discovering new concepts about living.

5. Gradually chaos yields to a preformative sense of emergent nucleation. It is important to stress that this is only a sense, but it does reflect a process of structural cohesion.

6. Suddenly the person discovers a fundamentally new perspective that generates many derivatives. This new vision is not the genera, but it is the first manifestation of its presence in consciousness and it will sponsor many new ways of seeing oneself, others, and one's work.

7. This moment will often feel revelatory, and although

it is a special experience it is not an occasion for a new theory of the sacred, but it does describe those seminal visions created by unconscious processes pushed by the life instincts, and is an erotics in form.

Intuition

Is it surprising that a generative internal object should provide us with a heightened mental capability? As we construct the skeleton of such an internal process, doesn't it enhance our perception as we go along? As the dreamer finds his first dream images to represent his dream thoughts, doesn't the dream content crystallize further imaging as its narrative structure becomes more plausible, bringing to it further condensation?

This seems obvious to me. A poet or scientist or musician begins with a notional sense of an undeveloped and inarticulate task. At first the ideas generated are trials, some seeming about right, others not so. In time, a set of ideas or representations feels more correct and as these ideas set in, they give back to the scientist, poet, or musician an increasingly specific vision of his object world, attuned to seeing things now with an enhanced eye.

What is this ability that derives from the incremental cohesion of a mental structure set up to think an as yet inarticulated idea? Is this not what we mean by a sense of intuition: the sense we have of where to look, what to look at, and how to look at it? Derived from the Latin *intuitus*, the past participle of *intueor*, to look at, its root suggests that intuition is a looking at or viewing of a phenomenon. Webster defines it as "the direct knowing or learning of something without the conscious use of reasoning; immediate apprehension or understanding."

What if we look upon intuition as an unconscious skill at least partly derived from the construction of genera? After the filmmaker makes his first film, or the author writes his first novel, comes an increased intuitional sense in the nature of such creations and in time this inner sense assists them in developing a special intelligence for work within this area. Build genera and out of such construction you get a new sense, enabling you to "feel about for the solution to life problems." Such feeling about is not an occult or mystical act, but a form of desire derived from the unconscious multimodal work of the different areas of the self acting upon an issue or problem. It is the sense of the pathway toward a revelation in one's perception.

Perhaps the sense of intuition is our preconscious experience of the ego's intelligent work, leading us to consciously authorize certain forms of investigation in thought which are not consciously logical but which may be unconsciously productive. It may emerge as a particularly strong factor in our decision making in ratio to the successful nucleation of a genera. "Prior to the writing of the poems I tried to have a sense of key areas that I'm watching, that are beginning to evolve as points I must know about," says Gary Snyder. These points may be similar to preconsciously understood areas of work in a psychoanalysis. "And poems will flow out of those in time," he adds, to which we may add that generative interpretations emerge in a psychoanalysis in like manner. An interviewer has asked Snyder if the genesis of his poems arrives from note taking or particular observations of reality. "I listen to my own interior mind-music closely," he replies, which may remind some readers of Freud's description of the multi-locular sense, derived from internal perceptions. "Most of the time there's nothing particularly interesting happening," he continues, "but once in a while I hear something which I recognize as belonging to the sphere of poetry. I listen very closely to that." Isn't there an equally special area in the mind of the psychoanalyst who listens differently, so that now and then he recognizes something that belongs to the sphere of psychoanalysis? (I should add, however, that such recognitions would derive from unconscious play work already long since applied to prior patient communications.) The interviewer asks Snyder if what he hears comes from "inside," and the poet replies, "But it's coming from outside, if you like. Maybe I have a radio receiver planted in my spinal cord" (284–85). A poet and the founder of psychoanalysis both use the metaphor of a radio receiver to address a particular form of listening, which in my view is the work of the intuitional part of the mind, one that knows how to receive messages (or significations) if it has crystallized points of attraction from a collection of psychic nodes that I term genera.

The fact that intuition seems to be an immediate knowing should not obscure the fact that it is the outcome of a sustained concentration of many types of unconscious and conscious thinking. Perhaps the inclination to differentiate intuition from reason is intended to stress the apparently effortless side to it. Working at an issue diligently in one's laboratory, studio, or consulting room is often hard work. How different intuitions seem, as first we follow an unreasoned hunch or clue, then we become deeply absorbed in it as it feels increasingly correct to us, and then suddenly we discover a new way of looking at, conceiving, or producing something. No wonder this process is subject to our mystifications. Perhaps we would like it to remain unlooked at; intuitive procedures seem so successful because they apparently exist outside of consciousness.

I would argue that intuition is a form of desire associated with the ego's notion of what to look at, what to look for, and how to do both beneficially. This sense is partly derived from the structure that evolves out of a multiformal contributing to the generative internal object from the many different types of self experience over a long period of time and owes much to that intelligence involved in the ego's selection of forms through which the subject's idiom may find its articulation. Our association of intuition with unintentionality and the irrational is testimony to the need for a relaxed nonvigilant effort of integration in the subject. Intuition works as successfully as it does precisely because the subject thinking in this way does not see what he is working on and what he is working with. In this respect, its strength rests upon its hiddenness. It may be so successful, then, because the intuiting person is unconsciously able to explore lines of investigation that would meet with incredulous disapproval if he were fully conscious of what was being considered.

Perhaps in time we will give increased attention to the self experience and mental processes involved in intuition. The fact that such inner proceedings are themselves the object of many convergent projective identifications—to which people assign magical wishes—should not deter us from investigating an important feature of unconscious life, particularly as it is such an important part of psychoanalytic experiencing. For although it is true that the analyst's evenly hovering attentiveness allows him to achieve a type of disciplined dispassion, much of his internal rendering of analysis depends on his intuitive capability.

Composed of the psychoanalyst's capacity to follow internal sensings when listening to the patient's material, such feelings are responsive to the subtle exercise of forms of experience and modes of expression in the analysand. Patient and analyst develop between them internal objects specific to the mutual processing of this self (analyst or patient) with this other (analyst or patient) in this particular place (the psychoanalysis). Just as a ship is constructed for sailors to sail the seas, or instruments are crafted in order to play music, patient and analyst construct internal objects to process the analysis.

As the patient conveys to the analyst the nature of his self (and objects), he uses differing forms of experience and modes of expression to represent his being. If he uses the iconic and verbal categories rather than the gestural, affective, and sonic, he conveys a perceptual structure with a particular character that will usually evoke structurally specific self experiences in the analyst. In this case, the analyst's visual and verbal abilities would be used, and his gestural, affective, and sonic capacities would not be directly played upon by the patient, although, of course, such categories would have their own independent existence. In other words, the analyst would feel his affects, move gesturally, perhaps convey elements of himself in his sound cadences, but not in dialogue with the patient.

Naturally the specific idiomatic contents processed in each category are communicated to the analyst, who builds pictures of, words about, feelings for, and somatic responses to the analysand. In time many factors contribute to a multilectical sensing of the analysand, which forms internal objects in the analyst and the patient that come to constitute core areas for the reception of and mulling over of the many contributions of both persons to the analysis.

An analysis is a creative process involving two subjectivities at work on overlapping tasks, and analytical genera are formed as shared internal structures. The respective significance of such complexes to the two persons will naturally differ; for the analyst such devotions are unconsciously sought after as part of his creative work with a particular patient, while such internal objects become part of the analysand's mental structure. But the psychic structure that will evolve out of psychoanalysis is the result of such a collaborative effort and its desires.

The Dreams of Psychoanalysis

The psychoanalyst and the patient construct a complex network of thinkings derived from a sequential multitude of categories of self experience, and over time play work condenses such thinkings into a structure (a complex) that has psychic gravity and desires further data that now serve both persons as a shared internal object. Such a psychic structure in analysis is homologous to the creation of dream content which is the result of a similar play work during the day when the person transforms "undigested facts" into psychic material. The unconscious scanning[5] occurs before sleep and reflects the dialectic between hermeneutic searching and aleatory evocativeness, as meaning meets up with chance to create psychic news. At night the dreamer nucleates many dream ideas (feelings, memories, day observations, theories, somatic urges) into condensed images which form a complex of ideas that work symbolically to bind the many contributing factors into a structure that may now generate new meanings.

This view suggests that the dream work, the factors working to assemble the dream in the first place, is as significant as either the meaning it yields or the experience it provides. If many different categories of self experience are utilized in the processing of life units, then many different modes of representation will be at work in the collecting of the dream. Dream content expresses a process begun long before the dream event—indeed, well before sleep. During the day a person's experiences are unconsciously assembled into different mental holding areas, incubating associative nuclei that evoke memories, serve to release instinctual drives, and satisfy the person's need to have "senses" of self. All these factors are none other than overdeterminants converging upon such clusters of assembled experiences to form increasingly condensed (psychically "weighty") internal states.

As the day proceeds, as new episodes accrue in these inner clusters, the condensed nucleations of experience sponsor a dream potential: psychic material has been gathered for dream experience. Do we need the dream to represent the condensing procedure? Has it become a type of ego excitation that needs discharge? If the individual cannot dream such

5. See Ehrenzweig, *The Hidden Order of Art.*

"dark embryos," then such work may need an alternative form of expression. Is the creative act, such as writing poetry, painting, composing music, an alternative means of releasing nucleations into representation? Is it also possible that psychotic hallucinations are violently radical means of releasing such internal objects, perhaps because the psychotic cannot use the dream experience to positive effect, and cannot find in creative work, or human relations, equally satisfying representations of the condensations of life gathered into nucleated internal objects?

In a psychoanalysis the clinician uses an intuitive sense to receive, play with, and work upon the patient's transferential actions, narrative contents, and free associations. When he claimed that psychoanalyst and analysand were on mutual wavelengths of the unconscious, transmitter (patient) to receiver (psychoanalyst), Freud suggested that analyst and analysand were in unconscious communication with one another.

This suggestive idea has played a considerable role in the clinical work of psychoanalysts in the British School of Psychoanalysis, who, through the concepts of projective identification and countertransference, have elaborated the methodological implications of Freud's statement. The patient unconsciously acts upon the analyst, as either a direct or a disguised internal object, or upon his actual internal world. If the psychoanalyst is aware of an inner affective and ideational shaping of his internal world which seems specific to clinical work with a particular patient, he may postulate that this shaping indicates his patient's projective identifications. Through a sustained self analysis the clinician works upon his own states of mind to see what object world the analysand is soliciting.

Although some British clinicians overuse the view that all patients' narrative content is an extended metaphor of the patient-analyst relation, this perspective nonetheless contributes to an important psychic capacity within the psychoanalyst. If we take the position that narrative content is a metaphor of the patient's internal state, then when listening to even rather ordinary material we find that it assumes a potential allegorical significance. Common statements such as "I am going to the cleaner's after the session" or "I can't stand the rain today" become encoded voices of unconscious states of mind (i.e., "I am going to have to clean the analytic shit off me after the session" or "I cannot bear your reigning over me anymore").

To use the metaphoric potential of an analysand's narrative content, the analyst must allow himself an imaginative inner play. His associations elaborate the patient's discourse, as narrative episodes sponsor the clinician's imaginings. Sometimes his associations are further displacements of the patient's latent thoughts. But even if the inner elaboration of a displacement moves the analyst further away from the latent thought, at the same time the derivative suggests its origins. In time, as the analyst elaborates the patient's displacements or defenses through his own inner associations, the structure of this elaboration will sometimes suggest the architecture of the defended latent contents. Unlike the patient, who is often dynamically driven not to discover such latent thoughts, the analyst is professionally motivated to find them, which in some respects he will do by collaborating with the analysand's wishes and defenses through concordant internal associations which allow him to internally "feel" the outlines of the patient's emotions, internal objects, ego defenses, and unconscious ideas. By internally elaborating a defense or by further articulating a signifier, the analyst follows the clues released through such associations to their points of origin.

It is difficult to describe how I listen to the analysand within the session. The endless slide of words, signifiers that evoke limitless associations just as they suggest specific links that imply precise meaning, the images that bring me to a formed world in that strange intimacy of co-imagining. Often patients indicate through diction texture, hesitation, body state, and expectation those moments in a session that are of particular significance. Most people take five to fifteen minutes to "settle in" to the hour, a devolution of socially adaptive wishings assisted by analytical silence. Then something happens. The patient is "in" the analysis. One analysand put it well: "This is the only place where I can hear myself speak." When the analysand reaches this place, he brings the analyst into deeper rapport with him, as the core mood of the hour rather naturally casts off prior rationalizations or defensive diversions.

How do we know such moments which Dennis Duncan calls "the feel of the session"? Is it possible to gain this understanding through psychoanalytic training? Certainly it helps when we learn how to be quiet and listen. Is knowledge of this ability to be found in the texts on ego psychology or object relations or theories of the subject? How could it be? And yet, knowing how to follow the analysand's moods in the session—dispositions that punctuate the hour with significance—is one of the most important clinical skills the analyst can possess.

I think the ability to move into the meditative state of evenly hovering attentiveness, to receive and articulate projective identifications, to elaborate the narrative contents through inner free associations, and to follow the analysand's mood in the hour contributes to the psychoanalyst's intuitive grasp of the analysand. Certainly this is what Bion means by the analyst's reverie when he takes in the patient's communications, contains them, works unconsciously to transform them into sense, and gradually passes them back to the analysand for consideration.

By containing, processing, and elaborating the analysand through the procedures described above, now and then the clinician is aware of working on something without knowing what that something is or what it might eventually mean. *Analytic work at such a point is in some respects like the dream work before the dream scene.* But the unknown area of work does yield a sense of its presence, and certain thoughts, feelings, object representations, memories, and body states somehow seem to link with the task at hand. Whether the manifest issue is a patient's refusal to sleep with her husband or a fear of traveling on the Underground, these issues eventually signify a very deep form of psychic work that may lead to genera. If so, then the analyst is involved in the construction of a dream not dreamed before, but one that is nonetheless based on the patient's prior self experiencings and the analyst's contributions.

For weeks and months I work with a patient, listening to dreams and associations, dispersed by the polysemous riots of language, gathered by the glue of imagery, attending to sonic punctuations and gestural suggestions, that dense moving panoply of communicatings uttered by the analysand, and I in turn associate, am moved to discrete affective positions, constitute the analysand and his objects in my internal world made out of them and yet of my own creation, offer interpretations, pose questions, and abandon many, many ideas and views along the way. Yet in the midst of all that I usually feel that this patient and I are at work on something. Something beyond our consciousness yet unconsciously compelling. Something that seems to draw us to it, so that ideas, interpretations, and associations that feel off center of this inner pull are discarded. Something we know but as yet cannot think. Some interpretations, views, questions, feel more in touch with that unthought known area being worked on, even though they seem no more plausible than the abandoned ideas. But the objectifying processes available to the analyst and the patient's corrections and associative directedness help the analyst to follow an unseen path, feeling the way as he goes.

Three years into an analysis, following scores and scores of dreams, thousands of associations, hundreds of comments from me, a patient discovers the pleasure of differentiated sexual desire of the other. At this very moment she has also reached a considerable new peace of mind with her internal mother, whom she now sees in a different light. Memories are de-repressed. She finds a new sense of her father. Her work becomes more creative. And so on. A new psychic structure is secured and the analysand's life is changed. Although she felt that she now had a new insight, originally expressed as a sense of herself as attractive to men because she had felt inner peace with her father, this point of view only announced that a genera was now in place.

In the months preceding this "discovery" I knew my analysand was at work on an important internal task. I knew it involved the mother and the father, but her transferential uses of me (and my countertransferential states) were so subtle, shifting, and unconscious that I could only sense the workings of a use-movement that I believed was her form of ego creativity. As she worked upon her disturbed states of mind, naturally my analytical acumen was involved, and yet the entire process had an inner logic of its own which I sensed but only partly understood. Resistances, false self movements, intellectualizations, hypomanic defenses, projective identifications, were analyzed, yet without the patient's continued contribution of the psychic truth pertinent to her inner work, the development of a new psychic structure would never have been forthcoming.

If the dialectic between the analysand's transferences and the analyst's countertransferences, between the patient's narratives and the analyst's associations, between the analysand's linguistic specifications and the clinician's readings, between the patient's declarations and the clinician's questions—and one could go on and on, listing the binary pairs that structure the dialectic—can be viewed as the labor of two separate yet deeply involved unconscious subjectivities, then much of the work of a psychoanalysis is a kind of dream work. Mutually agreed-upon core interpretations are, then, the dreams of psychoanalysis, constructed more through the interlocking logics of an unconscious dialectic than from the secondary-process delivery of a white-clothed surgical intervention.

It suggests, furthermore, that the play of two subjectivities at work on the formation of psychoanalytic genera is often as much an act of deception and disguise as it is an effort of understanding. One is not referring to conscious deception but to the evasion of organized consciousness which somehow robs the work of its integrity. Patient and analyst, through the necessary destruction of free association, collapse, conflate, and condense one another's communicatings. Consciousness is casualty to unconscious discourse, which in my view operates through the laws of unconscious distortion, not so much evading censorship as eluding premature consciousness. As I shall discuss further, the irony is that the analyst's misunderstandings of his patient as well as the analysand's distortions of the clinician's meanings are as essential to the dream work of psychoanalysis as informed understanding.

5

The Psychoanalyst's Use of Free Association

Freud's first reference to an evenly suspended attentiveness occurs in the case of Little Hans in 1909 when he says, "It is not in the least our business to 'understand' a case at once: this is only possible when we have received enough impressions of it." To receive impressions, "we will suspend our judgement and give our impartial attention to everything there is to observe" (23). In 1912 he identifies the suspension of judgment as "not directing one's notice to anything in particular and in maintaining the same 'evenly suspended attention' . . . in the face of all that one hears" (111–12). He describes a psychic screen peculiar to the psychoanalyst that registers significant patterns arising from the wealth of impressions.

Patterns do not form themselves, and clearly what impressed Freud derived from his own formation of the material. A pluralist, sometimes he was convinced by the trauma of actual events, other moments by the unconscious thoughts behind such manifest narratives, frequently by the word presentations deriving from the images, at times by the instinctual urges that spoke through the objects of representation, and now and then by the patient's transference. His theory of overdetermination allows for a pluralist vision to dictate that no one truth ever exhaustively explains a phenomenon, a symptom, or a dream: a person's character bears many truths.

Each of Freud's perspectives became an ideational holding space collecting impressions derived from his clinical work. His theory of instincts received the analysand's resistance to, or expression of, body urges. Slips of the tongue were referred to his linguistic model. Childhood distresses to his theory of trauma. One could go on.

This chapter explores aspects of the psychoanalyst's inner experience while he is working with a patient. In the previous chapter I argued that the analyst and his patient engage in unconscious work that leads to the formation of particular psychic structures (genera) and toward the end of this chapter I provide a clinical example which I hope will partly illustrate this process. In particular, however, I focus on the analyst's use of his free associations, as I believe that unconscious communication is enhanced if the analyst can disclose to the analysand mental contents of his own that are still unconscious, but seem of particular—and spontaneous— relevance to the reported mental contents of the analysand. Naturally, parameters to this extension of analytical technique must be considered, and I shall begin by reflecting on the forms of objectivity in a psychoanalysis that should always partner the analyst's inner free play of ideas and feelings.

Objectivity in Psychoanalysis

A psychoanalyst's subjectivity cut loose from the requirements of objectifying frames of reference is not only a wild analysis but a denuded subjectivity, since the analyst's inner experiences are only meaningful upon "objective" reflection. The analyst must, however, allow for his own simple self experiencing, when he scatters the analysand's material and works upon it through his own disseminating subjectivity, transforming the analysand's "data" into his own psychic news. He makes the patient's material into his own, not simply by containing it (to use Bion's metaphor) but by distorting, displacing, substituting, and condensing it. For this is the work of the unconscious. At regular recurring moments, however, he is the complex self, reflecting on his psychical re-creation of the material, and using the objectifying perspectives of psychoanalysis to assist him in his organization of—not *the* material, but *their* material: patient and analyst.

Some would no doubt argue that one subject could never achieve self objectivity, so the idea of a psychoanalyst achieving an objective relation to his own associations would therefore be an impossibility. But each discipline in life must work within the parameters of its own generative subjectivity and its own meaningful objectivity, and psychoanalysis does indeed have a highly complex, interlaced network of objectifying criteria for the continued assessment of the patient's and the analyst's states of mind.

In the first place, we have the basic rules of psychoanalysis, laws which precede and will outlive the analytical couple, and to which we adhere. Whether classical, Kleinian, Kohutian, Lacanian, or Independent, analysts have inherited a system of processing the analytical couple, and its subjectivity, and this system, among other things, supports the essential rights of the patient's free association, the necessity of the analyst's moral neutrality, and a considerable canon of rigor which we label technique that calls upon the analyst to listen to the material in a consistent manner. Although these canons could become imposing ideologies forced upon the analysand, they are more often ideational structures that analysts learn and adopt and to which they adhere. In this respect they are to a considerable extent outside the analyst's personal history or subjectivity.

Second, analysts have varying ways of testing a patient's

response to interpretation. They frequently listen to the patient's comments following an analytical intervention, to see if the patient unconsciously confirms or disconfirms the comment. This is a highly complex appraisal, as the analyst also listens to the analysand's emotional response, indeed places himself in identification with the patient, to see how it feels to have received the interpretation. A feature of my own clinical theory is to practice a dialectics of difference (Bollas, 1989): when I have given a comment and the patient seems hesitant, or goes into a type of silence that feels to me to be compliant, I will say, "Perhaps you would put it differently," or "I think you disagree." This may not always feel agreeable to the analyst. Indeed, given the ordinary narcissistic investment in making interpretations an analyst may not actually feel like hearing the patient's deconstructions of the comment; all the more reason, it seems to me, for the analyst to have a working element of difference as part of his practice, to counter his own narcissistic investments in interpretation.

Several important checks should be available to correct the analyst's wayward subjectivities, although, arguably, even the wayward idea is potentially relevant as a derivative of a patient's communications. After an interpretation, when I may say, "You might put it differently," I benefit from the analysand's correction and subsequent associations. This is an invaluable resource in the use of one's inner senses of the patient's communications because the analyst checks these ideational trains of thought with the analysand's difference of view. Even if the patient's corrections serve as resistances (assuming for a moment that this is aimed at putting the analyst on the wrong track), we know that such defenses would only be compromise formations with psychic truth, which would eventually be established through the chains of association. The analysand's corrections of the analyst can be extremely important, however, when the analyst has indeed developed a serious misperception; for this reason encouraging the analysand to put things differently is an important factor in the analyst's use of his inner associations precisely because the patient is encouraged to correct the analyst.

The psychoanalyst can also assess his subjective states by objectifying the transference (asking himself who in the patient is speaking and to whom in the analyst and why at that time) and by objectifying the countertransference (asking what he is feeling and thinking or who and what this resonates with in the patient's internal world and why now). Another vector of objectification is observation of how the transference and the countertransference form, if they do, an object-relational dialogue, such as when the patient addresses the analyst as a critical father, thereby soliciting a chastened-child experience within the clinician. By identifying the transference, objectifying the countertransference, and analyzing the relation between the two, the analyst can partly assess the meaning of some of his inner associations.

Finally, the clinician is likely to have the patient's detailed and complex account of his personal history, which, although a myth, nonetheless contains screen-memory representations of the actual past which can serve to orient the analyst, who will, from time to time, reconstruct the patient's history in the light of information emerging from his associations. As such, the person's history will also serve to process the dense movement of associations in the analyst as he matches inner states (of ideas, feelings, etc.) with historical accounts.

It is important to keep in mind that such objectifying criteria are always available to the clinician and therefore allow the analyst to give free momentary participation to immersion in unconscious processes. In collaboration with the objectifying factors of the analysis, the clinician uses his associations, conjectures, fleeting ideas, affects, and hunches to foster his interventions. The patient responds. He corrects the analyst. Or he elaborates the clinician's comment. A dialectic is established and the outcome of a patient-analyst intervention is a compromise between the two respective participants' original comments, both of which have been destroyed through the dialectic.

It is a dialectic operating between two different mental dispositions, as the participants exchange the positions of simple and complex self. One moment the analysand lost in narrative thought is accompanied by his analyst, who is also immersed in the experience of listening. Another moment the analyst moves to a reflective, complex-self position before reassuming the experiencing state. On occasion the analyst is in a simple-self state, following trains of inner associative logic, while the patient is objectifying himself, perhaps telling the analyst what he thinks his prior associations mean. In time, as both participants work on the main issues that arise, the dialectic constructs an emerging inner picture of the issue. It is inaccurate to say it is a picture, as it does not represent the problem worked on, but it is a sense of the eventual picture, and this sense is in fact derived from that internal object that is nucleating as a special psychic area for the collective reception of data and the development of a perspective sufficient to generate the lasting insights created out of these types of personality change. Genera become sensible long before the insight arrives, they are usable before then, and can be felt through intuitive (i.e., unconscious) perception.

An intuitive sense develops with the subject's trust in and facilitation of play work, in which ideas, feelings, and hunches are encouraged as long as they feel correct or seem to be on the right track. It is exactly this route that I think psychoanalysts travel when analyzing their patients as long as such inner sources are constantly checked by the objectifying factors available to the clinician.

Free Association

I shall take it as a maxim that all psychoanalysts who are silent for long stretches of time freely associate to their patient's narrations.[1] The "impressions" Freud wrote of are not, of course, undisturbed imprints of the analysand's associations onto the *tabula rasa* of the analyst's mind. Such impressions are those units of narration elaborated by the psychoanalyst. No matter what the patient talks about, or indeed how on occasion the analyst consciously assembles meanings among the patient's narrations, the clinician elaborates these narrations with his associations.

Indeed, the analyst's imaginative elaboration of the patient's narrations is often less organized, more the stuff of the primary process, than the patient's more cohesive narrative, as the analysand—however free in his associating— is still burdened with the sensibleness of speech. To talk is to cohere. But the analyst is free to be quiet. Much of what he thinks is rendered in the world of absolute silence, in an internal world which further maximizes free play of ideas: images, words, feelings, somatic states, body affinities, jumble together in a moving chorus of psychic apprehension. We come, then, to an intriguing point. The patient, encumbered with the task of narrating the self, is restricted in his or her speakings, while the psychoanalyst is permitted a wider range of free inner associating.

Hedges has written of the many "listening perspectives" in psychoanalysis, and Pine has cogently described in *Drive, Ego, Object and Self* the four psychologies available to clinicians in their work. Although models of conflict and development

---

1. Several psychoanalysts have written about the analyst's use of his own associations. The most far-reaching, and interesting, in my view, is that by Peter Thomson. Duncan's paper "The Flow of Interpretation" (1989) sensitively addresses the analyst's and analysand's mutual effect in a session. McDougall writes elegantly and directly about interpretations that are spontaneous utterances (see *Theatres of the Mind*). Coltart, Symington, and Casement also illustrate the intelligent use of free subjective states in their work with patients.

are important to the psychoanalyst's understanding of the patient, they do not sufficiently process that dense complexity conveyed by the analysand. Why? Because both participants possess an unconscious. Even as we organize a particular unit of material through a specific model, we do so in part unconsciously. More importantly, our conscious considera- tion of the meaning of a communication (dream, narrative report, mood) is only a small part of the mental contents we possess, as we also think of many interpretations we do not give. In addition, we often have a natural inner dialogical reply to what a patient is saying (i.e., "Oh yeah? I wonder," "Oh no, poor you," etc.); we dwell on some of the patient's narrative images, we daydream, we are moved by subtly changing emotions. I find, for example, that I may be absorbed in revisualizing a dream fragment in the minutes following the patient's dream report, and, as the analysand continues to associate, I may be having what we might think of as a free-associative daydream, working on the patient's material through my own kind of dream work. As this takes place, another part of myself has all the time been split off, listening to the patient's associations, and when I emerge from my daydream I will recall what has been said and take a more objective listening position.

Furthermore, we often disappear from the world of thought itself, into what Bion refers to as "O," a state of meditation, in which we seem to have no particular thoughts. These moments of inner stillness are continuous intermis- sions in the otherwise mentally productive world of inner experience. So, how useful is our consciousness in the midst of such a dense opera of inner states? How do any of our models organize this? Unless we are to discard our theory of the unconscious I believe we must conclude that we are only ever marginally conscious of the meaning of our own inner states and even less conscious of the significance of the patient's communications.

Perhaps we can find new ways to utilize our subjectivity—

in particular those private mental contents, affects, and relational responses that contribute to our self experiencing in our clinical work. But what is the value of such association? To a limited extent the analyst's inner experience shadows the dreamer's associative elaborations of the dream material, only in this respect the analyst associatively elaborates the patient's presence and discourse. As the patient speaks, the psychoanalyst associates. As the patient struggles with the rhetorical burden of narration, the analyst is often lost in thought. The patient organizes the material; it breaks down in the analyst's mind as he or she disseminates it through psychic pathways, exactly as Freud did with his own dreams and those of his patients.

However we look at it, the analyst is not neutral when listening to a dream, and however many associations the dreamer provides, each analyst is prolific, with his own inner associations moving in a complex psychic symphony of feelings, image gazing, word deciphering, recollecting, interpersonal assessments, story hearing, and meditative intermissions. Even if the analyst thinks much of such inner associating is lucid, it is not. The very laws of inner speech and internal representation mean that these associations are themselves condensations of prior work accomplished within the analysis. Our grasp of the patient's psychic reality is only partly thinkable, its logic more akin to the nature of poetry and music than to abstract thought or, to use the psychoanalytical term, the secondary process.

When the patient tells a dream, the analyst is "given" images to see in his mind's eye. He is also given something of a story and is a kind of reader. The dream report may convey the dreamer's affects, some of which will be felt by the analyst. Any dream report always evokes the analyst's curiosity, as he is now also partly a detective sifting through the clues provided by the manifest contents. He contracts a linguist part of himself to decipher word presentations, just as he delegates a part of himself to be the historian, collecting the dream into the many reconstructed contexts. An infant observer, he notes where, how, if at all, the dream expresses the infantile, just as the transference interpreter listens to the dream as an expression of the patient's experience of the analyst. Thus the analyst is moved by a dream report to many places within himself, rather like a psychic factory with a division of labor essential to the final construction of a dream interpretation.

However, if inner free experiencing is only partly thinkable, it is nonetheless the basis of our self experience and hence the inner foundation of thought. Inside us at any moment, but especially during intense units of experience, and usually when engaged with an object, we are "guided" by inner constellations of unconsciously organized psychic apprehensions which are part of a continuous, asymmetrical, creative response to the world.

In the psychoanalytical relationship there is a partnership of two persons who divide an important task but who often think in fundamentally different ways, at least when the one (the patient) is free-speaking and the other (the psychoanalyst) is free-experiencing. Fortunately each knows quite well the nature of this division, as sometimes the analysand's silence will be in the interest of free inner associating and the psychoanalyst will on occasion "make" an interpretation which of necessity is a secondary-process formation designed to be clear, sensible, psychological, and of a rational use to the patient.

But what of that vast cumulative inner experiencing in the analyst? Are there any ways in which this information can be placed before the analysand, particularly when such deep inner experiencing seems to sponsor thoughts which to the analyst feel relevant to the analysand's free speech? Perhaps to appreciate the *technical place* of this issue it is as well to see if other interventions by the analyst partly derive from his unconscious.

When a patient reports a dream and then exhausts the

associations, I often ask for associations to a specific dream image. Isolating a psychically specific object, like a dream image, often yields more unconscious information than the patient's association to the entire dream, where resistance is encountered, especially when the analysand tries to interpret the dream. I also seek day residue, questioning the patient about what happened on the day of the dream. Patients usually understand the spirit of the question and sometimes unconsciously recover the signifying day events. If the analysand speaks euphemistically about an event—i.e., "I had a horrible conversation with my sister"—and does not elaborate, I sometimes ask, "What was horrible?" or just "Horrible?"

I ask these questions because I lack sufficient information from my analysand, but in selecting a dream object (and leaving other props out), in asking for a clarification at one point in a session (and not at other equally possible moments), I work from a preconscious area within myself, where as yet I do not know why I pose these particular questions at their particular time and it is arguable that I am requesting more material for my own inner experiencing.

Most analysands become aware of the ongoing separate subjectivity of the psychoanalyst which is announced, as it were, through his questions, comments, and interpretations. Naturally, questions must be as infrequent as possible, as the analysand needs unhindered freedom of speech. So I usually do not pose them when the patient's free speech is in dynamic movement, when, that is, the analysand seems to be developing psychic material, or an insight, or a resistance.

In time the patient appreciates the analyst's focus on a dream or narrative object, as it releases further psychic elaboration. The psychoanalytic partnership becomes *unconsciously collaborative*. If the analyst's question sponsors a resistance in the patient, this needs careful scrutiny, as the reason for such opposition would need to be clear. Even on those frequent occasions when the analysand's subseqent remarks are elaborating resistances to the grain of psychic truth enunciated by the clinician, such resistances serve as compromised articulations that indicate the scope of such truth, by virtue of the network of denials, rationalizations, isolations of affect, and so forth. So too for the equally frequent false self compliances with the analyst when the patient may, among other things, try to elaborate the analyst's associations. In time the patient's true conviction—and corrections—of the analyst will emerge, if the psychoanalyst is relatively at ease with the inevitable errors he will make and is eager to hear from the patient's true self. If the patient's association to the analyst's questions are merely confirmatory and not dynamically elaborative, then it is likely that the analyst's question was not unconsciously in tune with the patient, and he may need to indicate that he can see that he has encouraged an effort of thought on the patient's part which was clearly not close to the core of what was internally significant to the patient at that moment.

Errors convey to the analysand the uncomfortable truth that the psychoanalyst's interpretive work is always flawed, and as analysts appreciate this they possess differing techniques which allow for the correction of error, misstatements, or "not quite right" formulations of the analysand's communication, which interestingly enough become a reliable matrix for use: in this case, something which is useful because it is wrong and serves the interest of a more accurate representation. Further, the analysand gains greater experience of the analyst's sensibility (his very particular way of working), and although this may lead to the disappointing realization that the analyst does not know everything (a powerful infantile wish in the analysand), it increases the patient's unconscious sense of the nature of human communication. The patient-analyst relationship is inevitably dialectical, as each participant destroys the other's perception and rhetorical rendering of events, to create that third intermediate object, a synthesis, that is owned by neither participant and objectifies the loss of omnipotent wishes to possess truth just as it situates the participants in that collaborative place from which the only analytically usable truth can emerge.

In time the psychoanalyst may decide to offer for mutual consideration something we could term a free association, as it is neither a question, clarification, confrontation, or interpretation. I believe the psychoanalyst's use of his inner associating to form a spoken intervention is far more widespread in analytical practice than has been acknowledged, such disclosed free associations being mistakenly named interpretations. When the psychoanalyst tells the analysand of a spontaneous thought or memory that he is having in response to the patient's material or presence, this is his *selective* disclosure of a free association. If he has assembled many associations and observations into a conscious understanding of the patient's material, this is an interpretation proper. But the disclosure of something that has just then occurred to him, that is not yet understood by him, that may prove to be of no lasting significance: this is a free association.

There are, of course, very important parameters to the disclosure of such inner associating. The fundamental rule, to my mind, is that reported associations should be related to the patient's material, to the transference, or to the emotional reality of the session. I most frequently disclose my associations when considering a patient's dream and its associations. Sometimes elements in a patient's dream and his associations remind me of a previous dream or session. What if the most "alive" material deriving through association occurs within the psychoanalyst? What if the patient is fairly stuck, or bogged down in listlessly adumbrated associations which in and of themselves fail to converge toward a meaningful area unless we include some image or memory evoked within the analyst? Is it not possible that the "missing link" lies in the analyst's mind, not in the patient's free association, so that when the analyst supplies this material something vitally missing (or split off) is now included? When this works, the patient recontacts his dream and the latent thoughts will eventually be as clear as they ever can be in this highly speculative work of ours. And later the analyst can consider exactly what it was that constituted the patient's resistance, or projection, and why it was put into or left to the clinician to facilitate the free-associative process.

It may be argued that the analyst should remain quiet to receive, contain, process, and interpret the unconscious factors operating the analysand's resistance. If the analyst feels this to be the case, then supplying an association would indeed cover over the analysand's underlying anxieties or depressions. But the analyst may feel that his inner association is, in fact, sponsored by the patient—part of the unconscious communications of the two participants—and if this is so, then speaking the spontaneous idea is partly to deliver the analysand's utterance.

When the patient struggles to work with my association or is only partly invested in it, I usually take it that I am out of touch and will often say something like "I've distracted you. Perhaps your thoughts take you elsewhere." Not surprisingly, my errors often sponsor the free-associative process by opposition, as if I have unwittingly provided a clear "untruth" to which the patient reacts, often revealing what is more truly the case.

I should make it clear that I always stress that reported associations are my own and not the same mental endeavors as interpretation proper when I aim to state something I believe to be true of the patient. I have found that partly because I am offering an association rather than putting an interpretation—and I do think there is an entirely different subjective state in the psychoanalyst during these two occasions—the patient is "freer" to use my associations, either as loci of collaborative elaboration or as forces for essential negation and developed opposition.

We do *make* interpretations, often as the outcome of

considerable intellectual synthetic work on the analyst's part, and inevitably as expressions of the psychoanalyst's creativity. Regardless of how dispassionately, calmly, or modestly they are offered to the patient, such makings reflect an essential narcissistic investment on the analyst's part, as the effort of binding the available data into an interpretation requires an energy, concentration, and commitment to the "truth" that could not be accomplished without this kind of investment. Even though I know my interpretations will inevitably be proved to be only partly correct, and a good many to be meagerly so, while still others are quite wrong, I am almost always pleased to make them. As I gather myself toward a sense of truly understanding something, I know that I bring a part of myself to the clinical situation different from the receptive, evocative, musing, and associating me. Perhaps when I speak my interpretation to a patient I betray a certain intensity of commitment which may be conveyed by the way I try to be lucid when speaking the complex. I do believe my analysands sense the difference in me at such a moment, something which of course is analyzable.

The reporting of an association, however, is spoken from a different place from the delivery of an interpretation. The analyst is less committed to it, it is not consciously understood, its "worth" is not verifiable, and its status is closer to the analysand's associative meanderings than an interpretation proper. An association is offered no less thoughtfully than an interpretation, insofar as the analyst will always consider its verbal appropriateness, but it becomes a different internal object for the analysand and a different intermediate object for the analyst-patient partnership from the interpretation proper. Analysts quite rightly expect patients to think about and comment on interpretations, and failure to do so may become an issue if the analysand seems to characteristically ignore them. However, the analyst does not expect the analysand to think about a free association; rather he hopes the patient will use it either to facilitate association, inspire essential and informative negation, or become the nuclei of defensive antibodies that enable the analyst to interpret unconscious resistances.

The psychoanalyst's mention of one of his own associations might appear to be an acting in of the analyst's needs of one kind or another: his need to give the patient a friendship of sorts, his competition with the patient's right to free imaginative speech, his expression of largesse: i.e., "You see, I am just like you in some ways." There are many possible reasons why a statement of association could be a corruption of the analytical process, but if the analyst is self aware analytically, he should know if his associating is usurpative. The report of an association should provide the analysand with a preconscious link to unconscious latent thoughts. If it is too clever, deep, or farfetched, it could only ever be an impingement that would arrest the patient's true self and promote a false discourse. Naturally it is important for the clinician to carefully assess the analysand's subsequent use of a reported association, which usually indicates its worth.

It is intriguing, however, that the psychic value of such mental contents and their selective reporting to the analysand are rarely discussed in the analytical literature, as clinicians sound the gongs of caution with deadening regularity: it is dangerous, it introduces a belief in the value of the irrational, it is an abreactive discharge of the analyst's inner life, it is a collusion with the patient's projective identifications. It is curious how at times we seem unduly afraid of our internal life, so that unthought-out associative contents must be kept entirely outside the analytical encounter. Is this mental apartheid not conveyed to our patients, whom, after all, we otherwise credit with sensing even the slightest private details of our life? Do we not convey a fear of subjectivity itself?

Surely Freud did not intend the analytic effort to render the id to the ego, or to make the unconscious conscious, to become a flight from such areas. Regardless of how well analyzed we may be, we shall always be a subject who only ever partly knows. Partly knows the other. Partly knows the self. Partly knows life. Most of our life is lived unconsciously, in dialogue with the other's unconscious, within the field of unconscious social processes. I believe there is great value in considering the representatives of the unthought known, even as much of this knowledge will forever elude consciousness. We should be less fearful and wonder more about the overdefensive employment of somber caution. Our analysands need to see us working in a *disciplined* way with our own internal processes rather than posing as dispassionate surgeons, calmly in possession of a cure that awaits the finally unresistant patient.

I shall now provide two clinical examples to indicate how and why I disclose inner associations to the analysand. The second example will be in greater detail and will, I hope, serve to increase the reader's understanding of how psychic genera are constructed in a psychoanalysis.

Clinical Example 1

Antal, 25, tells me the following dream: "I am walking along a cliff toward a cemetery and a loosely constructed boardwalk goes out over the cliff. I want to get to the graveyard but cannot climb over the barrier or wall and I am forced out onto the platform, which leaves me feeling very anxious. I manage to get to the graveyard; when I wake up I am still somehow anxious about the dream." He says that his family home is to be sold, as his father died six months ago. The day before the dream the estate agent rang to tell him of the sale. It was also his birthday and he makes the interpretation that he was struggling to get back to the scene of birth and death, which has so preoccupied him in his life. The family home is adjacent to a graveyard which holds a grave for his sister, who died at four months, one year before the patient was born. This sister was never discussed until the memory of her death occurred in the early part of the analysis—some years before the dream reported above.

As the patient reported the dream, an image came to my mind of Edgar leading Gloucester to the cliff to create the illusion of death in *King Lear*. I was conscious of this coming to mind because of the cliff image in the dream. I knew this patient had only recently had difficulties while writing a book on *Hamlet*, and I wondered if somehow *Lear* was there by association. The patient had, however, begun the hour by saying that his elder brother had called to ask how the sale of the house had gone and had not inquired after the patient's birthday, which may unconsciously have been a precursive *Lear* association, as in *Lear* two brothers compete to prove to the father who is the more loyal: a theme recurring in this patient's life. I also thought about Hamlet and Laertes fighting in the grave, but this association lacked weight. I found myself mulling over the word presentation "graveyard" and thought to myself how this patient seemed addicted to grave issues. "Boardwalk" left me wondering if he was referring to the boredom of walking along an addictive path. As he described his effort to climb the wall, his voice changed, its texture now thick with despair and body heaviness. I felt the inability to get over the wall and I was relieved that he decided to try the platform even if it went out over the cliff. Naturally I did not know why I felt this way.

I asked if he could tell me anything about his day. He had had people over for lunch and it was quite pleasant. Could he tell me more? I asked. He said it was one or two people from the publishers of his *Hamlet* book. This linked to Shakespeare, which slightly authorized my association to *Lear*. I then asked him if he had any associations to the cliff. He said not really, only to the concept of precipice. "Precipice" brought "precipitant" to my mind, leading me to wonder if we were being too hasty in coming to understand the dream. I wondered where the precipice was in the session for the patient, but I felt his association was not freely given but intellectually terminal.

The session fell flat at this moment. There I was with a rather vivid sense that *Lear* was involved, thinking now that it could have something to do with the patient's struggle to get to the despair and pain that he felt. At this point I said, "Coming so close to the cliff, I find myself not thinking of *Hamlet* but of *Lear*," and Antal broke in: "Where Edgar brings Gloucester to the cliff." Very hurriedly he then added somewhat apologetically: "I only realize now that I left out further details of the previous day. The night of the dream I saw *Ran*" (a film by Kurosawa on the *Lear* theme). Antal then proceeded to talk of his habit of breaking down into tears frequently, seemingly not in association to anything, and I wondered out loud, "But perhaps more so when a father and a son are involved?" and he paused and after a few minutes of silence told me that in fact it was this type of scene which struck him more deeply than others. He was silent for a time and then proceeded to talk about his birthday and his sense of just feeling guilty, as if he had to do something for the world. We both knew (because of the analysis) that a sense of devotion to the world was partly unconscious penance for the death of his sister, but his discussion of the brother who forgot his birthday and my association to *Lear* allowed me to conjecture why this patient was determined to absorb himself with the "graveyard": "Of course, in the end, Edgar proves he was the best brother, so I think it is partly gratifying to have your brother forget you, as you can say to your internal father, 'Well, you see, Dad, look at what a bad brother he is.' " The patient laughed and told me how he had thought that he would never be so thoughtless as his brother had been and how proud he was of this difference in their personalities.

But was this the correct emphasis? I do not know. That *Lear* came to my mind as a result of the cliff image indicates unconscious rapport with the patient, as the previous night he had seen *Ran*. The fact that in considering this dream I decide to use my associations, because of a strong inner sense that my associations were relevant to the dream, seemed justified by the patient's "forgetting" of *Ran*. Getting to this association, and the patient's resistance to it, raises issues of blindness amidst insight, generational succession, and a wealth of other Oedipal issues. Naturally I am "guided" in my associations by listening to this patient's dream life and I am also used by his affective states (and its sonic imagery) in the dream report, as indeed I am nudged along further toward Shakespeare by remembered day residue.

Clinical Example 2

In this second clinical elaboration I provide two associations within the space of a week and go on to examine an important moment in the patient's analysis one year later when she expressed a new psychic structure to which the free associations may have contributed.

At this point in her analysis she was in some respects a very cooperative patient, but interpretations in the area of her hysterical denigration of her husband (and all significant people) as expressions of extreme despair, derived from unconscious envy of her father, were unable to reach her. During one session, while she was describing in minute detail how wimpish and repellent her husband was, I said, "When is this frog ever going to turn into a prince!" The patient laughed. She said, "It's funny you should call him a frog, as last week, when I was in the bookstore trying to find a card for him for Valentine's Day, I could not find anything that was suitable. I looked and looked and looked and, as I just don't love him, nothing was right. But then I saw a card with a frog on the cover and inside it it said, 'You are a prince at heart.'" This was the card she purchased to give him.

A week later, while listlessly moaning about the many disappointments in her life—particularly her husband's ineptness and her father's remove—I imagined her in a particular way. This is what I said: "You know, as you are speaking I have a picture of you, a little girl of three in tutu and ballet shoes, asked by Mummy and Daddy to perform for guests, and who, warmed by the applause, believes the world will always be like this." Choked with intense feeling, bursting into tears for the first time in her analysis, she replied: "They dressed me up, put the clothes on me, and put me in front of their guests, but due to my father's criticisms I came out on the stage a frightened and frozen child, not knowing what to do!" An unnerving and unreal affective equanimity broke down in the patient as the image I constructed evoked intense feelings and became the nucleus of her informative opposition to me. The image was not historically correct, in that she had never taken ballet lessons or danced like this for her parents or her parents' guests. I spoke this image because it captured something about my patient that I had previously put in the abstract, but the image seemed much more representationally accurate. Her immediate oppositional use of it, the degree to which it sponsored both elaborative affective and ideational meanings, suggests to me its clinical value and eventually it helped her to see that her intense investment in an ideal self led her, during her Oedipal era, to really believe that her father would court her. His failure to do so became the object of intense disappointment both in him and in herself, which she alternately experienced either by denigration of her partners or by intense bouts of self devaluation.

In some respects the analyst's mention of a free association, in the form of an imagining as with this patient, can evoke a different psychic processing of mental contents from the more traditional category of the patient narrating and the analyst responding through interpretation. With this patient I *momentarily* resituated my place in relation to the unconscious, in that I produced an image which was highly evocative.

More than a year after this episode the patient reported the following dream. "I am attending a ballet at Covent Garden. It is either *Cinderella* or *Swan Lake*. I am dressed in a skintight, white leotard and I am enjoying being dressed in it and feeling good in my body. At some point toward the end of the concert someone on the production side of the event told me that they needed me to dance tomorrow afternoon, as they did not have anyone to replace one of the members of the cast who was unable to be there. I protested that I did not know how to dance. They insisted that I did. But I persisted and then it appeared to be an opera that I was to be in, and I said that I did not know how to sing. They said it did not matter, as I would only have a speaking part. The dream shifted then to the few minutes on the next day before opening curtain. A man dressed as a prince looked at me and said that I was not the right one, that clearly I was not the star. I agreed. But the other people insisted that I go on anyway, as, if I did not, they would have to cancel the production. I said then that they would have to cancel the production. I felt, of course, quite troubled, but equally quite sure that I was taking the right decision. And then the dream ended."

In the few moments prior to presenting the dream the patient had handed me a booklet that described her law practice and its sponsorship of a special training course. This was an important moment: she had never felt courageous enough to show me something of this course, which, in fact, had developed quite a good reputation in London. She thought I would disapprove of it and see through the holes in it.

In the previous three sessions a major change had occurred in this patient, which I noted and which alerted me to the emergence of something quite important, even though I did not know at the time quite what was happening. For a long time she had reproached herself for not seeking qualification as a barrister, and had hung on the fringes of that profession for years. Considerable work had been done in the analysis to understand this yearning, concentrating in particular on her belief that somewhere, someplace else, inside others certainly, was an ideal self to be achieved. This wishful belief was contrasted with her denigrated and depleted self, spent in its potential for realistic self valuation by the projection of her assets into the idealized objects; this interpretation was further confirmed by a constant feeling in the analysand that people were trying to rob her of her assets, something which I sometimes linked to her envy of others—a form of robbing the self via projective identification. Now, however, for the first time, the analysand told me she no longer intended to find some way to qualify as a barrister and had ended her efforts to do so. In fact, she had been recognized by that profession in an advisory role, something which she felt, looking back, was fine. That was enough. In that session I said, "And I think, in any event, that you rather like what you are doing," and she corrected me: "I don't like it, I love it." This was said with a passion that was really quite startling, as this was an analysand who for years had never let a week pass without complaining about being a solicitor, always feeling that it was second-rate, that she was a failure, and that greener pastures eluded her.

That session, two meetings before the reported dream, was then followed by two sessions in which there was now a marked difference in her self: more assured, less anguished, no reports of envy, no denigration of her husband. In fact, she talked about him in a tender way, not out of pity, but exuding a sense of his present interests in the world, conveying him in a manner that was quite important. During these two sessions I said very little, and during the silence the patient would talk about her practice, about her childhood, about her present relations, in a way that seemed transitionally affective, by which I mean that she seemed to be reporting derivatives of an evolving inner emotional reality that could yet not be reported, as it was *in statu nascendi.*

In her associations to the dream the patient said that she felt initially quite good in her body outfit, but acutely discomfited by the dance producers. I asked if it didn't seem to her as if she felt rather good in saying that no, she was not going onto the stage. She agreed but said that the moment inside the dream which felt significant was the first occasion when she was selected to do something she knew she could not do. It brought with it now memories of stage panic in childhood when she was asked to say something before the class; it further brought to her mind something she had not mentioned before: an event some years ago of acute de-realization when she had to go onto a stage to accept an award. She felt, as she put it, an "out-of-body experience" and said that she was watching the event from quite far away and actually felt a moment's acute panic, afraid that she might "lose myself right there and then."

Among other things, the dream report evoked my free association, reported one year before, of her dancing before her parents. Here now was a dream of dancing at Covent Garden. *Cinderella* and *Swan Lake* seemed obviously important as specified occasions of transformation, from the un-loved to the loved object. I thought to myself that the patient may have been unconsciously at work not so much on that free association, but that my association had itself been part of a type of unconscious work, preconsciously considered by me and then reported to her, turning up in her dream. In the months prior to the dream the patient had for the first time been able to tell me of her love and affection for me, of her wish that I think well of her, her disclosure having been painful to speak, but also yielding, I thought, a sense of personal accomplishment. It became clear that she was afraid not only of being rejected by me but more to the point, and more fearfully, of being idealized by me as a result of reporting affection, something which led toward an extended period of association to her mother's idolizations of her.

It is intriguing, I think, how certain images or events in a dream seem to the analyst particularly laden with meaning. I found myself feeling that her dressing in a skintight outfit represented a child's narcissistic investment in her own body, and indeed, that such an investment in the dream appeared to initially echo her identification with the figures on the stage. The entire way that she reported this first part of the dream seemed, if I can put it this way, a memory of being a child at play.

But in the middle part of the dream she conveyed a fear of being appropriated by the other's desire. The people in the dream now wanted her to do something she could not do, but clearly something that was within the realm of her own wishes. However, as the analysand had in the previous weeks been telling me of feeling appropriated by her mother's idolization of her, I found myself thinking of a child of about three, having a wish, enjoying her own body, but then being intruded upon by a mother who insisted that the daughter's private wish was in fact a realizable reality.

At the same time the patient expressed in the dream a wish to be embodied in relation to myself. Nascent exhibitionistic urges were clearly announced, but so too was her resistance to dance for the analytical production, particularly for a princely analyst who could be more enamored of analytic productivity in spite of the psychic truth. But the recognition in the prince's face that she was not the right person for the role was not accompanied by depressive or denigratory affect: quite the opposite. She seemed grateful for his assistance in declaring, implicitly, the difference between private wishes and public possibilities, and it was his assistance that enabled her to resist the production's demands, in this case by using reality orientation, or the sense of reality, and by expressing it, as the means of deterring grandiose ambitions.

I reminded her of our free associations of the year before and said that now she seemed to be correcting them. It was not that her parents failed to dress her up and were critical, but that both she and they adored the girl self that she was so much that they did not attend to the steps in reality necessary to the accomplishment of wishes. She could not, even now, step onto a stage to receive recognition of her work without feeling, somehow, that she should not be there.

She then told me for the first time that throughout her childhood her mother had insisted upon dressing her. When I first heard this I found it almost unbelievable, but she went on to describe the morning ritual in which the mother, calling her her little doll, would dress her up in an outfit that the mother wished. She would also take her to dress stores and ask the shopkeepers if they didn't agree with her that her daughter had a wonderful figure (to which they invariably agreed), and then she would be fitted out by her mother. Her description of these events, or rituals, was not saturated with hate or denigration, but almost tenderly conveyed, as if speaking the memory was to forgive the mother.

I said I thought we could now further understand why she felt her husband, and others, were always trying to rob her, to take things from her: it seemed that her own ordinary love of her body was taken from her by her mother's extraordinary love of it. She agreed and then there was a silence for some ten minutes, in which it was quite clear to me that she was engaged in some deep inner work on something. She then said that it seemed important to her that she got caught up in agreeing to the production, by appearing at Covent Garden. After this she faltered a bit, then said she thought the ending of the dream was important, but she could not see why. I felt she was very close to seeing its meaning, and I said that I thought the ending of the dream partly expressed her child self's collusion with her mother's ambitions, but that she now had within her an internal father who could help her with reality, and though she could not dance onstage with this prince, she actually felt reassured by that fact, as, told she was not suitable, she gained a valued sense of personal reality.

She was silent for a moment. Then she told me that when she went to conferences, and hesitated slightly, she felt I was somehow with her, as if she were clothed in a kind of "protective mantle" that was me, and that it was a secret, and yet it wasn't really me, but her organization of me into something that was hers. I cannot pretend that on first hearing this I understood exactly what she was telling me. I certainly felt its significance, and I felt like responding to it rather than sustaining analytical silence. I also had a kind of immediate conjecture. So I said that the protective mantle me, like the her dressed in the white leotards—an identification with those onstage—seemed to be a kind of essential use of the other, a use that would be for her a secret of sorts, but one that she felt in the past might be taken from her were it not secretly sustained. I think my comment was only partly correct, but close enough to the latent ideas to keep this element of the session moving in association. I also thought that work at this level was progressing as much from unconscious-preconscious intuitions of significance than from conscious understanding of precise mental contents, so by saying what occurred to me I was somewhere, now, between association and interpretation.

The patient then talked openly about a change she felt had occurred in me several days before and which she felt was significant. She did not know how to describe it, and now, upon thinking of it further, she did not think it was, in fact, a change in me, but a change in the both of us, or rather, as she proceeded to correct herself, a change in her, which changed both of us. She thinks that she had always regarded me as a kind of Olympian figure and analysis as a sort of oracular situation in which I was the god, and she was the supplicant, somehow beset with the problem of having to get something out of this. Now she felt me to be, actually, a person at work. Quite intensely at work. On the analysis. This recognition seemed to make a true difference to the way she perceived herself in my presence.

I knew her comment was very important, but it came as a surprise. To be sure, I had thought in the hearing of the dream that the producers of the great ballets that depicted transformations from deficit to glamour must be transferential communications. I thought she was saying she believed I expected great things of her, but we had worked on this many times before, and the prince in the dream seemed to be a part of me telling her that she was not suitable for the grandiose role she assigned to herself.

However, I also was preoccupied with thinking through to myself the felt difference between her resistance to the opera staff and her many resistances in her life: to her husband, to friends, to her mother, etc. The plethora of anal material had suggested its instinctual valence: she would retain her feces to defy her mother; she would not give them up, even though many dreams depicted scenes of being covered in feces. But now the resistance to grandiose ambitions seemed to be represented in a logical or realistic mode. But within a dream! In other words, she had found a way to use the father as a principle of reality, and then to use the principle to find a way to say no without doing so in a pathological mode.

I told her that the dream seemed to announce a change within, that she had now found a part of her that could say no both to her own grandiose wishings and to the internal parents who seemed to adore her to excess. This meant finding her own body self, made up of her own figure, but also clad in elements of her own identifications with mothers and fathers, all of which was an essential secret.

There was a sense within both the patient and myself that psychic change had occurred and we were seeing evidence of it now. My task, I thought, was to announce it realistically, which can be seen as a form of celebration, but obviously I was aware of her understandable fear that I would make her an object of my own idealization. So I told her that her mantle was her private use of me, but that she must be worried that I would now see the significance of this session as an occasion for my appropriation, as we would now come to adore this change in her. She laughed with relief and said that as long as we both continued to talk about it she didn't reckon that would happen. And the fact is, I felt a change had occurred that, although obviously having to do with analysis, was now quite independent of myself and definitely in the patient's possession.

Psychic genera constructed in analysis are the outcome of types of play and forms of work between analysand and analyst. I think my free association of the patient in ballet costume was somewhere in touch with the patient's unconscious inner reality, although it was not historically correct. It was a small but telling contribution, in my view, to the dream which occurred one year later, when the patient was dressed to dance. That dream announced a new psychic position in the analysand in which she could stand up to princes (including the analyst-prince) and say no to the restricting effect of idealizations of herself.

The Error of Our Ways

Psychoanalysis is not a relation between equals. The patient comes to the analyst because of suffering, and the analyst offers a procedure for the investigation into and the possible cure of such suffering. The analyst's recurring mention of his inner associations is not intended to establish a more equal relation to the patient, although by using some of his associations he is slightly more participatory in the process. But he will continue to decide when and why he will or will not report his inner associatings. Technical use of such association must be a disciplined act, designed to further the course of the analysis. The analyst will need to make this clear to the analysand at the beginning of the analysis. It is most certainly not an occasion for a free disclosure of events in the psychoanalyst's life, nor is it the foundation of a new type of dialogue in psychoanalysis: i.e., "You say what comes to your mind and I shall say what comes to my mind in response."

When the analyst uses one of the free images, words, or memories (of former analytical material) to speak to the patient, although he will not be conscious of its meaning, it has been selected for mention from the vast range of inner associations and has therefore been partly processed by the analyst's therapeutic and technical intelligence. Such reportings are more like preconscious mental contents, temporarily intermediate between unconsciousness and consciousness. Frequently it will be the patient's elaboration of such preconscious contents that renders such inner associatings conscious. This for me is one of the great values of such a discipline, as once the analyst knows technically how to "put" associations to the patient—and it does necessitate expertise—the patient's unconscious has at its service the collaborative work of *occasional* analytical preconscious contents that are often evocative.

For a number of years—during my American training in ego psychology and my English education in object relations theory—I believed it was possible to acquire a technique that could only fail if I failed to utilize it properly. I believed there was at least a model which, if grasped, could set the clinician on the correct path to comprehending his analysand. In some ways I am not disappointed. Both models do indeed yield techniques highly useful to the clinical task. But work with any analysand is far more complex than any theory about psychic life. The Hartmann, Klein, Kohut, and Lacan models usefully orient the clinician in a narrowed focus achieving an essential tautology, as the psychoanalyst uses such models as nets to catch his own shadow. But what about the extraordinary amount of our work which is beyond our comprehension? Is it irrelevant because we do not understand it? Are we not liable to make a considerable number of mistakes in our work, from allowing too much silence on one occasion to not providing enough on another, from an interpretation which is substantially off the mark to one that is partly correct but wrong in essence? Do we conclude that there is a technique somewhere which we can learn that will absolve us of this proneness to error?

The above suggests that it is possible to comprehend our patients. I do not agree. I think we fail to "grasp" them, because anyone—including oneself—is substantially beyond knowing. In certain important respects, however, such as conceptualizing the person's transference, deciphering certain symptoms, noting defenses, and analyzing Oedipus complexes, the clinician does gain effective if limited understandings of his patient. But the unconscious never ceases its work and the psychic material in which it plies its trade is profoundly beyond our knowing. Each analyst and his patient must come to terms with the limitations of psychoanalysis if they are to sustain a truthful relation to the human condition.

Naturally I strive to find what is true of my patient at any one moment. I take my task seriously and I believe there is some truth to most of my comments. But I mistrust my ambitions. I know that important as it is to seek the truth, it is this urge to get to the "heart" of the matter that proves to be the greatest potential misfortune for the analysand. It is only a slight step from the somewhat self-righteous feeling that one is searching for the truth to the imposition of one's views (i.e., models of the self) upon the patient.

In this respect, every psychoanalyst seated in the analytic

chair betrays the process he invites. His training, his relation to his analyst and supervisors, and his models of the mind saturate him with preconceptions that counter the idiosyn-chromes of the analysand's free establishments of self. Freud's invention of the analytical process, an enormous step forward in the evolution of human freedom, was understand-ably resisted by Freud himself (as with all of us) because he absolutely had to organize the material. Not only must we employ models of cure, but our patients rightly expect this: their suffering can only be cured through our efforts of organization. But the paradox remains: as we bring our models of cure to the clinical space, we invariably resist the very process that frees the analysand to escape through the polysemous movements of unconscious expression.

Of course we impose our models of the mind, the self, and object relating upon the patient. How could it be otherwise? As Pine argues, it is impossible for us not to organize our patients into frames of reference. So is it not possible that our very ignorance is the matrix of freedom for the patient and the analyst? In *Forces of Destiny* I claim that we must "unknow" our patients, to which I would add that if we are honest with ourselves, we have no choice; there is vast evidence of the failures of our knowings, inevitably displaced by increased complexity and dynamic signification as when a unit of analyzed material changes its prior latent meaning as it is now reinvested with new latent thoughts.

The analyst's selective reporting of unthought-out associ-ations to the analysand's material serves the continual rep-resentation of the mass of unconscious thinkings with which we live. But it also honors our relation to the unconscious as bearers of a significance that eludes us. Our errors of association, corrected by the analysand—or "destroyed" through a use-change of them—assist in the ordinary essen-tial deconstruction of analytical certainty. If we impose our models of the mind upon the patient, as we cannot fail to do, let us equally bear a shared witness to the reliable deconstruction of such authority. Therein lies a potential balance, between the necessary ambition that authorizes our search to find the truth and the ineffable movement of unconscious processes that keeps us as democratic representatives in the assembly of consciousness rather than monarchs of an imposed truth.

Part II

6

Cutting

A Monday morning at an open psychiatric hospital. The therapy staff, medical director, and various nurses sit around a large conference table, its ceremonious presence dotted acne-like with plastic cups of coffee, as the psychoanalysts self stimulate to wake from the night's slumbers. A senior nurse reads the customary lengthy report of the patients' deeds and misdeeds during the day and at night, from poignantly meaningful insights that seem newsworthy to fistfights, from complaints about the food to stolen sexual moments; each event never entirely free of the dialectic between the perceived and the hallucinated that keeps all the inhabitants of a mental hospital slightly on edge.

Today the nurse reports several incidents of cutting, the word itself stabbing into our peace of mind. "Who?" "How many?" "How deep?" we wonder as another female patient is named as the latest cutter. In the last month, six of our fifty patients have begun to cut themselves on different parts of the body but mostly wrists or thighs. We always seemed to be capable of dealing with a single cutter, but now a new anxiety emerges: the women have opened a competition, daring each other on, cutting deeper, spreading the wound to the body politic, as we all worry if one of *our* women—I now speak of course of our patients—will cut herself and mark our coupling with this act of . . . Act of what?

"Well, clearly S cuts because she is testing limits. It is boundary testing. How far can she go before we step in to say, 'Enough. Either you accept the rules against self mutilation in our open hospital or you go elsewhere.' " / "Obviously S cuts because she poses the question 'Who is to control my body, the body in question? Is it to be you? How dare you.' We should ask her to speak of her feeling that this body of hers is no longer in control." / "We must ask the analyst, or S, or both, 'What is happening in the transference to inspire the analysand to cut her analyst at this moment?" / "Cutting is a relief. The patient cuts to free herself of her persecutory inner contents, which she lets out concretely by bleeding, thus uniting the ego with the super-ego in an alliance of pleasure in pain."

"S"

"My cut is secret. I create it in stolen moments. In a private place. No one is present when I do this. I slice my skin with a fine razor. I cut deftly so no one can see the finest works of this forbidden craft. I place one cut next to another, each a valley of incisions. I tell Nurse, 'I want to show you something.' She likes me. I speak to her about secrets. 'I have cut myself,' and she takes me to her room, where she bathes my inner thigh with soft light. She cannot find the cuts. Where are they? *There*, and I take her finger and put it on the place where the cuts live. She can feel them and I am relieved that she believes me. She frowns, lectures me wordlessly, gives me some soothing cream. Will she tell our secret? I hope not.

"I hear A cut across her stomach. All the way across it. A deep cut. She bled through her analytical hour, but Dr. Z knew nothing as she sheltered beneath her lovely Scottish sweater, its heavy braid soaking up the sacrament. Moments before the session's end she lifted the sweater to reveal the cut and Dr. Z's face became horror. He closed his eyes. Pathetic cuts sutured by his petty anxiety. A went to the hospital and took thirty stitches across her belly, but she refuses to speak about what it means.

"I like to cut myself. It is my private séance. Who owns this razor I use? With whose hand do I make these incisions? Is it my hand? Who cuts me? I cut deep now, to bring blood. It spurts out. Sylvia Plath cut herself in 1962:

> What a thrill—
> My thumb instead of an onion.
> The top quite gone
> Except for a sort of hinge
> of skin . . .

What do I celebrate when I cut? I love the passing of time, the interval between the incision and the arrival of the blood. I wait. Have I cut deep enough to bring up the blood? Or is this a virgin's cut, no menarche here? I must wait. I am used to such waiting. The cut in my body did not bleed until I was twelve; so I know all about waiting for a cut to bleed.

"Up it flows, up and out, spilling over my skin. Pure. No effluence of eggs. No dead babies here. No smelly stains that problematize my relation to that other cut: this blood is pure.

"How deeply have I cut? Will it run out and stop? Will it congeal, gather itself up into little balls of resistance, to arrest itself? Or do I have to stop it? Shall I mix it with pure water? Not the mixture of blood with urine but with pure spring water? Does it still flow? Shall I take my body, then, my hospital body with its new wound, to a doctor for attention? Will the mama nurse barely see it and give me her soothing female creams, or has it gone too far? Have I lost her, this pure mummy who soothed me? If the blood

flows I shall lose mummy nurse to a new world, the place of
Dr. Z, who frowns and puts his touchless fingers against the
wound. Am I to be sutured, sewed up?

"Fuck it. It's rather nice, that. A deadening injection, no
pain, and swift nimble fingers that stitch it up. Back then to
mummy nurse, who removes the pieces of string, like the
tiny cotton of a doll's world, and then the gentle stares and
womanly kindnesses.

"Not the look of fear upon the man's face. I have not
done that yet, but A did it to Dr. Z with that wonderful
great cut across her belly. 'Have a look at this, you coal
miner of the unconscious, open your eyes to this fearsome
cunt, with no pubic fleece to protect your gaze from its
object: a hole that bleeds and bleeds and bleeds. Look at
this, you coward!' I am not there yet. L cut herself on the
upper left arm, just below her shoulder, in a very special
secret place, and the blood flowed all the way down her arm,
trickling off her finger into her bowl of cereal, mingling with
the milk and cornflakes. She stirred and stirred. What a
shock! Who could dare to look at this! It was enough to
bring a horrified silence to the breakfast room. A mummy
nurse led her away from her bowl of milk, but the men—
ha!—they could not move. They can't take this blood, they
can't deal with this, our cunt, that moves around our bodies
to new secret places.

"Ah, the times I have looked and looked at my cunt. I was
pure and simple, a girl, no problem, and my fine black hair,
their shy locks hiding my pound of vanished flesh, grew and
grew, and even my first blood was not so much a big deal.
Perhaps I fool myself. I needed to see myself there but I
couldn't. A man has no problem cock spotting. He can just
look down, any old time, and there it is. But I can't. I tried.
Many, many positions. I would just catch sight of the vulva,
but I could not have a nice long, relaxed look. I was always
aching in my body trying to look. I needed a long, long,
relaxed look at it.

"So I borrowed a small hand mirror from my mother's closet. I lay on my bed, pillowed up from behind, and spread myself. And there it was. The famous French psychoanalyst Jacques Lacan has written an article on the mirror stage. He says the baby looks into the mirror and sees an image of pure bodily organization, a whole that unites him in the image, and divides him from his inner sense of being in pieces. What does he say of this secret mirror stage, when I gaze at my cunt and find there a gap, a hole, a wound, a . . . ? Is this not the return of the *corps morcelé*? Is this the image of unity? Where do I find representations in the icons of my civilization for such a hole, an o-ffense? Greek and Roman men still walk the museums of our world with representational arrogance flaunting this penis, but where are our vaginas?

"Perhaps in the ellipses, the gaps in consciousness. The holes in minds that do not represent. In the closed eyelids of the doctors when we flash our wound. The cunt is the negative hallucination of an entire civilization. Is it?

"My cunts aren't the real thing, are they? Usually I just scratch my surfaces. Sometimes blood comes and I turn it into pretend surprise: Oh! Blood. But I control it. My cunts shock the analyst. I flash my bleeding wound and force his lids shut, but this cunt is only a cul-de-sac, it has no interior to it, no complex foldings of skin layering its way to my insides. I present the doctors with a medical model of my cunt, a cut version, with no inside to the body, just a surface representation for diagnostic familiarity.

"If my doctor knew me he would know when I felt like cutting. He would know before I bled myself. When I get my period, well, a day or two before it actually happens, I change. We all change differently. I feel cross, irritated by small things, and I cut myself off from my friends, as I don't want to be a pain. I get an unpleasant full-body feeling, a container stretched to its limits, about to burst its skin. My breasts, tender. Pain. It *is* pain. Every bloody month. And my close friends, one or two, they *do know*. I needn't even tell them. 'That time of month, eh!' or 'Curse time again?' and I nod, all of this just as I start to change. But my doctor, he is an ignoramus. He knows nothing. Never once asked if I was on the rag. Occasionally he sniffs oddly, so perhaps he has smelled me, but it's far too late. He never says a thing. And they think they are so clever, these doctors. They write about psychic pain, but do they know it when it sits in front of them! Not a chance. There I am, bitchy, grouchy, tenderized by pain, and he doesn't say or know anything. I don't even think he knows when I am bleeding. Why should I tell the ignoramus? I bring my purse with me, packed with Tampax, sit it down before his very eyes, every month for a few days. Does he say anything? I keep him waiting while I linger in the women's toilet, just to make the point, but does he notice?

"He does not know me. He knows nothing of the signs of my pain, so I am delighted to shock him with my *cul-de-sacs*, my little cunts, which he takes very, very seriously. These are true signs of pain. Indisputable marks. Inscriptions. Texts written all over my body. He reads and reads these petite cunts with all the earnestness of an anthropologist whose only fieldwork among the natives will be in the library. It gives me pleasure to laugh when he takes my little cunts so seriously. It gets him all twisted up inside. I can see his worry, his *uncertainty*. He is no longer so sure of himself. Perhaps I will create a really massive cut. Perhaps I will go to a motel, cut my wrists, get in a warm bath, take some Xanex, and go to sleep.

"So I am cutting him up. He tells me so. Well, good. That's what I desire. I want my cut to signify him. 'Oh, Dr. Y,' his colleagues inquire, 'how is S doing?' The doctor whose patient cuts. Ha! The doctor defined by cunts, the doctor who does not know so much, who does not know when the blood comes. Let him be a cunt. A little cunt. I bleed: he bleeds. I bleed a lot: he bleeds a lot. I shallow-cut: he breathes an invisible sigh of relief. Let him be a cunt. Shall I bleed him every twenty-eight days? Shall I go all moody and silent and mysterious every twenty-eight days and see him turn into a cunt: sliced up by his anxiety? Shall I ask him if he is okay? How about 'You don't look so well today, Dr. Y. You look pale. The blood has left your face.' Shall I? 'This seems to happen to you once a month, Dr. Y. What is it?' You would call this projective identification, wouldn't you? I worry you to death every twenty-eight days or so, you thinking I shall kill myself, and yet you having this period of your month for me. Poor man. Shall I tell him this?

"No. He has no insides for me. No place for me to look inside him. Just that phallic externality, that compost heap of exposure, that medicality embodied; so why should he see inside me? Why should I open myself to him? Why show my true opening to him? He is ignorant anyway. These little cunts, these false incisions, false pains, are for him and his false cures.

"We women of the hospital should unite. We have them scared. One, two, three of us to the hospital for stitching up in one week! They say it's a record. A stream of blood from this false hospital to the true place, where they stitch up pain. We had one heck of a chance to unite; we did until R, that competitive fucked-up bitch, cut herself. In the grand manner, of course. No secrecy. No art. Just walked into the living room, cut from shoulder to wrist, and handed herself to the handsome Dr. P like the beautiful hysteric floating in Charcot's arms at the saltpeter hospital for impotent psychiatrists. She set us all against each other. A war of cunts. Who has the most hideous cunt? Whose is biggest? Widest? Longest? Whose is attractive? Repellent? Ah. Now it is all lost, we are all hostage to our silly competition for these men, all except A, who cuts into her Carrara body with the certainty of a Tuscan: her mass was meant to be cut and she wields the razor with a sculptor's knife."

7

Cruising in the Homosexual Arena

An intense and thoughtful man in his early thirties, Bruce lies on the couch twitching with eroticized self loathing as he tells me he does not know if he can resist going to the sauna this afternoon. He knows only too well what it will be like. As he enters the building, he will feel the grip of numbing excitement. In the changing room, he will glance furtively yet suggestively at the fifteen or so men in states of vestimentary transformation: some going, some coming. Once inside he will find a position in the steaming room, hopefully a good place where he can be viewed, in a pose he prefers, with towel draped loosely over his genitals. Will someone emerge from the mists to give him a close inspection? Will that person be right? Will he know that Bruce does not want to give suck or be entered from behind, at least not there? That a gentle masturbation under the towel, while being comforted, perhaps looked at with loving eyes, will suffice? Few seem to know this. He must reject so many would-be suitors, and usually he leaves the scene feeling deeply alone, filled with self disgust, and littered with the afterimagery of varied cocks, buttocks, smooth chests, hairy arms, balletlike legs, or any of the parts in this body shop.

Well, is he to go to the sauna, or can he wait until the evening to visit a very particular disco? There he feels certain he will find a more suitable lover. The men there are more animated, dancing to the throbbing boom of the music, striated by flickering strobe lights, passions realizing themselves in perspiring bodies which gleam in the night light, lending a supportive background to those pulsating eyes, those quick-to-the-soul teasing looks that fellow dancers flash to each other. Now?'Now do we pop down to the john for a quick one-two? Is it you? Are you the one for this?

For weeks at a time, when Bruce is "outside" a relationship he abandons himself to the lure of the disco, his lovers changing each night, metamorphosing before his very eyes from wonderful expectant objects to spent strangers who vanish in the seconds following orgasm.

Bruce's recurring accounts of this particular scene of gay life occupied many of his analytic hours, and was a feature of his existence which gave me pause to think about it from many different points of view. I now believe that particular theaters of the gay life, those devoted to impersonal sexual encounters with a stranger, sometimes represent an important issue in the unconscious mental pain of certain male homosexuals. To be sure, the specifics of any homosexual's fantasy life are as different, no doubt, as heterosexual erotic interests. A gay bar bears no obvious behaviorally objective difference from a heterosexual pickup place. Heterosexuals are certainly not uninterested in the erotics of body parts; they too practice the self-other deception of intense driven interest in orgasmic exchange with an other that can end so quickly in flight from the spent object. Nor can we view homosexual life as entirely separate from heterosexual life; later I shall argue that the particular depersonalizing affliction that besets some homosexual men (especially the cruiser) is an ailment participated in, and partly sustained by, the heterosexual community. Indeed this chapter could as easily be about a different type of mental anguish were I to focus on the heterosexual bachelor's temporary immersion in fleeting relations, or were I to discuss the psychodynamics of an affair.

But it would be a falsehood to argue that the gay disco, theater of homosexual promiscuity, is no different from a heterosexuals' singles bar. There may be common elements, but there are important and essential differences which can, I think, enable us to better understand psychic pain in certain homosexual men. In researching this traumatic "scene" I have supplemented my own clinical findings with a reading of gay novels and diaries. I did this because I thought it highly likely that some homosexual writers would describe the setting of the gay disco scene, explore the experience of being a participant observer there, and no doubt reflect on the psychology of the act. I was not wrong. Indeed, I owe a very special debt to a group of writers whose extraordinary self scrutiny and depth of self understanding testifies to a remarkably raised consciousness. I have, I think, learned more from their literature than from psychoanalytical writings on them; indeed, their works—from James Baldwin's deeply moving *Giovanni's Room* to Alan Hollinghurst's recent first novel, *The Swimming Pool Library*—reflect a literary-psychological investigation of what it can mean to be homosexual, an exploration of the self through fiction that I am sure serves therapeutic aims.

Although homosexuals suffer the stigma that arises when any group of persons "comes out" of the closet of the internal world to declare their erotic fantasies, they have benefited from a collective thinking-through of the nature of that erotic life and in this respect know a good deal more about themselves than do other sexual groups, including the "normal heterosexual."

The Act in the Setting

The theater of gay promiscuity is usually housed in the disco, bar, or sauna, but it can be in a park or public toilet. Johnny Rio, the promiscuous hero of John Rechy's novel *Numbers* migrates from darkened movie houses to parks in Los Angeles. "There is here something of pantomime, something of a frozen dream, a trance, of something dazed, traumatized, unreal" (98), he muses, as he sits in the park amidst fellow prowlers. Baldwin describes a scene in which one of the novel's characters created "among the people at the bar, a *troupe*, who would now play various roles in a play they knew very well" (54). What is the source of the excitement here, in this dreadful place? Certainly not the tense incremental erotics of interrelating; this is more often a theater of strangers. "I have never desired another man, I'm aroused only by what another man does—and not by him," says Johnny Rio (45). Is the disco scene the place of action, of the act, where what a man does (to himself and to and for others) is particularly exciting?

We know of the apparent excitement of place, but equally, as so many homosexual writers insist, this is also the location of "an internecine clash between [a] charged body and [a] numbed mind" (*Numbers*, 74). Why are such encounters shameful? one character poses to another in *Giovanni's Room*. "Because there is no affection in them, and no joy. It's like putting an electric plug in a dead socket. Touch, but no contact" (57). Perhaps this is the particular place for the presentation of an element of such deadness, disguised, ornamented into its sickly opposite, a lurid caricature of life and joy: a "gay" scene to conceal intense lonesomeness. As Johnny Rio says: "And so it is a game—but a game that can't be won because it's limitless. Only it can win—the game itself . . . and the park" (190), the park: that special place that Johnny Rio inhabits. Later Johnny says he will only be "with people with identity—men or women—people I know

. . .The park was all about . . . losing control and losing identity" (245). Why should this act be so compelling? Why is it such a crucial symbolic place in the gay world?

The It

The scene of cruising, as much a place for the angry evacuation of desire ("He quickly removed his mouth from Johnny's cock, stood up—spitting contemptuously," *Numbers*, 104), as for orgasmic intimacy, haunts the promiscuous homosexual who must go there. When Bruce would tell me of his experience in the disco, it was clear after a while that in this place his identity was suspended, as indeed were the identities of those who participated in the act. It seemed a place for an impersonal third person singular, a transitional sexual self, or an "it" to exist. Some homosexual writers capture this sense of an indeterminate object emerging from within the place of desire.

The main character in Baldwin's *Giovanni's Room* experiences that moment when he sees a figure emerging out of the scene:

> Now someone whom I had never seen before came out of the shadows towards me. It looked like a mummy or a zombie—this was the first, overwhelming impression—of something walking after it had been put to death. And it walked . . . It carried a glass, it walked on its toes . . . (41)

Someone emerges from shadows into identity:

> He's been sitting there only a few minutes when a shadow melts from the darkness, flows along the row where he's sitting, and materializes as a man only one seat away. (*Numbers*, 77)

or a person in the scene is a pure form:

> Warm from exercise I showered in water that was almost
> cold, and observed the strange variety of physical forms which
> were making their lingering transit back to the clean, clothed
> world. (*Swimming Pool Library*, 25)

The other may seem to embody strangeness itself:

> . . . the creature who, for a reason I could not put my finger
> on, fascinated me more than any of the habitués of that place
> came in the door: Sutherland. (Holleran, *Dancer from the Dance*,
> 37)

The place of this act can be a world of profound imper-
sonality, of an eroticized estrangement, where the stranger's
un-identity is the very source of excitement, just as the
cruiser's anxiety bears the print of his own suspended self.
Sometimes it seems to be a meeting place for "it-to-it"
encounters, a rendezvous of personified desires, ironically
close to Freud's theory of instinctual object relations. The
object seems conjured in order to rid the organism of
excitation. Hunting his objects like the master of instinct,
the cruiser scans the object world to find a thing best suited
to discharge the instinct's energy. In turn, he knows he too
is sought as an object of discharge and the tense anticipation
of being sighted heralds the moment of an orgasm that
eliminates interrelating itself.

"Everything reduced to the physical act!" screams a character from *Numbers*: "The localized sensation. Instead of the
mind and the heart stimulated, it's the *penis!*" (103). The
preoccupation with the penis objectifies the displacement of
interrelating, the id's object, it usurps the ego's pleasure:
"his eyes shot to Peter's crotch to see if there were any telltale
signs of excitement there, but he saw nothing" (Merrick, *One
for the Gods*, 35). The penis becomes the sign of intention, of

the aim of any subject in the presence of any object. "My dear, whole *lives* have been wasted chasing dick," exclaims a figure in *Dancer from the Dance*, neatly summing up the loss of life that can follow upon this preoccupation (39).

Alternately, however, if the act erases and dominates the subject, one of the aims—to find a love object—is an effort to arise out of the ashes of it-to-it erasure into love, mutual knowing, and possession of identity. Merrick puts it well:

> Little wonder that he wandered in these ghostly places late summer nights: He was half-waiting to be born. Having vanished from his former life, having shed his previous self with the suits he left behind in a basement in Washington, he was a ghost, in fact, waiting to come to life through love. He fell in love with people he did not know how to meet. (73)

Looked at from this perspective, the gay place for some homosexuals is, as Rechy calls it, an "arena" for the gathering of deadened selves looking for some erotic salvation for their plight. But the arena itself functions as an uncanny theater in which some of the participants, while seeking love, compulsively portray the scene of death and annihilation.

An altogether different mental state prevails in those men who do not feel deadened by the pickup place, a perspective that I shall only briefly mention here, as it does not figure in my examination of the arena as a deadening space. Mike, a homosexual patient, is an isolate who never felt embodied as a child, but felt marginalized by the mother's demand that he be her angel, and by the father's indifference, which suggested a schizoid scheme for the child as father's son. Well into his twenties his erotic life was discharged in masturbation as he remained fortified in his flat far removed from contact with anyone. In his late twenties he went to a disco and "had sex" which lasted a matter of a few minutes. He felt an enormous personal relief that was, in some ways, part of the erotics of this situation. Here, he imagined, were people like himself who did not feel confident in their sexuality, who felt disembodied, and who had always somehow been misfits. The arena for Mike was a secret rendezvous of fellow men, who although always nameless and unknown, were nonetheless secret sharers of common pasts. For Mike, the arena was a reassuring place which he visited from time to time to have some sexual, bodily, and "personal" encounter with the other, even if the personal dimension was achieved through prefabricated mannerisms unfolding in predictable ways.

I do not claim that people like Mike have no sense of the spirit of personal erasure in the arena—I am sure that some aspects of it are haunting—but I think it is important to establish that for a good many gay men the arena no doubt fulfills important sexual needs and represents significant efforts to be embodied.

Inside the Mother

Like many psychoanalysts who listen to homosexual patients' accounts of childhood, I am struck by the overwhelmingly consistent preoccupation with the mother, who is usually seen as compassionately encompassing, powerfully persuasive, and personally absorbing. But what is one to make of this? Some patients describe a mother's personality with such acute detail that one is left convinced that she actually was a domineering figure who dictated the child's personality to him. Yet other homosexuals' mothers seem quite different, objects of preoccupation because they seem to offer reliable refuge from an otherwise anxiety-provoking world, often supplying the love and affection unavailable from a distant or remote father.

The dilemma confronting an analytical understanding of maternal contributions to homosexuality is further complicated by the fact that clinicians only see homosexual men who are suffering—an inadequate measure of the homosexual community at large. In this study of the promiscuous cruiser, therefore, I am limited in what I believe I know by the accounts of homosexual men who have sought psychotherapy and psychoanalysis, by the writings of homosexual novelists and essayists, and by the psychoanalytical literature. Any effort to constitute an encompassing theory of homosexuality might well only be achieved by serious distortions of the discrete and important differences between homosexual men, an act that could in the extreme constitute "intellectual genocide" (see Chapter 10).

I shall assume, therefore, that there are as many factors determining the homosexual boy's relation to his mother as there are with the the heterosexual child. Some mothers may occupy a powerful place in the child's mind because they were powerful. Others because the child made her powerful in order to project parts of himself into her for safekeeping. Or to seek refuge from an actually distant and cold father. Or to contain an ideal self inside an ideal other while the father contains a bad self inside a negative other. Or, or, or, or. The causes are potentially endless.

Bruce, however, was sure that he was a child held captive in his mother's internal world. She devoted herself to him, gained a leisured obsessive pleasure in dressing him in feminine clothing, took him for long exhibitionistic walks to display her son to the neighbors, shopkeepers, and friends, and played idiosyncratic private imaginary games with him. It was an enchanting theater entirely directed by her desire. This sense of being inside the mother's internal world, as her object, is occasionally represented in the homosexual literature, I think, by a common reference to the ambience of the arena: it is likened to being inside the other's dream:

> Johnny stands up dizzily—bewildered by what he's done—as if he acted in another's dream—another's nightmare. (*Numbers*, 254)

Although it had seemed an endless nightmare while it was going on, he realized that the incident hadn't taken much more than five minutes. (*One for the Gods*, 48)

All this occurred in a state both trancelike and sharply conscious; as if another being had momentarily occupied the physical shell that was Malone. When he got home, and emerged from this dream-play, like a man who has just murdered someone and returns to his apartment and sits down to a bowl of soup, Malone took a shower that lasted over an hour and washed his mouth out with soap. (*Dancer from the Dance*, 67)

Bruce's visits to the sauna or the disco were trancelike. In some cases, does the arena re-create the homosexual's experience of the cumulative moments when he feels erased by the mother's usage of him as her "it" within her own fantasy world, even if he empowers her authority by projective identification? This may be an overt and severe erasure, as when a mother dresses her son as a girl, or it may be an intermittent usage nonetheless distinct as a self experience for the child, who does not know who he is to the mother, and consequently loses his sense of who the mother is. She becomes an intimate stranger. Perhaps this homosexual represents this mother in the arena when he seeks a stranger for it-to-it erotics.

Devolution to simple self experience inside the arena, then, is a particular type of loss of complexity, as the cruiser senses he is inside an object world that will absorb him, so this loss of reflectivity is, in fact, only a ritual experience. There is no true abandon to a process of projective investment of one's world with parts of oneself, because the world is already perceived as too eager to transform the subject into its terms. Thus cruisers, apparently giving in to the simple self, are in fact exceptionally self aware and vigilant, creating a kind of perspirational sexuality.

Perhaps unsurprisingly there is an ever-present sense of near panic as the cruiser enters the arena:

> Having taken a wrong path, moving deeper into the area, Johnny feels an instant of panic—illogical, of being lost in the park, of remaining here forever . . . wandering. (*Numbers*, 119)

> For that is the curious quality of the discotheque after you have been there a long time: In the midst of all the lights, and music, the bodies, the dancing, the drugs, you are stiller than still within, and though you go through the motions of dancing you are thinking a thousand disparate things. You find yourself listening to the lyrics, and you wonder what these people around you are doing. They seem crazed to you. You stand there on the floor moving your hips, wondering if there is such a thing as love, and conscious for the very first time that it is three twenty-five and the night only half over . . . you are thinking, as grave as a judge: what will I do with my life? What can any man do with his life? And you finally don't know where to rest your eyes. You don't know where to look, as you dance. You have been expelled from the communion of saints. (*Dancer from the Dance*, 126)

If the arena objectifies the child's sense of isolation as an "it" inside the other's theater (whether appropriated by it or seeking its refuge), it also represents the subject's effort to gain control of the theater: to produce it, direct it, and act within it. In the more sublimated ways this may be why a homosexual genius goes into the theater, opera, or film world, which may creatively master something previously victimizing. But for a cruiser in the arena, the panic and dissociation is still very present, and the struggle for mastery over this erasure of self takes the form of finding an erotic victim into whom this loss of control can be passed.

Numbers, as the title suggests, indicates the cruiser's need to conquer as many men as possible. If an orgasmically discharged former love object shows up again in the arena, the cruiser does not want him: he is among the vanquished, evidence that the cruiser is in control of his sexual destiny. "Johnny doesn't want the same person. He wants—needs—someone else" (82). Rejection can terrify a cruiser: "One rejection—real or imaginary—can slaughter Johnny Rio, even among 100 successes" (82–83). "Imagine a pleasure," muses Malone, "in which the moment of satisfaction is simultaneous with the moment of destruction: to kiss is to poison; lifting to your lips this face after which you have ached, dreamed, longed for, the face shatters every time" (*Dancer from the Dance*, 69).

The domination of a fellow cruiser is not simply an effort to achieve limited power within the arena. For as is frequently noted, the other is often sought for its lovely attractiveness, for "its" intrinsic and specific object appeal. Youthful appearance is almost always preferred. Working out in the gymnasium, cruisers bring their bodies closer and closer to that ideal self they aim to achieve. A substantial part of the effort to build such a body is determined by the market economy of the arena: the prettiest objects have a higher value, and the cruiser is more likely to be the dominant figure in an exchange of body value. "And Jacques threw a delighted look in the direction of Giovanni, rather as though Giovanni were a valuable racehorse or a rare bit of china," writes Baldwin (34). Is this sought-after object simply a narcissistic reflection of the cruiser? Does he seek that lovely boy he once was? This side of the equation is often stressed in the psychoanalytic literature: the homosexual searches for his ideal body self to perpetuate relation to an immaculate body, loving himself in an essentially worshipful way as the mother adored him. But this lover object is rather violently discharged along with the instinct.

Freud (1922) was perhaps unwittingly very close to defining one essential feature of the destruction of the object in the arena. He considered that most homosexuals envied an older brother in the family, the destructive side of homosexual erotics reflecting such envy. There *is* a rival that often becomes an object of envy. In my view, it is the *internal object* held inside the mother which mother and child see as the essential child. Sometimes it can be the child's rival and double. When feeling in rapport with the mother, all seems well and the self and the mother's essence-child feel identical. But during times of misrecognition, the child feels infuriated by the mother's treasuring of her object and a power struggle may ensue between them. The homosexual child may then become a false self created by mother and child, a double set up to conceal the true self. Looked at from this perspective, the arena may be a theater of breakdown where some homosexuals release the true self to a drama of fragmented part objects (penis, buttocks, anus) that objectify a self fractured by desire.

Whatever the reasons for the sense of being separated out by a rift with a mother or father, often (but not always) the homosexual child's anguish emerges from some perhaps hidden break with the parents. This break is a terrible loss of the parenting skills needed by a child growing up in the world; this child cannot be the parent's boy, and is unsure if he can become his own person. In my view, as he experiences this loss, he often loses the authorizing force of his true self and projects its strength into an ideal alter self. As he cannot maintain his personal strength in the face of blocks to his evolution, he projects it into an ideal boy that may later in adult life be adored back into reality. Love of the boy or the ideal body is a reclamatory love, an effort to unite with the divided half, to overcome one's deficiency and isolation. Needless to say, this alter being that possesses lost parts of the self is the object of intense need, the objectification of anguishing loss and, when it is acted out with the other, of a most ironic envy and hate.

Perhaps the cruiser seeks his double in order to vanquish him and gain control of this destructive rival. Is this why occasionally people are represented as emerging from the mists or shadows into recognition, just prior to the cruiser's erotic encounter? Does this emphasize the strange journey taken by the other, who comes from the misty world of the mother's fantasy, out of the shadows of other places, and into the light where this double can be seen?

Out of the shadows of a park, a bar, or a cinema anonymous others casually embody the transient nature of the psychic world, meeting up in an intermediate space where actual self and the internal object-rival encounter one another. Dominating the hapless psychic object (obviously out of its element now) is at least a pleasure if "it" keeps reappearing, in different disguises, from its other world. "I was in that movie about four hours," Johnny Rio thinks, "and three people came on with me, and many others wanted to, and two sucked me, and another tried to, and I came three times! He thinks that victoriously" (89).

But the paradox of seeking the psychic double while simultaneously materializing as another cruiser's internal object does not escape the ego's recognition, and is a source of continuous anxiety. For the cruiser "knows" that just as he seeks an out-of-closet rival, he is viewed as an escaped phantom, sought by the embodied force of sexual instinct, hunted by an urge to use him as the object of excitational extinction.

The Cruiser in Love

If cruisers sexually execute each other, they also seek love in the very place of its eradication. Love may triumph over the death instinct, as the object survives to become an other, so the erotics of it-to-it encounter may partly be an effort *to recover* the self from the annihilating ambience of the arena. If the cocksucking is dismissive, it is also simultaneously an effort to recuperate from the wasteland.

I take the view that recovery from the traumatic conditions of the arena often occurs in and through successful homosexual coupling. It is by finding a steady partner that the homosexual cures himself, and his lover, of the sexual muggings to be had in the arena. To be sure, even among the steadiest of couples there may be a nagging fear that the partner will break out of the couple to go off, secretly, to the arena. But I do not think steady homosexuals regard this as a betrayal of an alternative object choice, but sometimes as a sad capitulation to the scene of eradication. Thus it is much closer to the gambler's surrender to the casino— to the scene of his erasure—than it is to the need for another partner.

Nonetheless, for many homosexuals the arena may be a place of some exciting yet dreadful existence, whether frequented or not. It remains a point of anxious reference. As the airplane may haunt a person whose fear of flying results in total abstention from taking to the skies, the arena may still worry some gay men.

If the arena haunts the man, as the place of erasure, where the urges of and for the body cancel out the self in a punitive orgasm, it also objectifies that appalling lonesomeness that permeates the subject who has lost his actual sense of self to the other's internal object, who has lost the pleasures of interrelating to the prison of internal object relations serving the somatic-narcissistic requirements of the other's psyche-soma. The dread of being rejected is well described by a Baldwin character:

> I knew . . . that Jacques' vaunted affection for me was involved with desire, the desire, in fact, to be rid of me, to be able, soon, to despise me as he now despised that army of boys who had come, without love, to his bed. I held my own against this desire by pretending that Jacques and I were friends, by forcing Jacques, on pain of humiliation, to pretend this. (31)

The false self that Baldwin's character erects to protect himself from Jacques is that very persona that contributes to the destructive deceptiveness of the body as the bait that beckons the object to its annihilation. Himself an executioner, the victim carries knowledge of death to the sexual pit and sponsors a sense of horror at what he conveys that leads him to profound concern over the fate of the other. Baldwin again:

> He looked at me and I saw in his face again something which I have fleetingly seen there during these hours: under his beauty and his bravado, terror, and a terrible desire to please; dreadfully moving, and it made me want, in anguish, to reach out and comfort him. (61)

As Johnny Rio sits in his parked car "an enormous loneliness is choking him," a loneliness always vertiginous to fright (38). "No matter what I was doing," muses Baldwin's hero, "another me sat in my belly, absolutely cold with terror over the question of my life" (80). Lonely terror, for some a psychic ticket to the arena, gives combative place to the otherwise mute sense of cold remove from the essays of desire. Despair transmutes into a dissociated force that seems to shove the closeted self to abortional sexings:

> He set his suitcase aside. He got into his car, and it was suddenly as if a force beyond himself was pulling him physically to the park.
> And he felt:
> That coldness. And:
> A sadness. A heavy weariness. A breathtaking pain. A terrible resignation. A bottomless emptiness.
> And then, as he entered the arena:
> A terrified excitement, screaming. (*Numbers*, 244)

Surely the registration of the killing off of the other parts of the self, the coldness occasions a grief that metamorphoses to terrified anticipation of sex death.

The transformation of being (from self to it), and the succession of feelings, from dread to coldness, from sadness to excitement, may encapsulate that very movement in the child who participates in the yielding up of his true self to the double imagined by the other. Does this dreadful erasure also become a moment of excitement? Does the alteration of one's being, the flight of true self potential into the other's imaginary, congregate an excitement derived from this very movement?

Homosexuals and Heterosexuals Together

Perhaps there can be no homosexual without a heterosexual, by which I mean that heterosexual ambivalence toward the homosexual has, over the centuries, become an intrinsic contribution to homosexual psychic pain, and, as I hope to show, partly supported the homosexual's arena. Michel Foucault says that as expressed homosexuality was forbidden in the Western world, all the vitality of homosexual life had to be concentrated on the act of sex itself: "Homosexuals were not allowed to elaborate a system of courtship because the cultural expression necessary for such an elaboration was denied them—the wink on the street, the split-second decision to get it on, the speed with which homosexual relations are consummated: all these are products of an interdiction" (18). The true moment of homosexual encounter is after the brief orgasm is over, when, according to Foucault, the lovers recall each other, dreaming of the smell of their bodies, conjuring the focus of the lover, recalling the tone of voice. Foucault maintains that in heterosexual courtship issues of domination and submission are so enacted and settled in the leisure of time afforded the heterosexual, while the two lovers get to know each other prior to intercourse. The homosexual, on the other hand, must wait until the act is over before he discovers the lover's identity. Paul Robinson maintains that "the structure of gay sexual life is rather the reverse of straight life"—love grows out of sex, as "gays begin having sex at a much lower level of emotional commitment" (30). What Foucault says of retrospective love may be true of the homosexual's move toward object love, but is not true of the cruiser. There is no such lingering pleasure, but quite the opposite, a deadened and erased state.

Foucault and Robinson raise an important issue, it seems to me, which points to heterosexual oppression as a factor in the homosexual's sexuality. This does not contravene my argument that the arena is sometimes a place of self erasure; indeed, I now want to examine in just what way the heterosexual is complicitous in homosexual psychic pain.

James and Harry

I shall begin with what I consider to be unfortunately still a common response in the heterosexual to another human being who is assumed to be of like kind. Let us speak of two men who have recently met professionally. I shall call them James and Harry. James likes Harry, and after a second meeting asks where Harry lives and whether Harry has children. No, says Harry: no children; indeed, not even married. As conversation turns away from the personal, James has a slightly uneasy feeling about Harry, whose comradeship he has enjoyed. James wonders. Could it be that Harry is gay? Naw! No chance. But doubt sets in. In another meeting James cracks a joke about his boss's affair with his secretary, an open invitation to Harry to join in as a choral member of the heterosexual chase. Harry demurs, later discussing how this weekend he will visit his mother and also mentioning his love of opera. James's doubts set in more firmly. "I think Harry is queer," he muses to himself. Elsewhere he chats with a colleague, or a mutual friend, or his wife. "Do you think Harry is a fag?" he queries. "Could be!" replies the other. As the two heterosexuals scan their memories for corroborating information, all pointing to Harry's being gay, James will be in a different position the next time he meets Harry. So what has happened?

As one of my observations of the cruiser's experience in the arena is of being an "it," where love objects are partly his double—the object either introjected by or projected into the mother in her dreamy internal world—it is pertinent to consider just how the heterosexual converts the homosexual into an "it" before his very eyes.

Is he? Is he gay? Is he a fag? Is he queer? The epithets bear less force than the very question itself, which depersonalizes. Customarily, at least in the heterosexual community, one's erotic wishes and sexual identity are private. But under the pressure of the heterosexual's depersonalization, some homosexuals will indicate their sexual identity. Perhaps through a hint, a slight effeminate gesture—a discreet though distinct sign to the heterosexual of their homosexuality. "Oh, I just luuuuve Looociano Pavarotti; he's so fabulous, don't you just think!!" is enough to tell an anxious heterosexual: "Yes, I'm gay. Don't worry. I do it at the opera." In other words, some of the effeminate discourse becomes a signal to the heterosexual, answering latent anxieties without too abrupt a breach of privacy.

For the homosexual such moments may provide a rather uncanny experience. For as the heterosexual begins to sense the other's homosexuality, he converts the terms of this self-other situation from interrelating to his own internal object relation. He transforms the other person *into* a *thing*: a fag, a queer, a homo. And there, before his eyes, the homosexual experiences the creation of yet another double, the heterosexual's internal object. Not the idealized private object of the mother, but a despised figure evoking anxious and hateful feelings. What does the homosexual do? Does he say, "Please forgive me my sins, I confess"? Does he reply, "I'm in analysis, working on this"? He might. More likely he will either accept this defeat, knowing that his status as the heterosexual's internal object is crudely dismissive of his inner sense of self, or he may play the fag to the heterosexual, bringing this out into the open in a certain way. The point is that heterosexual objectification of the homosexual, which arrests interplay and spirits the person of the homosexual into a private if predictable inner space within the heterosexual, is sometimes an ironic continuation of this person's experience of being captured by the other's internal world.

James and Harry again. James has rendered Harry into an "it," and Harry has re-experienced that loss of true self to the other's internal world, an act of incarceration of the double so familiar to him. Let us slightly change the script with the passage of time. After business meetings, at the end of the day, Harry lets it be known to James that he is popping off down to a local gay bar for a quick one. This appears to happen every day. Indeed, after a business dinner James hears of Harry's plans to dance through the night, and Harry may make reference to his sexual conquests. Sometime in the course of this evolution, James may feel repelled by Harry's promiscuity. Were Harry heterosexual, were he fucking one woman after another, at some point James might confront him: "You're a jerk, you know that!" or "What! You just fuck them and leave them?" Initially James might convey a kind of old boys' envy: "Gee, how many you doing it with, you old cruster!" But eventually this will give way to a sense of outrage over this sordid expression of sexuality. In other words, a true expression of *feeling* would be present in that situation. But in the world of heterosexual-homosexual unrelatedness a James might more likely think, "Well, he's gay!" and write it off as something gays do. In other words, Harry would be treated at the affective and aggressive level as a self-defining "it," outside the bounds of human interrelating. This creation of false self unrelatedness re-creates something of that disconnection that prevails in some homosexuals' childhoods, with the heterosexual de-subjectifying himself in order to accommodate to the gay.

Readers of homosexual fiction will find a searing, often moving, and frequently tough-minded critique of the arena and its cruisers. I have no doubt that many in the homosexual community of writers often appraise the arena and the erasure of the subject as an affliction, perhaps as an illness of place. The resolution to the false self adaptiveness on the heterosexual's part does not lie in a misplaced pluralism which results in viewing all aspects of gay culture as simply a different order of things. Ironically, those heterosexuals who do shrug their shoulders when considering the arena —blithely claiming it is a matter of a comparative cultural anthropology—simply academize the false self, ensuring that some homosexuals remain an "it" to whom one grants a reserved space in an apartheid bounded by genial unrelating.

Finally, I trust that the spirit of this text makes clear what I consider problematic to the cruiser's world: an erasure of self that is relived in the arena, a place which seems to symbolize an inner experience endured by some homosexuals in relation to the mother, even though some may only rarely be cruisers. Through steady relationships, with the support of the gay liberation movement (particularly in men's groups), and in psychotherapy and psychoanalysis, distressed cruisers have been able to work through unconscious partic-ipation in their own elimination. I do not believe that any homosexual going to a sauna, disco, or park seeks the cruiser's death sex; if the search is to find a partner or to seek intimacy, then the homosexual is simply courting. Rather than being characterized by the aesthetics of space, the arena exists in the cruiser's frame of mind. A cinema for one homosexual is a place to watch the film; for another it is the arena.

8

Violent Innocence

During the McCarthy era, when left-wing and liberal writers and artists were brought before the House Un-American Activities Committee (HUAC), Arthur Miller wrote his play *The Crucible*. He used the Salem witchcraft trials of some two hundred and fifty years past to voice outrage over a persecution taking place in the present.

From the congressional investigator's point of view, the issue at the HUAC hearings was whether or not those subpoenaed before it had ever engaged in activities that were un-American. Were they guilty of holding views and participating in meetings which in any way expressed the cause of other than American ideologies? If so, they should confess and redeem themselves before the nation by recalling the names of those people with whom they had discussed their ideas, in some cases thirty years before.

In *The Crucible*, when the Reverend Parris's daughter takes ill some townsfolk discover that she and several friends have been dancing in the woods and conclude that this must be the work of the devil. The Reverend Hale is called from another town to determine whether Betty Parris's symptoms are the devil's work. The audience knows that the Reverend

Parris has happened upon the girls, one of whom was dancing naked: an erotic realization, shall we say, not beyond the realm of his dreams. Within moments of the opening scene Parris confronts Abigail, the girl who will ultimately lead the persecution and hanging of her elders. He tells her that he "saw a dress lying on the grass," and Miller has Abigail reply, "[innocently] A dress?"—forcing Parris to repeat his perception: "[It is very hard to say.] Aye, a dress. And I thought I saw—someone naked running through the trees!" Abigail protests vehemently, "[in terror] No one was naked! You mistake yourself, uncle!" The more Parris asserts what he saw, the more violent is Abigail's innocence.

Abigail is lying, and in a brief meeting with some of the other girls she demands that they "shut up." Her deviousness is somewhat understandable, as she fears a public whipping for her erotic dancings; but, as we discover, she is also the victim of a denial, when John Proctor—the man who ultimately leads the opposition to Abigail and who is hanged for it—disavows any knowledge of their having had sexual intercourse when Abigail lived with the Proctors. One can sense her fury, impotence, and bewilderment over his apparent innocence.

In the third act of the play, to my mind the most harrowing moment in American drama, Abigail is confronted by Mary Warren, one of her girlfriends. Mary reveals the girls' culpability, and an infuriated Abigail assumes the position of innocent witness to the presence of evil, as, stricken, she says, "A wind, a cold wind, has come." In the seventeenth century this signified the presence of the devil, and everyone looks at Mary, who—"terrified, pleading"—yells, "Abby!"— knowing now that Abby is setting her up to embody evil. Eventually Mary joins the now hysterical group of young girls who mime the devil's somatic influence.

Those of us who are American may do well to consider the functions of innocence within our history, from the time when the first Puritans were to found a "city upon a hill" to cast a saving light across the Atlantic and deliver the Europeans from doom, to something as recent as the 1988 presidential elections, when the leadership of the Republican party used the gesture of the simple pledge before the flag as a sign of one's Americanism, of one's innocence of un-American elements. It was interesting to see how this simplifying of consciousness—a trait of the innocent position—led to the successful location of disturbing phenomena (the debt, the homeless, pollution) in the Democratic candidate, who then represented the disfigurement of innocence: he was a gloom-monger, only focusing on what wasn't consistent with innocence; he was, in short, un-American.

The Types of Denial

All psychoanalysts are familiar with denial: the analysand's unconscious need to be innocent of what is often most troubling. Freud introduced it as a defense when discussing the boy-child's denial of the absence of a phallus in a girl, possibly a first step in a move to psychosis, as this affects the subject's grasp of external reality. The psychoanalyst's effort is directed toward uncovering the distressing ideas and affects that mobilized a denial in the first place, and although this is one of the most primitive defenses—in that very little ego work (i.e., symbolization or substitution, etc.) is employed—the analysand will of necessity resist the analyst's patient work, and over time the resistance will lessen and the denied content will enter consciousness.

Each of us is aware in ourselves of the workings of denial, of our need to be innocent of a troubling recognition. And although it can be frustrating for the other who aims to bring a denied content to the subject who "does not want to know," denial is not ordinarily considered within the framework of object relations theory. This is often as it should be. If a subject denies a perception, he does so because it troubles him. Abigail initially denies any knowledge of dancing naked in the woods because this recognition disturbs her, although here we are not dealing with unconscious denial. Her denial of what took place troubles the Reverend Parris, and we can see how her refusal to validate what both of them in fact saw forces Parris to struggle: he does not really want to talk about this. If only she will admit to it, and apologize, then he can explain to his neighbors that the disturbance in his household is nothing more than the miscreant work of adolescence.

But Abby changes the scenario when she becomes a radical innocent, disavowing responsibility for her actions, accusing the village elders of acting on behalf of Satan. When she becomes what we might term a violent innocent, she passes her crime into the other, who now stands accused. A denial of reality has now entered the field of interrelating at a dynamic level as the subject insists that the other bear an unwanted perception. The transitional moment from simple denial to violent innocence can be seen, in my view, when Abby's denial compels Parris to say more. As Parris speaks about what he has seen, Abby subtly suggests that Parris's perception derives from his desire. As he struggles to get her to own up to her actions, she uses the theater of innocence to identify him with the very accusation he brings. Indeed, he barely escapes persecution when Abby blames Satan for having them dance in the woods.

Violent Innocence

What takes place in the act I term violent innocence? In some respects the elders and adolescents compete to repudiate the experiencing self, each side claiming the authority to objectify the crisis in the collective mind of the closely knit village. But John Proctor has given in to his lust, just as the girls have yielded to shared erotic enactments, and it is such simple self states that are now condemned, indeed blamed on the work of the devil. By being innocent the subject provokes the other to speak the truth and sometimes sustains innocence in order to maintain some contact with the repudiated content. By provoking the other, the violent innocent stirs up distress, ideational density, and emotional turbulence in the other, a simple self sponsored by the sadistically cool and "objective" complex self, detached from the other's anguish. Later I will examine this situation in terms of the psychoanalysis of a particular individual, but vignettes of this process, in ordinary situations in life, may help to bring my topic into sharper focus.

(A)

Mary and John are sister and brother. Mary is fifteen and John is nine. As a recurrent expression of her sibling hate Mary stirs John up, out of sight of the parents, in order to get him into trouble with the mother and father. "Come, John, let's play army. Take your peashooter and see if you can hit anybody," she says, and then leaves John to shoot at an "enemy" while removing herself to another part of the house. "What are you up to?" queries her mother, passing by the sewing room, as she sees her daughter there. "Oh, I'm making some napkins for the table," she replies. "What a nice thing to do," says the mother, who now proceeds up to John's room, thinking she had seen something that looked like beans dropping from his window. Upon entering the room she finds John, head out the window, "shooting" at cars and people passing by. "What are you doing?" she cries. Caught in the act, he whirls back into the room. "What is that in your hand?" she yells. "It's . . . I . . . was . . . Mary and I are playing army." "No, you aren't! You are shooting peas at people, and anyway Mary is busy being helpful, not mischievous." "Ask her! Ask her! She said for me to do it."

In another place, the three of them together: "Mary, did you get John to do this?" Now, a good enough sister might at this point confess, and her younger brother, although having been the devil, will no longer be a solo venturer in crime. A not good enough sister might innocently say, "John, don't be silly. I've been sewing this last half hour." If so, Mary will have passed her impishness to the brother by eliciting his criminality in order to get him into difficulty (as well as to express her instinctual life) accomplished by her absolute innocence.

(B)

At a dinner party seated near Veronica, Isabel, and Harold, Edward is irritated by the attention being given to Harold. He knows that some five years ago Veronica and Harold (now married) had been close to ending their relationship because, at a professional conference in São Paulo, Harold and Isabel nearly had an affair. Over time, however, the three have managed more or less to forget about this episode. Earnestly requesting Harold's attention, during a lull in the conversation when Veronica and Isabel turned to attend to Edward's inquiry, Edward says, "Harold, Harold, Harold. Tell me. I have to go to São Paulo next month. I think you have been there, if I remember. What is it like?" If we assume further that Harold is not sure whether Edward knew of the episode, Edward may successfully appear perfectly innocent and Harold may suddenly find himself, as will Veronica and Isabel, in a rather tough situation. Harold may try to evade this by saying, "Oh, it's quite nice, Edward. Super place. Do go there. Be a good chap and pass the salt, will you?" And Edward may let it drop at that if he is satisfied that he has passed his discomfort, irritation, and vulnerability into Harold. Perhaps his sadistic intent is greater, however. "Would you like the pepper too? Some more wine?" See how helpful he is! "But you seemed a little ill after your trip to São Paulo. Was it an unpleasant experience for you?" "No, Edward. I was fine, just tired," etc., replies Harold, now clearly being pinned to this position by aggressive innocence.

Perhaps these stories have at least indicated the object-relational phenomenon which I wish to study. Now for Jessica.

Jessica

A stocky, red-haired, and assertive woman of thirty, Jessica came for analysis because she had been referred by a colleague of mine who found her behavior in a professional setting difficult. This, at least, was the pretext. In fact, she had had a period of psychotherapy with an analyst some years before, but she was convinced that he gave up on her because she was so deeply frustrating.

The cause of the previous analyst's frustration was not at all bewildering to me: some two months or so into the analysis I noted that Jessica corrected and eliminated virtually all of my comments, though occasionally they lived a short while when she would say nothing disconfirming in reply.

In the consultation I had found her pleasant, although very formal, even rather arrogant, but I assumed this might be because analytical encounter is anxiety-provoking. At the least, I thought, she is very proud and not very pleased about the way that she has been referred to analysis. In the first sessions she talked in a highly self-composed way about her upbringing and her marriage. She had grown up in the Lake District in an upper-middle-class family. Her mother was a well-meaning but anxious woman who had devoted much of her life, it seemed, to Jessica, and toward furthering her husband's modestly successful political career. Jessica had been the favorite of five children; she was the second in line, with a brother two years older, two younger sisters, and a youngest brother. Her father had thought well of her when she was a young girl, and she often preoccupied herself with his career and his interests. For example, he became semi-expert in the politics of Northern Ireland, and Jessica read up on this and was even invited by an Irish youth group to participate in a conference on Irish affairs. Her father thought this unwise, and because he was worried she might be abducted, he forbade her to go.

In early adolescence she began to do poorly in school, and although she passed her O levels, she never achieved the level of ability anticipated either by herself or by her family. She recalls feeling proud of herself for being at school and admiring the way she looked in the school uniform, but she could not get to work because she often felt quite blank. Her greatest passion during this period was her disgust with her older brother, whom she considered physically repulsive and socially uncouth. In sessions she would complain about his personal ineptness and describe in vivid and near-photographic detail his habits, mannerisms, and personal appearance. She fought back tears with vengeful sarcasm as she detailed her efforts to get her brother to shape up enough so he could accompany her to important social events.

Because she was disappointed with the "losers" who constituted her social set, she cast her gaze far afield, and one day it happened upon a solicitor whom she courted because she could see that he was going places. She did not find him attractive and was not in love with him, but to marry him would be a victory over all that she despised in the world—not least her family, who by her late adolescence were all disappointments.

Session after session was taken up with graphic details of her husband's ineptitude. She would take twenty minutes to describe his efforts to do the washing up: how he spooned the leftovers into the bin with a wimpish fear that he might splatter himself, contorting his body to avoid such a mishap; how he pathetically tried to engage in a conversation with friends at dinner, utterly misunderstanding the essence of the conversation and ruining the meal.

In describing these events she conveyed her contempt for him (or the brother), but whenever I endeavored to identify her feelings, she always disowned my comment. She once took some ten minutes to tell me how pathetically incompetent her husband was when he tried to fix the car. "He infuriates you," I said. "What makes you think I am infuriated by him?" she replied, quite taken aback. "You would put it differently," I replied, and she said, "I don't see that what I've said has anything to do with my being infuriated, as you say." On another occasion I said to her over a similar account, "He disappoints you." She replied, "Disappointment doesn't come into it. He is the way he is, and I am a rational person who simply sees things as they are. I don't see where what I've said leaves you thinking I'm disappointed in him." "Perhaps I overstated it," I replied. "It's more accurate, do you think, to say you were disappointed in his actions at the time?" She replied, "I wasn't, no. I simply think he was inept, it's the way he was, but I didn't have any feelings about it."

These interchanges between us were frequent, and I was left perplexed by her seeming inability to acknowledge what appeared to me to be clear expressions of feeling. I also found her denials irritating, particularly as she became even more arrogant and condescending in her manner, although she was manifestly polite and formal with me. When I collected her from the waiting room, she arose from her chair as if descending from a throne, did not look at or acknowledge me, and passed to the consulting room like the Queen walking through Westminster Abbey. I had never seen such a condescending person, yet so totally unaware— apparently—of the idiom of being and relating that way.

From the point of view of analysis the situation could have been dire, as in some respects she seemed to lack any degree of psychological-mindedness; but in other respects, even if unintentionally, she was quite self-revealing. Early on she told me that she invariably thought the most awful things about people and was pleased that she could keep things to herself. She assessed herself as a person with no personality, just a false self, who had never loved anyone or really felt that life was truly worth living. And, as I said, her descriptions of events (at home and work) were not only vividly recalled but rich in unconscious communications. It was simply that whenever I tried to identify her feelings, she always denied them.

I must say now what we all know: a clinical example must pass up so many important details. This is no exception, as I want to focus on a particular feature of her personality and its realization in the transference-countertransference dialectic.

I found that the analytical partnership was the occasion of a split. Jessica would describe an event that was vivid and affectively evocative, but as she denied all knowledge of feeling, I was continuously left to note the feelings derived from her narrations. In time her polite but contemptuous corrections of my reference to feelings quite irritated me. When she described her husband's rather sad yet moving effort to communicate, I identified with his pain and felt cross with her coldness and triumphant destruction of him. I mused how she refused to let him enter her life as she refused me analytical entrance into the world of her feelings. I puzzled, however, over the paradoxical nature of this transference-countertransference dialogue, as Jessica continued to provide me with reports that were virtually to ensure my self state, of which she was apparently innocent.

In the seventh month of analysis she drew my attention to a comment she had made many times before: to the effect that she suffered "fogs" or "blanknesses." "I have a feeling," she reported, "that I am now entering a fog. It's the strangest thing. I have many things on my mind yet I can't think here," whereupon she gave me convincing notice that she was very likely now to be in silence for months, "and I hope you can tolerate it," she said. I replied that for some reason she made her way into relationships (with her husband and her colleagues) which she sustained as empty shells of life— which I did not understand—but that the analytic relationship was a working partnership and I wondered openly if she really wanted an analysis.

I had never spoken to an analysand like this before. I am accustomed to working with patients who do become silent for long periods of time, but there was never any doubt in my mind that I would not facilitate this for Jessica. This was a considered view, but I felt angry with her announcement and I felt maneuvered by her use of London psychoanalytic lingo about the need for true self states to evolve in an untroubled holding environment. Jessica's announcement came on a Thursday after earlier sessions that week when she had begun to contact some early memories of her relation to her father. I linked her announcement to the previous sessions and to how unsettling they may have been for her, but of course I knew she would deny having any feelings.

In time I was able to see how Jessica's blanknesses were losses of awareness following quite meaningful self disclosures, but my efforts to attend to her anxieties over such disclosures were for a long time refuted by her insistence that such blanknesses were meaningless. Instead I found myself concentrating on the transference, how she provided me with considerable information that authorized my comments but which she turned into my authoritarianism by claiming to be innocent of the knowledge present in my remarks. I was able to link this enactment to the relation to her father, whom she initially admired, then envied, then scorned. I indicated that her moments of innocence left me the seemingly omnipotent father. For a period of the analysis we considered how she found such authority on my part exciting—once again she was dominated by a powerful father—but later we turned to the unconscious contempt she held for him: if I was content to assume my power from an innocent and helpless child, what kind of a man was I? Jessica responded to both interpretations. She knew that she hoped I would be a masterful analyst and she also knew that she enjoyed watching me struggle against her denials, as she then felt in a place of power with me a kind of helpless fool.

During the course of her analysis these processes and characterological states were meaningfully linked to her ambivalent relation to the father. But I thought I could not leave it there; there was a peculiarity to my countertransference that I mulled over again and again and which brought me back to considering the transference from its pre-Oedipal frame of reference.

The Recipient's Experience

To examine the structure of my countertransference I will exaggerate its overall significance in the analysis of Jessica: what I shall describe will sound more vivid and defined than it was. In fact, recognition of its structure was slow to form and took many sessions before I could grasp it and then put it to the patient.

1. The first feature of my inner state is to be with an other, Jessica, who seems pleasant and cooperative. I am pleased to be the analyst and I look forward to working with her.
2. I note a formality to her person in the first session, but I take this to be a sign of anxiety. Over time, however, this formality becomes a deep contempt which elicits states of doubt in me about my analytic competence.
3. I am mildly shocked by the patient's denial that her

descriptions of events suggest the feelings I ascribe to her. These cumulative shocks sponsor a tentativeness in me in relation to the obvious.

4. As the patient often describes a sequence of sadistic thoughts or actions (usually against the husband or a colleague), I find I am privately angered by the patient's gloating descriptions. But as I am in doubt about my grasp of this patient's communications, I am at odds with my affective registrations. The other suggests that my affective response is idiopathic.

5. As time passes Jessica suggests that my comments on her communications are not simply imperceptive but imaginary. But they seem to me to be the very foundations of perception itself. Was I seeing things?

6. Jessica then invariably wanted to know how I had come to my comment. What had she said that led me to my remark? At times this was internally confusing for me, as she intended that I account for what she more or less claimed to be hallucinatory percepts on my part.

7. I felt stirred up by her, transferentially acted upon to a precise effect, but then isolated by her to be the victim of my own affects, which I was invited to see as endogenously bizarre.

8. When I rephrased my comments, I realize, looking back, that I felt as if I was almost pleading with the patient as the manageress of the doors of perception. Would I be admitted? Did she agree that my sense of the situation was linked up to reality?

9. I sensed that the terms of my inclusion into the world of the confirmed—the ordinary—were wholly arbitrary, determined by a power my patient had either to include me or not.

10. In time I found her repeated statement that she had no idea why I thought the way I did was moving me to face the cold terms of her innocence.

11. I was aware of an inclination in me to retreat, exiting through the analytic door marked "neutrality," but I knew this was a halfhearted rationalization for backing away from an intensely organized transference.

In time, a picture did emerge of who or what the patient was in the transference and who or what I was in the countertransference. We reached this recognition fundamentally through my descriptions of the relation between the transference and countertransference. I puzzled out loud over what it meant that she disclosed important information, leading me to virtually certain comments, which were met by a seemingly innocent self who had no idea why I thought the way I did. When she was eventually able to split off a portion of her ego to join me in this observation, she could see that the relation that typified this scenario was the relation to her own mother.[1] At first she had characterized her mother as a nice but somewhat inconsequential

1. How do we know, however, that Jessica's mother was the person she describes? Psychoanalysis quite rightly regards such memories with suspicion. I tread a middle path between the view that such recollections are correct and those positions that inevitably hold that parental object representations are either wish fulfillments or projected parts of the self. For a very long time, indeed, I usually accept my analysand's accounts of maternal or paternal behavior as valid, in order that I may assess whether or not pathologic maternal or paternal behavior seems to consistently serve as the vessel of an unwanted part of the patient's personality, or whether the analysand acts out said aspects of the parent in the transference. In time the analysis refers less and less to the mother and increasingly to the patient's self. References to the past become less significant. As reconstructions decrease, and as the patient's character is increasingly understood within the transference, the question of what the mother actually did, or who she actually was, fades into its proper place: into the areas of speculation and hypothesis, profoundly tempered by a forgiveness intrinsic to the more important realizations of one's own generated disturbances. I intend to address this important question, of the invocation of the name of the mother in psychoanalytic reconstruction, in a future essay.

woman—a bit of a worrier—but it became clearer that Jessica had diminished the significance of the mother to deal with the mother's lack of rapport with her. I could see that as a child she felt affected by a mother who was disinclined (for many reasons) to assume any responsibility for disrupting or disturbing her child. The mother seemed innocent. Jessica partly resolved this dilemma in relation to her mother by taking aspects of it—a form of early transference from the mother-child relation to the father-child relation—to the father. In particular, she took the child self who was deeply confused and frustrated by a maternal absence (and denial) to the authoritarian father who knew it all and apparently had a reason for everything. By identifying with the father's parenting of the child who is so puzzling (the mother's girl), Jessica placed the dilemma into the structure of a classic interchange between some fathers and daughters: he was to find her a "silly little girl" who could become admirable by following in Daddy's footsteps.

In the transference-countertransference re-creation of this complex family situation, Jessica played the mother to my experience of her child self, inviting me to feel deeply confused, angry, and isolated in the presence of maternal denial of contact. This is to be resolved (according to her) by a role reversal, in which the patient tells me she is really rather stupid, I am a highly esteemed analyst, and I am invited to be the powerful father who with this daughter-patient seals over a very disturbing and disturbed object relation.

Jessica's unconscious representation of the history of her violent innocence eventually revealed her presentation of the effects of a primary object upon her ego, but I do not wish to suggest that this repetition of an early object relation is the sole means of developing a radical innocence. Indeed, another patient, Teresa, in a deep rage over the birth of her younger sister, developed a hatred of reality that evolved into a malicious antipathy toward her father, who seemed to her to embody the relation to reality. She clearly felt provoked, confused, and isolated by the unwanted arrival of her sister. In her adult relations, and in analysis, Teresa would act upon the other in subtle but persistently aggressive ways, yet whenever confronted she would plead absolute ignorance of the provocation and then proceed to accuse the recipient of bringing disturbing mental contents into her life. We can see that by provoking the other she gives birth to the recipient's injury, stirring up the other to an isolated and frustrated position, accomplished by her refusal to acknowledge her actions. Thus the recipient's isolation within the realities of interrelating is a transference-countertransference invention of Teresa's isolated hatred of reality, as the victim of Teresa's enactments comes to feel an intense discomfort and eventual repudiation of that reality created by Teresa. In this case, a violent innocence develops from the child's own intrapsychic processing of a lived experience, rather than, as with Jessica, from the child's possible repetition of maternal action against the self. Of course, there is always an interplay between the intrapsychic and the intersubjective, and a risk in presenting vignettes such as these about Jessica and Teresa is that a psychoanalysis is oversimplified in order to convey a certain distinction. This inevitable hazard, regrettable though it may be, is an unavoidable feature of any effort, in my view, to isolate single factors contributing to the psychic texture of any person in an analysis.

"Never Mind"

I hope the stories and brief clinical examples have set the stage for a deeper understanding of what I mean by violent innocence. Clearly it is a form of denial, but one in which we observe not the nature of the subject's denial of external perception, but the subject's denial of the other's perception.

We are looking at denial in an object relations frame of reference to see how an individual can be disturbed by the actions of the other that are denied. The analyst can differentiate between an internalized denial that is part of an object relationship and endogenous or simple denial by analyzing the transference and its countertransference. If the patient's denial of perception of reality gradually yields itself to insight through free associations and analytic interpretation, then we are witness to endogenous denial, even if we can trace this denial back to family attitudes. Denial that is part of an object relation works in the transference according to a split, in which the patient induces the analyst to entertain feelings and ideas of which the patient denies any knowledge. It is a dynamic whereby the patient uses the analyst to struggle with feelings that are split off, not in order to have an unwanted mental content detoxified by the process of interpretation, but to inflict upon the analyst a relationship which sometimes re-creates the patient's experience in childhood of facing parental denial.

The violent innocent sponsors affective and ideational confusion in the other, which he then disavows any knowledge of—this being the true violation. The recipient is invited to sink into an intense lonesomeness, where feelings, thoughts, and potential verbalizations have no reception. Here the recipient sits at a doorway, between intrapsychic life and intersubjective existence, where a fundamental question is posed: "Am I alive to the other to whom I speak, or am I to be dead there—in intermediate space—to live only in my carefully managed and dehydrated internal world?" To be the recipient of the other's provocation, an aimless intent until formation occurs through the definition of the object relation (when chaos becomes pathological order), is to be strangely caught up inside the other, then dropped as a dumb dream object that has served its purpose.

The recipient of violent innocence knows little. He has been disturbed by the actions of the other who projects something into him, or who evokes an unprocessed mental content.

"Never mind," we say often enough as we begin to articulate an idea or feeling. "It's nothing, forget it," we may add. A common enough event in life which may elicit a grunt from a companion who has, perhaps only mildly, been stirred to curiosity. Whatever "it" was that might have reached representation sinks back to its place of origin. But the act of violent innocence stirs the mind, tumbles it about, forces the mind to experience its uselessness, as whatever it is that is being conveyed is unknowable in its form. A mind in action, yet a never mind: a mind that is not to know its own contents. The other who has caused the mind this predicament could clear things up through an explanation of the provocative action. But the innocent gaze, the refusal, disavows assistance and the mental life of the recipient is to have a disturbed useless mind.

This seems to me to be one of the unconscious aims of violent innocence when enacted in the analytical setting. The analyst is coerced into a position where his inner mental state is useless as a means for processing self-other relating. To be there, where mind is useless, is to be in a place occupied by the child whose mind was of no use. As a self state, then, what is a uselessly active mind?

If I am a child of five and unselfconsciously at play, expressing, let's say, my instinctual life, and my mother enters my space, frowns, and indicates irritation but refuses my question as to what is wrong, where am I? Perhaps I will reprocess actions, ideas, impulses, and feelings of the last moments and try to find the cause of irritation. But what if this intrapsychic research meets with no recognition when reported to the mother who remains removed?

Is not intrapsychic work useless? Am I not invited into a speculative projection, a scrutinizing employment full of "mights": it might be this, it might have been that. Then where am I? Am I not slightly at odds with my own mind as an object? Do I not, then, distance myself from the nature of mental processing as this world of speculative projections, of "ifs" and "mights," fails to relieve me of the psychic pain caused by the other? If I am a child, am I not liable, then, to blank myself, to fog out mental life, to dull my evocative response to the actual object world?

So Jessica's "fogs," which she intended to be our fate, were her traditional response to meaningful sessions which I think elicited desire (and awakened mental life) in relation to the other.

Or, as in the case of Teresa, and returning to the child of five whose mother enters the room, perhaps the child denies maternal comment on the self, and, furthermore, accuses the mother of odd and idiopathic perceptions. As the years pass, the child refuses to accept anyone's mental objectifications of her personal affects, eventually denuding her own mind of its capacity to process her own aggression. In this respect, then, "fogs" or "blanknesses" are the psychic outcome of continuous projective identifications of the child's own mind into the other, who is momentarily left to process the self's aggressive states, and given that the child furthermore repudiates the other's mental processing of the aggression, mental processing is further attacked, eventually leading to a massive lack of contact with the inner contents of the self.

Innocence and the False Self

The psychodynamics of violent innocence are a commonplace, often seen in marital relations, families, and groups. "Whatever is the matter?" "You don't seem content," are the musical chords frequently played as instruments of violent innocence, when a subject assumes the posture of false wonder to disturb the other. Indeed, this is often one of the more perverse dynamics of pathological group processes.

Imagine an institution of a hundred people. Like so many places, it may be strife-ridden; there are unpleasant rivalries, vicious gossips, and powerful people jockeying for positions of authority. Imagine that its shared fantasy is that it is an admirable place, a cut above comparable institutions. Perhaps I should term this a shared false self that conceals the true states of mind, as the place, let's say, believes it could not survive the truth about itself. But in such a place, though everyone knows how awful some of the dynamics are, each also believes that part of the price of continued admission is to collude with a collective false self. Although privately, to one's closest colleagues and spouses, one could say how it really feels to be part of the place, in the public domain one reckons it is best to say that it is "inspiring" or "stimulating" to be there.

We could say that a violent innocence is present in that each appears innocent of the more disturbing truths that are a part of the place. And those who are exceptionally gifted at false-self technique will contribute to the structure of innocence that climatizes the institution.

Inevitably, though, one, two, or twenty people will at times breach the false self and express views about some of the unpleasant realities. "I see, do you really find it so here?" an innocent may reply to the subject who slips up and speaks. The speaker may be invited to say more, and in a sense actually partly process the conflicts indigenous to the place, but in a split-off manner, as the subject's expressions of feeling are regarded as idiosyncratic formations of feeling and thought.

I recall an institution's group process in which the group would characteristically invite one of its members to express her view whenever the suppressed conflict was in frightful collision with the group's false self. X was the group's "feeler," who could not disguise how she felt, and whenever the assembly needed a type of relief, X was invited to express her pain—which she always did—although the group sustained its functioning false self by nursing X through her affective distress, ensuring that she continued to serve as a split-off receptacle of suppressed psychic pain. Whatever X's personal dynamics were, there was an underlying cruelty to the group's innocent questioning of this member, as she was always stirred up to ideational confusion and affective turbulence by such seemingly thoughtful inquiries into her view of the situation.

To be sure, if one "knows the score," if one knows that the rules of place inevitably involve negative hallucination, then the split between false self and true self in institutional life can be lived with. One must sometimes falsify one's response. "How do you find it here?" "Oh, fine. Invigorating place." Two innocents whose mutual gaze blithely erases the truth which will be its own casualty.

The Illusion of Understanding

The analysand who commits acts of violent innocence does not simply impose an isolation upon the analyst and bring about a disturbed and useless frame of mind. Beneath the structure of the projective identifications that place the analyst, there is a profound despair and an insidious cynicism. How can I describe this?

Winnicott wrote about how the mother facilitates an illusion that the infant creates the world (mostly the breast and the mother herself) out of his own needs and wishes. From this practice comes a sense in the child that the world understands and is shaped by him. This illusion is quietly sustained by the language we hold in common that cultivates an assumption that what we mean when we speak is what the recipient understands through our speech. If I say, "Would you please pass me the paper clip?" and the other does so, I am assured that I am understood. Countless simple transactions of this kind sustain the powerful idea that people understand one another. In this belief lies a freedom to assume reception that facilitates communication and creativity.

The idea that we understand one another through the different orders of communication is, in my view, largely illusory. In the first place, as Freud has taught us, the conscious self is inevitably only a partly present creature, his unconscious voices speak up now and then, reminding us how little we understand of ourself. Harold Bloom, the literary critic, has argued that literary history is a tradition of creative misperception, as poets and novelists distort, alter, and misread the works of their masters. Norman Holland's research of ordinary readers' responses to literature convincingly demonstrates how we misread the literary object.

These observations might serve a rhetoric of despair, employed to argue that we are hopelessly removed from one another. If we don't understand each other, whatever is the point to communicating? Yet this does not seem to me to be true, even though each of us has repeated conscious experiences of not being understood. How can this be? Why is it not the inauguration of a comprehensive doom?

At the heart of this factor in human life is an extraordinary paradox. Because we do not comprehend one another (in the discreet, momentous conveying of the contents of our internal world) we are therefore free to invent one another. We change one another. We create and re-create, form and break our "senses" or "understandings" of one another, secured from anxiety or despair by the illusion of understanding and yet freed by its impossibility to imagine one another. This is, I suggest, a double paradox. Because we do not comprehend one another we are free to misperceive—an act of creativity—and so, out of this gap emerges unconscious mental life, or intersubjective play, which brings us closer together. We do not thoughtfully understand one another any better, or at least not much better, but as we play we come closer to one another.

Two paradoxes and now an irony. It is likely that we are compelled to know more about the other when the illusion of understanding breaks down. During such breakdowns we are forced into reobjectifying one another, renegotiating the terms of conscious understanding of each other; while if the illusion of understanding prevails, we are lulled into countlessly creative, subjectively determined misrecognitions of one another in the interest of deep play.

We have, furthermore, a highly restricted understanding of one another, as so much of what we unconsciously know, about ourself and the other, will remain unthought. Freud cannily realized that the rule of free association employs this paradox: that if we cease the search to discover our hidden thoughts, simply relax and unselfconsciously speak what's on our mind, we shall release meaning into limited understanding through the work of displacement, condensation, symbolization, and so forth. Nowadays I think we must add to this view of free association that interplay of ideas and affects exchanged in the transference and countertransference between patient and analyst. The play of interrelating, the free association of two distinct subjective idioms, will remain largely unthought, though what does reach consciousness (such as through a good interpretation) is prized partly because of its unusual status as a valued fragment of thought knowledge.

We are, however, engaged in unconscious communication with one another. Messages conveyed to a recipient will be unconsciously perceived, and certain deep understandings —those, for example, that constitute the intuitional dialectic of genera formation, where patient and analyst construct a new vision together—are possible, but the very ingredients of unconscious life, the displacing logic of primary-process thought, the distorting effect of ego defense, always mean that unconscious communications between people are as likely to mislead consciousness as they are to lead it. This is especially so if the recipient tries to convert the subject's unconscious communications into premature conscious sense, as often—though not always—the subject will respond to such effort by further more elusive displacement, condensation, and defense, if the subject senses that too much consciousness of the latent mental contents is close at hand. It is as if the patient's ego, sensing the recipient's ego working to move an unconscious content toward consciousness, resists it, unless the subject is wishing to be understood—in which case there will be a kind of dance of mutual displacements, distortions, affective reciprocities, and psychic gravitational attractions that assist the continuation of shared communicating. In a sense, if the recipient plays with the subject's unconscious messages, a dialectical intersubjectivity is established, as the subject feels free to send his latent unconscious ideas and feelings to the other, as the other will reply in like language, rather than in the imperial palace of conscious logic. It may seem absurd to say that unconscious communication is unconscious, but in this day and age that term is often used to specify the patient's unconscious expression which is consciously comprehended by the analyst; here, though, I wish to emphasize a type of discourse which eludes consciousness for both participants. Certain conscious understandings do, however, emerge from unconscious communication, but these will be less comprehensions of precise mental contents than mutually constructed understandings limited to distinct episodes shared by the participants.

Unconscious communication does not mean surreptitious conveyance of a clear message. It means that the subject engages the recipient in the language of the unconscious, which means that part of the aim of such a language is to deceive and mislead the other. The irony is that such an intentionality is precisely understood by the recipient's unconscious, which thinks in exactly the same terms; it is rather like two Balkan merchants shrewdly misleading one another toward a sale in which each feels certain that the other has been well and truly cheated. So, as the other receives the subject's unconscious communications, he will not be able to consciously understand what is conveyed, but he does understand the dense logics of deception, and in this regard he can engage the subject in a similar language. What a curious paradox it is that unconscious communication takes place as acts of conscious misunderstanding ensuring that unconscious discourse survives. But do we not all know this? Have we not all had the experience, in the midst of talking and working our way through some only partly known subjective state, of being brought up short—and suspiciously so—when the other nods and says, "Ah yes, I understand perfectly!" All the more odd, isn't it, when we discover that they have indeed understood our manifest text, and yet we feel that somehow we have not really been heard.

Characteristically, we do not arrest each other in such moments to demand exactitude of thought. Certainly, we may stop each other, question one another, "correct" a misperception (for the sake of the functioning of the illusion, I should add), but human discourse would be the first casualty of exactitude, as the urge to ensure exact understanding would either paralyze the playful creation of one another or lead to a formalization of exchange that expels misunderstanding as it legalizes the exchange of thought.

Inter-knowing, then, is only ever an act of part understanding; its dialectic, in fact, is generated more out of the creatively misperceptive play of imaginations that meet up continuously if enigmatically through the nature of this dialectic. To know, here, is not to understand or comprehend; it is to play, especially *to be played* by the evocative effect of the other's personality idiom, a correspondence between two unthought knowns.

Unconscious communication is thus a dialectic between two subjects who distort, displace, and condense one another's received communications in the spirit of unconscious play that, like the dream work, only ever represents a part of the psychic truth through a complex medium of wonderfully inventive repudiations. In this sense, not to gather the other into one's consciousness is, strangely enough, to be in touch with the other's otherness, to remain in contact with the inevitable elusiveness of the other who cannot be known, a vital factor in marriages, deep friendships, and good analyses.

The person who becomes a violent innocent may have suffered a rupture in that essential early play with the other in which creative misperception is allowed to be perceptive understanding. (All children need to seriously distort "reality" for a very, very long time in order to "make" the world into a true "psychic reality.") Jessica was not free to play with the mother, who compelled her child into premature realization that we are not capable of understanding the nature of the other's inner self experience, and therefore, by extension, we too are not understood by our primary objects. Infants and children need to believe that the mother knows them from within, a powerful illusion that partly authorizes speech and play, the progressive investments in representational audacity. Forced into a telling isolation by the rupture in the illusion of understanding, Jessica lost the love of speech and play.

Or, as with Teresa, a violent innocent may create a rupture in interrelating in order to take revenge upon reality for "its" injurious provocations of the infant's narcissistic equilibrium. This child will then attack reality by refusing to play with it, accomplished by a continuous assault on the other's attempted play with the self's communications. A Teresa will incessantly point out that the other has distorted her statements or misconstrued her intentions, and by breaking down units of communication into scrutinized segments of mutual analysis, she can sufficiently deconstruct dialectics in order to prove that she is correct and that the other has wrongfully submitted a perceptual distortion of her exceptionally precise meaning. In a relatively short time the other will abandon the play of interrelating, defeated by the militant presence of a fine-print mentality.

A further casualty of this catastrophic disillusion is the corresponding loss of affective life (in particular the feelings between people) as a secret compensatory alternative to understanding. Sometime in the future we may understand more about feelings as a nonlinguistic system of communicating that generates powerful senses of understanding, even though what is known between any two feeling persons is likely to be ideationally misconstrued constructions. The violent innocent destroys the analyst's feelings that he is in rapport with the patient and so cuts off this partnership from the rhythmic progression of affective interplays that sustains and inspires the participants to creatively misunderstand one another. The life of feelings, a vital constituent to the interplay of two persons, sustains the illusion of comprehension, authorized by the dialectic of unthought knowledge between two subjects and maintained by a degree of realization in all of us that to live a life is to be in some place of inevitable solitude which is unsharable as an idiom, though shared by us all as a common factor in human life.

The violent innocent provokes the other to a uselessly disturbed frame of mind that is left to a defining isolation through the refusal of recognition. In the analytical setting such a patient may provoke the analyst to interpretation in order to deny the analyst's associations, to stir up the analyst's inner life in order to isolate him. In so doing, the analysand communicates through the transference and countertransference that experience of being with an other who provokes and then departs, innocent of the act of aggression. Finally

such a patient may be attacking the essential illusion underlying human discourse that we understand one another
through speech. By forcing the analyst to mind his speech,
to eat his words, this analysand unconsciously seeks to
represent either his or his parents' failure to play with misrecognition.

9

The Fascist State of Mind

"Our program is simple," wrote Benito Mussolini in 1932. "They ask us for programs, but there are already too many. It is not programs that are wanting for the salvation of Italy but men and willpower" (185). "What is Fascism?" asked Gramsci some ten years before Mussolini's spartan statement. "It is the attempt to resolve the problems of production and exchange with machine-gun fire and pistol shots" (82).

Fascism seemed to simplify the ideological, theological, and cultural confusions that emerged from the failure of the Enlightment view of man to comprehend human existence. It was, argues Fritz Stern, a "conservative revolution" constituting "the ideological attack on modernity, on the complex of ideas and institutions that characterize our liberal, secular, and industrial civilization" (xvi). Where the Enlightenment had partly emphasized the integrity of individual man, twentieth-century Fascism extolled the virtue of the state, an organic creation driven by the militant will of the masses, a sharp contrast indeed to the federal republic encumbered by checks and balances dividing power so that the people remained individually free to speak their minds in a pluralistic society.

While Freud reconsidered the dark side of man's self, this id never was free as a virtuous agent of the innate will of man. It became part of an internal federation of complex checks and balances, of ego working with superego against id, or id with superego in compromise negotiations with the ego. Freud rethought man and maintained some considerable belief in the power of reason to influence the id, and even if his theory of the death instinct accounts for the possibility of a mass negation of life, he remained a Bismarckian with a sense of real politics: life was to be an endless series of compromise solutions between the parts of the self. At the end of a Freudian life it is possible to be a Montaigne, rendered far too wise by the mayorial negotiations of existence to characterize ontology as a "pursuit of happiness," but nonetheless continuously respectful of the individual skills of man to negotiate a good enough life.

Like many Europeans of his time, Freud deferred recognition of a deeply troubling factor in human culture, an element which preoccupies us now with its haunting relevance: the related issues of terror and genocide. In February 1915 the Ottoman government decreed that its Armenian population would lose the privileges of the ordinary civilian, and immediately the slaughter began. In that year 800,000 Armenians were massacred, and although the *entente* nations (Britain, France, Russia) protested to the Ottoman government and Arnold Toynbee collected a volume of essays testifying to the atrocities against the Armenians, this was to be a massacre that could not be inscribed in the symbolic orders of Western thought; references to it were scarce indeed. There is no mention in Freud's work of the elimination of 75 percent of the Armenian population. Nor indeed does he make more than a single reference to the pogroms that preceded it in European history.

Although the genocide against the Jewish population in Nazi Germany—the Holocaust—seems an irreplaceable icon to evil in the twentieth-century mind, we may wonder if its ironic function (the Jew now used once again to serve as a point of projection) is to serve as a continued mental negation of the continuation of genocide. We seem to know this, as citizens of the Western world do try not to eliminate from their thoughts the re-emergence in Cambodia of the Khmer Rouge which put to death millions of people. "Never forget," the cry of the Holocaust victim, seems a tellingly apt injunction: we seem all too able to forget.

"Terror is the realization of the law of movement: its chief aim is to make it possible," writes Hannah Arendt, "for the force of nature or of history to race freely through mankind unhindered by any spontaneous human actions." Is genocide, the mass implementation of terror, social license to remake the world according to one's vision? "Those who are not of my species are not my fellow men . . . a noble is not one of my species: he is a wolf and I shoot" (O'Sullivan, 49). So spoke a French revolutionary. And from 3 executions a week in 1793 to 32 a week in early 1794, the revolutionaries executed, on average, 196 people a week in the summer of 1794.

But a noble is not man but wolf, so is this the destruction of a lowly creature? In genocide a person is killed for who he is, not for what he does, which prompts Kuper to pose an uncomfortable question: as there is a "thoroughgoing dehumanization of the bourgeoisie" in the Communist manifesto, is it possible to see this intellectual act as a precondition for Stalin's elimination of such bourgeois elements in his death camps (95)? In other words, is this famous act of Marxist objectification, the vilification of the bourgeoisie to which thousands of intellects since that time have paid lip service, the "warrant" for killing some 20 million human beings in the years between 1919 and 1939 (59)?

In the *perestroika* world created by Mikhail Gorbachev it now seems not only possible but equally essential to think not only about what we have done but about who we are, or what we are, when we license genocide. As a psychoanalyst

I turn my attention to that frame of mind which is the warrant for the extermination of human beings. I term it the Fascist state of mind, knowing that in some respects this is historiographically incorrect, as Fascism was a particular movement in world history with highly unique features to it, but I justify this license by playing on the double meaning of the word "state." There was a Fascist state. The coming into being of that state and its political theory can tell us quite a lot about another state: the state of mind that authorized a Fascist theory. Furthermore, like it or not, "Fascist" is now a metaphor in our world for a particular kind of person, and I wish to reserve this ironic scapegoating of the Fascist from the convenient movement of its person-ification of evil, as, like Wilhelm Reich and Hannah Arendt, I shall argue that there is a Fascist in each of us and that there is indeed a highly identifiable psychic profile for this personal state.

Noel O'Sullivan, a political theorist and author of a fine study of Fascism, dismisses the psychoanalytical literature on Fascism as "dangerously complacent . . . since it merely explains Fascism away by pushing it out of sight into a psychiatric ward." He disagrees with Martin Wangh's view (247) that the idealization of Hitler relieved homosexual tensions through submission to the leader, and objects to this and other analytical studies of Nazi pathology as failing to "explain why other nations whose children were left fatherless in the First World War did not produce successful Führers and Nazi-type mass movements." Psychoanalytic studies, he continues, "explain everything, and therefore tell us nothing"; they assume that any sane person would be a liberal, and "once this hidden postulate is granted, it naturally follows that those who dislike parliamentary institutions, respond to nationalistic appeals, and show a taste for heroism and self-sacrifice, are the victims of some psychological disorder." The psychoanalytic argument, O'Sullivan concludes, ultimately claims that Fascists are the insane, and liberals and psychoanalysts are the sane (27).

Some analytic studies of the Nazi movement may have suggested that there was an illness peculiar to the Germans, and if such a disorder is regarded as an idiosynchrome of culture and history, then I would join O'Sullivan in regarding such psychoanalytical positions as worryingly simplistic. It is my understanding of a prominent feature of psychoanalysis that the pathology found in the Fascist movement is inside each of us, and that one aim of a training analysis is to provide the analyst-to-be with the evidence of neurotic and psychotic processes within the ordinary self. Indeed I shall argue that it is possible to be both a liberal believing in a parliamentary world and yet capable of developing a Fascist frame of mind. I thus find no contradiction between a belief that a world of checks and balances mitigates genocide and the view that as the Fascist state of mind is ordinary, it can indeed subvert the democratic mind.

There is a view now fairly common in psychoanalysis that the subject is composed of varied parts of the self. These parts are the ordinary functioning parts of the mind (i.e., the workings of the mind according to Freud, Klein, Fairbairn, and Winnicott) and the differing selves and objects represented in this internal world. It is rather like a parliamentary order with instincts, memories, needs, anxieties, and object responses finding representatives in the psyche for mental processing. When under the pressure of some particularly intense drive (such as greed), or force (such as envy), or anxiety (such as the fear of mutilation) this internal world can indeed lose its parliamentary function and evolve into a less representative internal order, particularly as differing parts of the self are projected out into other objects, leaving the mind denuded of its representative constituents.

To see the mind's move to Fascism, we need to consider just how this democratic order is changed. How does one become Fascist? Eric Brenman suggests that "the practice of cruelty" is a "singular narrow-mindedness of purpose" that when "put into operation . . . has the function of squeezing out humanity and preventing human understanding from modifying the cruelty" (256). In object relations terms, humanity is presumably represented or representable by the presence of different capacities of the self (such as empathy, forgiveness, and reparation) which had been squeezed out of the self.

Kleinian psychoanalysts frequently refer in their literature to the "killing off" of those parts of the self, thereby emphasizing the factor of murder as an ordinary feature of intrapsychic life. Rosenfeld, for example, describes an aggressive aspect of the narcissistic self state achieved by "killing their loving dependent self and identifying themselves almost entirely with the destructive narcissistic parts of the self which provides them with a sense of superiority and self admiration" (248). Compare this psychoanalytic observation to the terrorist credo of Mikhail Bakunin's *Revolutionary Catechism* written in 1869.

> All the tender feelings of family life, of friendship, love, gratitude, and even honor must be stifled in the revolutionary by a single cold passion for the revolutionary cause. (67)

Bakunin's statement is a conscious articulation of what the revolutionary must do to achieve his cold passion, and perhaps because he knows (has made conscious) what must be squeezed out, we can feel the horror and sadness of this psychic movement. Rosenfeld, however, addresses the unconscious equivalent of this process, and in a passage strikingly relevant to our subsequent considerations of political genocide, he likens destructive narcissism to the work of a gang:

> The destructive narcissism of these patients appears often
> highly organized, as if one were dealing with a powerful gang
> dominated by a leader, who controls all the members of the
> gang to see that they support one another in making the
> criminal destructive work more effective and powerful. (249)

The death camps of Buchenwald and Dachau come to mind,
the training ground for the SS, a gang dominated by a
hierarchy of Hitler clones who watched each other commit
atrocities in order to ensure that no one in the gang stepped
outside the ethos of terror. There could be no internal
opposition to the gang's operation of the death camps,
organized by their "death work" (Pontalis, 184). "Terror
becomes total when it becomes independent of all opposition," says Arendt. "It rules supreme when nobody any
longer stands in its way" (464). Other psychoanalysts (e.g.,
Kovel and Federn) have addressed certain mental mechanisms that are useful to an understanding of the Fascist state
of mind.

It is incumbent to very briefly outline the extraordinary
study by Robert J. Lifton, who believes the key to understanding how Nazi doctors committed acts of genocide yet
remained ordinary family men lies in the psychology of
doubling: "the division of the self into two functioning
wholes, so that a part self acts as an entire self" (418). Such
doubling may be ordinary—for example, when a surgeon
needs to be his ordinary doctor self in order to perform
operations. Nazi doctors escaped the sense of guilt arising
from their evil actions by transferring the guilt from the
ordinary to the "Auschwitz self." Nonetheless, argues Lifton,
the Auschwitz self must become psychically numb to commit
atrocities, something partly achieved by refusing to name
the act of killing, finding instead many alternative words.

Lifton brilliantly illustrates the link between these Nazi
doctors' sense of being inside the atmosphere of death and

their increased omnipotence and mechanization of self as they transcended the death feeling. German genocide, argues Lifton, emerged from the sense of death that followed on from the First World War, a war that left Germans with a "profound experience of *failed regeneration*" (468). A sense of collective illness pervaded the country, leading to a "vision of total cure" (470) which the charismatic Hitler provided. The cure that becomes genocide, according to Lifton, must be total, invincible, transcendental. The victim of genocide is designated a disease that could contaminate the self and must therefore be eliminated, sponsoring a "genocidal necessity" that is a "fierce purification procedure" (482).

The Fascist State of Mind

Whatever the factors that sponsor any specific social act of genocide, the core element in the Fascist state of mind (in the individual or the group) is the presence of an ideology that maintains its certainty through the operation of specific mental mechanisms aimed at eliminating all opposition. But the presence of ideology (either political, theological, or psychological) is hardly unusual; indeed it is quite ordinary. The core of the Fascist state of mind—its substructure, let us say—is the ordinary presence of ideology, or what we might call belief or conviction. Arendt finds the seeds of totalitarianism in ideology because ideologies "claim . . . total explanation," divorce themselves from all experience "from which they cannot learn anything new," insisting therefore on the powerful possession of a secret truth that explains all phenomena, and operates from a logic which orders facts to support the ideological axiom (470–71).

Thus something almost banal in its ordinariness—namely, our cohering of life into ideologies or theories—is the seed of the Fascist state of mind when such ideology must (for whatever reason) become total.

To achieve such totality, the mind (or group) can entertain no doubt. Doubt, uncertainty, self-interrogation, are equivalent to weakness and must be expelled from the mind to maintain ideological certainty.

This is accompanied, in my view, by a special act of *binding* as doubts and counter-views are expelled, and the mind ceases to be complex, achieving a simplicity held together initially by bindings around the signs of the ideology. Political slogans, ideological maxims, oaths, material icons (such as the flag), fill the gap previously occupied by the polysemousness of the symbolic order. When the mind had previously entertained in its democratic order the parts of the self and the representatives of the outside world, it was participant in a multifaceted movement of many ideas linked to the symbolic, the imaginary, and the real—Lacan's terms. Specifically, words, as signifiers, were always free in the democratic order to link to any other words, in that famous Lacanian slide of the signifiers which expressed the true freedom of the unconscious (this Other) to represent itself. But when representational freedom is foreclosed, signifiers lack this freedom, as ideology freezes up the symbolic order, words becoming signs of positions in the ideological structure. When Michael Dukakis tried to introduce complex issues in the American presidential campaign of 1988, George Bush made the word "liberal" a sign of weakness visited upon the certain mind by doubt and complexity. To supplement his destruction of the symbolic order Bush made the American flag the sign of the difference between Dukakis and himself; sadly, it signified the end of discourse and the presence of an emergent Fascist frame of mind.

As the empty binding of the order of signs constitutes an act of de-semiosis, it enables the mind to function in a highly simplified way, cushioned initially by the success of such binding.

O'Sullivan believes there is a "marshall sense" to Fascism, which I shall define here as a binding of mental forces to create a sense capable of murder. In a way the elimination of the symbolic, of polysemousness, is the first murder committed by this order, as the symbolic is the true subversion of ideology. The slide of signifiers will always dissipate a bound meaning and subvert any act of solidarity, a fact which Freud showed so very simply in his numerous demonstrations of how the parapraxis subverts the position of the conscious subject.

Aware of the pathological functions of certainty, Freud wrote in *The Future of an Illusion*:

> An enquiry which proceeds like a monologue, without interruption, is not altogether free from danger. One is too easily tempted into pushing aside thoughts which threaten to break into it, and in exchange, one is left with a feeling of uncertainty which in the end one tries to keep down by over-decisiveness. (21)

Ideological certainty, then, in spite of its binding of the self through simplification and the exile of other views, is threatened by the sudden breakthrough of the pushed-aside thoughts, which now must be dynamically ordered by an overdecisiveness.

This will work for some time, perhaps for a long time. Stuart Hampshire claims that the Nazi movement created "a dizzying sense in German minds that all things are possible and that nothing is forbidden . . . and that there is an infinite moral space now open for natural violence and domination" (69). The psychoanalyst Janine Chasseguet-Smirgel sees this infinite moral space as the pervert's accomplishment eliminating (at first Oedipal) opposition to desire and gaining objects without opposition. Hampshire argues that the violence inherent in the Nazi moral space has left "a great vacancy . . . a moral void" (69), which psychoanalysts such as Chasseguet-Smirgel, Khan, and Stoller, who study the perversions, would agree lies at the now empty heart of the pervert.

The moral void created by the simplifying violence of an ideology that brooks no true opposition is also an essential consequence of this stage in the evolution of the Fascist state of mind. For although the binding of signs and the power of certainty dull the subject into complacency, the moral void created by the destruction of opposition begins to make its presence felt. At this point the subject must find a victim to contain that void, and now a state of mind becomes an act of violence. On the verge of its own moral vacuum, the mind splits off this dead core self and projects it into a victim henceforth identified with the moral void. To accomplish this transfer, the Fascist mind transforms a human other into a disposable nonentity, a bizarre mirror transference of what has already occurred in the Fascist's self experience.

As contact with the moral void is lost through projective identification into a victim, and the victim now exterminated, the profoundly destructive processes involved are further denied by a form of delusional narcissism which is constructed out of the annihilation of negative hallucination, an idealization of self accomplished by the negation of any alternative (and thus enviable or persecutory) self or environment. As the negation of the qualities of the other are destroyed via the annihilation of the other, a delusional grandiosity forms in the Fascistically stated mind.

It is at this point that the process of annihilation is idealized in order to supply the Fascist mind with the qualities essential to delusional narcissism. Mental contents are now regarded as contaminates, and the Fascist mind idealizes the process of purging itself of what it has contained. The cleansing of the self suggests the possible birth of a new, forever empty self to be born with no contact with others, with no past (which is severed), and with a future entirely of its own creation.

The foregoing mental processes can be seen, in some

respects, in Nietzsche's semi-autobiographical *Ecce Homo*. At a time when he suffered from continuous episodes of vomiting, traveling about Europe he became preoccupied with "the question of nutriment," by which he meant not only literally what one ate but also what sort of national culture one took into oneself. He proclaimed, for example, that "the German spirit is an indigestion" while extolling the virtues of Italian culture and life (52).

Ecce Homo is, by any account, a deeply anguished text, full of contradictions, which, if they evoke our interest and compassion, are nonetheless remarkable actions of split consciousness. "I am by nature warlike," he proclaims (47); yet elsewhere he claims: "no trace of struggle can be discovered in my life . . . I look out upon my future as upon a smooth sea . . . ruffled by no desire" (65). Perhaps this is a sea of vomit, accomplished through a continuous warlike spirit that leaves him feeling serene.

I refer to Nietzsche because at times he defines quite precisely the unconscious idealization of the self as an empty, and therefore pure, container. "I possess a perfectly uncanny sensitivity of the instinct for cleanliness," he writes, adding that this instinct has given him a sense of smell for the unclean "innermost parts, the 'entrails,' of every soul" which are the cause of his "disgust." No doubt in such moments he would have to vomit up these noxious internal objects in order to maintain his sense of inner purity: "As has always been customary with me an extreme cleanliness in relation to me is a presupposition of my existence, I perish under unclean conditions" (48).

Such a state of mind extols the virtue of being pure, uncontaminated because nothing is taken into the self, the psyche living from its sense of antiseptic accomplishment by maintaining purity in its own right, achieved by the continuous oral evacuation of the noxious. We can find this phenomenon, however, in ordinary life, whether it be spoken by those who attempt to claim the position of pure Christianity, pure objectivity, pure science, or, dare I say, pure analysis!

The greater the annihilation of the opposition, the more delusionally narcissistic the Fascist mind must become, a psyche now empty of ideas other than those performing a pure sign function—to bind the state of mind—a mind that idealizes itself as a cleaning process. It is not difficult to see, then, why the Fascist did not share the Marxist's belief in a logical history, but supported a movement that idealized struggle (or riddance) in its own right. As Mussolini wrote:

> War alone brings up to their highest tension all human energies and puts the stamp of nobility upon the peoples who have the courage to meet it. Fascism carries this anti-pacifist struggle into the lives of individuals. It is education for combat . . . war is to man what maternity is to the woman. I do not believe in perpetual peace; not only do I not believe in it but I find it depressing and a negation of all the fundamental virtues of man. (185)

But this so-called struggle is, in fact, no combat at all. How far we are indeed from that "noble" warfare found in the chivalric code of the *Song of Roland* when the virtue of one's opponents ennobled the act of physical battle. What is this male maternity to which Mussolini refers? Is it not the death camps, where the living are brought to a container, stripped of their culture, their loved ones, their adult characters, and turned into bizarre fetuses eventually to be killed in this deadly womb?

Some who opposed Fascism, such as Giovanni Zibordi, were able to diagnose the Fascist need to be at war. In 1922, in "Towards a Definition of Fascism," he wrote that after the First World War "the officers sympathize with Fascism because it represents a prolongation of the state of war internally, and of a possibility of war externally" (89). Psychoanalytically considered, this permanent war is actually against struggle, against the conflicts brought on by continued engagement with opposition views. The idealization of war and of the warrior is a call to a state of mind that rids itself of opposition by permanent violence.

Cotta suggests that there is a "circuit of de-personalization" conducted by the person who submits to domination by passing on to another victim his own circumstance. "Violence has its origins and triumphs within the circuit of de-personalization thus actuated, which ultimately leads to a dispossession of oneself" (63).

This loss of self seems to me to be that loss of humanity to which Brenman referred, and which leaves in its place an idolized skeleton, a figure (leader, ideology, or state) revered for its militant capacity, in the end an idealization of the capacity to murder the self.

Thus the concentration camp, a metaphor of the psychic process of Fascism, is the place where, as the humane parts of the self are dehumanized and then exterminated, the death work is idealized in the death workers who cleanse the body politic of the undesirables. As Susan Sontag argues, when illness is used as a metaphor for the opposition, then the act of elimination is viewed only as a necessary surgical intervention. Reference to the opposition as a disease or cancer that must be removed from society (and mind) is a frequent feature of the Fascist mental state, leading eventually to an idealization of the anti-human. Writing of the mobile killing units of the SS, Leo Kuper muses that "the 'ideal' seems to have been that of the dispassionate, efficient killer, engaged in systematic slaughter, in the service of a higher cause" (122). "Higher" here is a metaphor of that grandiosity that achieves nobility by rising above the human: Kuper quotes from an address by the chief of the SS to his top commanders in October 1943:

> Most of you know what it means when 100 corpses lie there, or when 500 corpses lie there, or when 1,000 corpses lie there.

To have gone through this and—apart from a few exceptions caused by human weakness—to have remained decent, that has made us great. (122)

Intellectual Genocide

"Genocide" is a word coined by the jurist Raphael Lemkin in 1944, from the Greek *genos* (tribal race) and the Latin *cide* (killing). Lemkin found a word that linked up with "tyrannicide" and "homicide" and thus inscribed itself in the symbolic order, enabling us finally to think about this crime.

The process that leads to a Fascist state (of mind, group, or nation) is unremarkable, and evidence of its emergence is easy to detect. I intend to list the features of what I shall term *intellectual genocide*, to name the mental processes precursor to, and eventually part of, the genocidal act. I do so, as will be clear toward the end of the chapter, not only out of interest in this problem but because I think identification of ordinary genocide (the genocide of everyday life) may lead us toward self scrutiny and confrontation of others when we see that an individual or a group has taken on this form of representation of the other. Because it is so ordinary, it is easily identifiable but, equally, because of its unremarkable status, it is also capable of emergence into mass murder.

I start by differentiating between committive genocide, identifying its visible traits, and omittive genocide, which is an act of omission.

Committive Genocide

Distortion. In the early stages of a possible move to a Fascist state of mind, the subject subtly distorts the view of the opponent, rendering it less intelligent or credible than hitherto. This is an ordinary part of debate, but in the extreme manifests itself as slander.

Decontextualization. A point of view held by the opposition is taken out of its proper context, which recontextualized would make the content more credible. This is an ordinary part of debate and the victim of decontextualization will naturally struggle to fill the gaps created by this rhetorical violence. The extreme of this act is the removal of a victim from his tribe, home (i.e., context), isolated for purposes of persecution.

Denigration. The belittling of an opponent's view combines distortion and decontextualization, rendering the opponent's views ridiculous. This is a door through which affects (of scorn and belittlement) move and displace ideation as the machinery of conflict with the opposition.

Caricature. This is the move from the denigration of the opponent's views to cartooning of the individual who presumably holds the views. Again, it is part of ordinary rhetoric to caricature the opposition's view and yet it is a transfer from the view held to the holder of the view. It therefore represents a significant step in the identification of a person or group with ascribed undesirable qualities.

Character assassination. This refers to the attempt to eliminate the opposition by discrediting the personal character of the holder of a view. An unacceptable form of debate, it is an ordinary part of discourse, usually referred to as "gossip." This perfectly harmless act of character assassination ("Oh, I do love gossip! Tell me all about it!") which discredits an opponent by conveying fictions or facts in a nonjudicial place—notably where the victim cannot speak for himself—can eliminate a person from the scene of consideration.

Change of name. Again, this is sometimes an acceptable part of debate but with obviously more disturbing manifestations ("kikes" for Jews, "gooks" for Vietnamese) that form part of the act of elimination of the proper name, precursor to the elimination of the person himself (from the scene of consideration or from life itself). It is ordinary ("You know, what's his name. Thingy"), sometimes acceptable, if tiresome (when a person's name is consciously distorted for humorous purposes), and may be an unconscious parapraxis when the name is unknowingly altered.

Categorization as aggregation. These terms, used by Kuper, are useful to define the moment when the individual is transferred to a mass in which he loses his identity. It may be ordinary: "Oh, but of course she is Freudian." It may be permissible, if dicey: "Well, of course she is ill" or "Well, he is a psychopath." Or it may be an extreme act of lumping together: "He's a Jew."

Omittive Genocide

Absence of reference. This is an act of omission, when the life, work, or culture of an individual or group is intentionally not referred to. Again, this is an ordinary feature of life: one group may get rid of the contributions of another group by never referring to them, or a writer such as Solzhenitsyn may be removed from bookshelves, or in the extreme there are no references to crimes against humanity.

When a person or a group addresses the opposition in the terms outlined above, alarms should ring in the witnesses to such action, who may respond by not engaging in vicious gossip or by directly confronting an individual who distorts, decontextualizes, denigrates, or caricatures the holder of different views. Such confrontation aims to arrest, at the very least, intellectual genocide. It is ordinary. Yet even in its purely rhetorical expression it can be extremely destructive. If an individual or group, previously participant in discourse, is a ceaseless object of intellectual genocide, then the recipients will show the effects. Some will simply leave the scene, no longer partaking in the group—a kind of voluntary exile in the face of persecution. Some may be pushed to express extreme views, victims of a violent innocence (discussed in Chapter 8) who appear to have gone over the edge. Others may somatize the conflict: a heart attack, we know, is often the outcome of extreme duress in one's place of work. Others may attempt to form alliances with the persecutor in an effort to gain some form of protection against their own potential destruction.

My point here is to raise intellectual genocide within our consciousness as a crime against humanity. Since it is ordinary, we can do something about it in the simple Freudian way of talking about it in the here and now and therefore partly divesting the act of its potential by addressing it.

The Vicious Circle

We could say that until Lemkin created a word for mass murder, "genocide" managed to elude the signifier and thus escaped its representation in a symbolic order. To this list of obstacles I wish to add a few more.

One of the most perplexing features of the success of intellectual genocide is that its most gifted practitioners not only seem to achieve places of prominence by viciously attacking others; indeed they also seem to become objects of endearment to those who otherwise—one would have thought—would be horrified by such behavior. I recall a right-wing political figure in my hometown in Southern California, a person who vilified the opposition, spread vicious gossip, and damaged many, many people. Yet he was almost loved as a kind of cute monster. I also recall, only a few miles down the road, another person known for his viciousness who was finding himself the object of endearment: Richard Nixon. And though we knew of Stalin's monstrosity we still turned him into good old Uncle Joe.

The puzzle is why we "love" these monstrous monsters

rather than oppose them. Why are they allowed to climb so far up the ladder of success, sometimes to a place of leadership where they continue to eliminate the opposition in vicious ways? Perhaps they represent us. Perhaps we fear to challenge such an individual. There must be some truth to that, but I also think we observe an interpersonal sleight of hand in which the monster person is "the impossible loved object" because love here exonerates the subject from re-sponsible opposition: "I wish I could stand up to Mary, but you know she's just impossible and I'm afraid I love the old monster." Presumably confrontation of the monster must be reserved for those who don't love the monster, and yet almost everyone gives the same shrug of the shoulder: "How can Mary be challenged? She is Mary and her very monstrous qualities, darn it, are what we kind of love about her." In some ways this seems to me to be the interpersonal equivalent of creating a type of joke. Aggression—the anger or outrage evoked by such a person's behavior—is turned into humor: Mary becomes the basis of our laughter about the atrocious. But such an obstacle to confronting viciousness in a person, and in some cases the practice of intellectual genocide, is no laughing matter and deserves our continuing study. I con-sider this further through a personal vignette.

I attended high school in Orange County, California, during the 1950s, and for a limited period of time it became compulsory for the students to attend Christian anti-Communist crusades in—of all appropriate places—Disney-land, and usually with a visiting speaker, who now and then was Ronald Reagan. I particularly admired one of my history teachers, who struck me as an intelligent and very decent man. Yet in the weeks approaching such events and most intensively at the crusade itself, he became rabid in his hate of the liberal conspiracy that was plotting to overthrow the U.S. government.

I had not known his politics until then and I recall being shocked at the utter transformation in his character whenever contemporary politics entered his mind. I think most of us were bewildered by him and by what I would now term a local psychotic state. But what we did is of interest: we turned this aspect of his behavior into a joke. He became our loved madman, and occasionally one or another of the group would "push his button" and send him across the boundary from the sane to the insane part of his personality.

Discussing the vicious behavior of a person, people will often say, "But you know, she really is quite a lovely and kind person" or "Well, you know, removed from her pulpit she is really quite a different person." And this is true. But it is not the point. In fact, this opposes the point: humanity (the good parts of the self) is now used to excuse the destructive side of the self. The joke, as always, now borders on the perverse. The humane now authorizes the inhumane as Mary's viciousness is loved, in the economical exchange between the Fascistic and the non-Fascistic parts of her personality.

Even if we accept that compliance with a Mary is in the interests of vicarious support of one's own viciousness, which will always be partly true, the act of dissociative acceptance (the "how Mary is really privately a nice person" story) colludes with the function of genocide. In this case, however, it is the witness who, by tacitly accepting Mary's viciousness, accepts the eradication of the humane as a joke: the world will then be full of monstrous Mary stories, tales of her beastliness.

When we excuse the destructive behavior of anyone by citing their humanity, we commit a crime against the function of humanity. When we distance ourselves from collusive responsibility for the destructive effects of the vicious person by turning them into a joke of sorts, we pervert the truth. It is this corruption in the citing of humanity that perverts truth and that constitutes essential contextual support for any vicious person's successful establishment of the Fascistic parts of themselves in the successful movement of the social group to its own Fascism.

The noncollusive witness to that personality change that occurs when the person crosses over from the sane to the insane parts of the self, is initially shocked by this transference. We all know how stunning it is, when discussing an issue with someone, to witness the person's vicious espousal of a doctrine that derives part of its energy from the intellectual annihilation of the other. We may be speechless. Such a rupture also occasions a sense of dissociation: we feel immediately separated out from the conversant's insanity. And following this dissociation, part of us will feel deadened by the eruption, as now it is clear to us that the other is subject to an internal Fascistic process. In a way our response is our victimage. It is in feeling shocked, dissociated, and deadened that we share elements in common with those who are more severely traumatized by socially operant Fascism.

We may also share responsive qualities in common with a collusive witness, whereby we may try to recover from this trauma by reminding ourselves how, in so many other ways, this person is not only sane but likable. In this respect we use our humanity and its link to the humane parts of the other to recuperate from the trauma, but, as suggested, the irony of this is that it ultimately excuses, and finally supports, the destruction of humanity. Often we feel a certain dread as we sense our responsibility to those who are the objects of this person's intellectual genocide. We must say something that at the very least marks our opposition to the Fascistic state of mind.

When we exonerate a vicious person's actions by citing elements of their humanity, I think we create a perversion in logic itself—in thinking—that is part of what we may consider the vicious circle. It is of interest that from the seventeenth century the word "vicious" was used to describe a fault in logic, when a conclusion was realized by false means of reasoning. Webster's third definition of the vicious circle cites this fault in logic: "an argument which is invalid because its conclusion rests upon a premise which itself depends on the conclusion." The argument that Mary is really a good human being, in spite of her nefarious actions, because she is at the same time a human being, is a circular argument, a flawed logic that perverts the truth because it comes round full circle. Indeed, I use the word "vicious" to describe the person in a Fascist state of mind not only because this word signifies one who is "full of faults," which seems an apt description of one carrying moral voids determined by massive evacuations, but because we may also speak of a particular process—the vicious circle—which is definitionally affiliated with the vicious person, that suits my analysis of such a person as involved in a particular mental process.

A vicious circle is also defined as "a situation in which the solution of one problem gives rise to another, but the solution of this, or of other problems rising out of it, brings back the first, often with greater involvement." Another definition states: "a situation in which one disease or disorder results in another which in turn aggravates the first." It is exactly this type of process which, in my view, takes place in the Fascist state of mind: whatever the anxiety or need that sponsors the drive to certainty, which becomes the dynamic in the Fascist construction, the outcome is to empty the mind of all opposition (on the actual stage of world politics, to kill the opposition), a process that ironically undermines the vicious person. It does this by creating a moral void which further increases the underlying uncertainty which set the mind on its pathological track to certainty in the first place.

It is a procedure which Nietzsche regards as a virtue: "the doctrine of 'eternal recurrence,' that is to say of the unconditional and endlessly repeated *circular course* [italics mine] of all things" (81). The cycle of purification through violent expulsion leaves a void which Nietzsche tries to fill with a

notion of tranquillity derived from the liquefaction of opposition: "I swim and bathe and splash continually as it were
in water, in any kind of perfectly transparent and glittering
element" (48), which is possible until he meets up with any
human element which fills him with a sense of disgust (48).
To the extent to which Nietzsche portrays early on the
process of thought subsequently peculiar to the Nazi movement, we can see how the Fascist sea of inner tranquillity is
mirrored by those horrid seas of internment camps that
contain the Fascist's vomit: the place that purifies them
because it contains the indigestible opposition.

For a person incarcerated in the concentration camp, it is
hard to find any vestige of the humane that could possibly
offer resistance to the Fascist state. In *The Informed Heart*,
Bruno Bettelheim tells us that humane gestures expressed
by one detainee to another were punished by death. One
eventually could not help the other. Nor indeed could the
subject express any of his feelings about the treatment meted
out to the other and to oneself. Expression of feeling led to
further torture and sometimes to extinction. Thus those
qualities we value so highly as expressions of humanity—
helping others in need and expressing our feelings and
views—were eliminated. In that situation, incarcerated in
Buchenwald, Bettelheim knew that to lose one's humanity
was to risk personal madness. How could he remain sane?
He discovered that it was through an ironic act sponsored
by his extreme state: he would observe the SS, study them,
consider at an intellectual remove what was taking place. "If
I should try to sum up in one sentence what my main
problem was during the whole time I spent in the camps,"
he writes, "it would be: to protect my inner self in such a
way that if, by any good fortune, I should regain liberty, I
would be approximately the same person I was when de-
prived of liberty" (126). He had to accept, therefore, a split
in his personality between the private world of his own
thoughts—which ultimately were unreachable by the SS—

and "the rest of the personality that would have to submit and adjust for survival" (127). This is an extreme state of victimage in which the subject can only retain his humanity by preserving his sanity, which he accomplishes by accepting a split of sorts in his personality. It is interesting that thought and memory, the capacity to perceive reality, to think it, and remember it, become the core of potential recovery to a humane future.

We can see, then, why any person or group which has suffered a genocide must reach a point in the process of recuperation when remembering what actually happened is crucial. It is not only an action aimed at objectifying the crimes committed against the self, but, as Bettelheim hints, to recuperate from one's own destruction of the humane parts of the self in the interests of survival. As the victim seeks his own safety and deserts his fellow man, there will be an enormous loss of self respect. Only through further self analysis and self expression can the victim recuperate that love of himself that is an ordinary part of the generative narcissistic structure of human relations. I suggest, therefore, that the ultimate human response to genocide is self preservation: following physical liberation from the terms of aggression, this curiously inhuman side of the preservation of one's humanity (the will to survive) will move toward its abandoned humanities first by memory, then by speech, and finally by true grief. There is a triumph, here, of the seemingly inhuman (our Darwinian move) that is curiously more humane than the collusive acts of humanizing the monstrous parts of the self.

If a person, group, institution, or country truly wishes to recover from the traumas of intellectual or physical genocide, then it will have to remember the crimes it has committed. The act of remembering is the antecedent to forgiveness (of self and others) and instrumental to the reparative rehumanization of the group. This painful process is often bypassed by denials ("it is water under the bridge") aimed to thwart recollection, and by transfers to the next generation, which is somehow meant to naturalistically displace the crimes of the older generation and absolve that generation from its collective responsibility. And as we know, a new generation, though seemingly possessed of its own displacing vision of the future, is highly liable to inherit the sins of the fathers.

10

Why Oedipus?

When Freud designated *Oedipus the King* as a theatrical metaphor of the crucial psychic conflict of the individual, linking the worlds of politics, literature, and psychology in one fell swoop, like Sophocles he dramatized the many factors that constitute human complexity, as he was astutely aware of the mythic, civic, psychic, and cultural elements that contribute to the living of a life.

There is a vast, intelligent, and compelling critical literature on the play and on Freud's view of the Oedipal scene in the life of the individual, which I shall not review here. Instead I shall consider the Oedipal dilemma as a complex that is independent, if that is possible, of any of its singular participants, including, of course, the child Oedipus who kills his father and sleeps with his mother. This is not to diminish the solitary significance of the Oedipal horror or its psychic place in the life of every child whose desire threatens him with terrors and whose father is essential to the survival of such fears, but I think Sophocles explores a more tragic fate than the frame of mind constituted by the Oedipal dilemma.

The Planes of Reference

Hesiod's *Theogeny* was the fundamental oral version of the Greek myths passed from one generation to the next. Curious forms of condensation, myths often derive from specific historical events, and when they do they bear some link to reality; but the persons who form the tableau of a myth exist at different times with represented events from diverse unrelated cultures yoked into one false unity, occasionally populated by fabulous creatures and fantastical events. Versions of a myth are also subject to change, in what Robert Graves terms "iconotropy": the moment when a mythographer deliberately misinterprets the visual representations of a sacred picture (the pictorial place of myth as a visual condensation) by weaving a verbal picture that changes it (21).

The legend of Oedipus was well known to Athenians. The audience knew the outcome of the hero's future, and even though differing playwrights and storytellers changed the inner details of the legend, Oedipus always slew his father and slept with his mother. As Knox points out, Sophocles used this fact to place the audience in the position of the gods who could see the full course of events and yet, by identification with Oedipus, be drawn into the inner texture of his specific dilemma: a mirroring of that oscillation we all endure in life between our complex reflective self states and the location of the simple experiencing self.

What are some of the elements that Sophocles weaves into what I term the psychic context of his play?

In the Greek middle ages, to which some of the play refers, kingship was the universal form of government. With the collapse of trade, kings could no longer afford their retinues and gradually their power was usurped by a regent, then a council, then a group of judges, to form the nine Archons of Athens which formed the structure of Greek democracy. The kings were not abolished, however; they served a ceremonial function closely allied to the temple and the patron god of the city, an ironic affiliation as the temple took the place of the palace.

The Greeks also had in mind—in some part of their mind—the transition from the world of the warrior-king (the Achilles figures of Homer) to the world of the figure of discourse—a Pericles—who could participate in democracy. This evolution is not total or absolute. In Sparta, only a hundred miles from Athens, was another society that continued to revere the patriarchal. Shall we speak, then, of Athenians knowing of two structures: one monarchial (or dictatorial) and the other democratic?

At the same time they would have had in mind the legendary transition from a matriarchal world order to a patriarchal one. It is unclear whether there ever was a matriarchal society in Crete before the invasion by the Greeks, but even if there was, it is hard to believe that such a culture was, in fact, known by the Athenians, as surely it would have spawned a rich mythological elaboration. But the Athenians certainly did have a powerful myth of a matriarchal line, as in their mythology Gaia was the founding god of all the gods and mankind. She was a kind of primordial element who gave birth to Uranus without coupling with a male, and then coupled with Uranus to propagate the gods. Greek mythology is in large part the saga of conflict between men and women. So, if there was in fact no matrilineal culture, there was certainly a powerful myth of an originating maternal power out of which men emerged and eventually took power. This evolution, if one can put it that way, was very much in their mind, and certainly Sophocles played upon its ontological resonance in the life of each child who was born from the mother and who became subject to the father's law.

If we believe Robert Graves, however (whose work on myths is open to serious question), there *was* a matriarchal society in Crete which was dominated by a queen who annually appointed a king. In prehistoric Greek culture this king was allegedly appointed annually (a probable representation of the seasons and of fertility), while the queen ruled until her death, passing on her power to her eldest daughter. Occasionally the king substituted for the queen and wore false breasts. At the end of his annual reign the king was "sacrificed" and there were many and varied symbolizations of his death. Commonly, he endured a symbolic execution, yielding his kingship for one day to a boy-king who "died" at the end of the day, although sometimes he remained as alternative to the king. Note how he might be killed:

> His ritual death varied greatly in circumstance; he might be torn in pieces by wild women, transfixed by a sting-ray spear, felled with an axe, pricked in the heel with a poisoned arrow, flung over a cliff . . . or killed in a prearranged chariot crash. (Graves, 18)

Perhaps audiences attending *Oedipus Rex* identified Laius's death by chariot and Oedipus's immediate reign as partly symbolic of a legendary annual ritual, practiced within a matriarchy, a mythic trace of an alleged prior social structure considered now within a democratic society which was still bearing traces of its more recent patriarchal power structure. Thus the mother, the father, and the group are part of the psychic texture of this play, layered into the action at different points of symbolic reference.

The audience also knew of a legend that Tiresias had once seen two snakes coupling and had intervened to kill the female. He was immediately turned into a woman and could only regain his masculinity some seven years later when he returned to kill the male serpent. Indeed, he was responsible for a small war between Hera and Zeus, who were quarreling over which sex gained the greater pleasure in intercourse. They called for Tiresias to settle the matter, as he had been both a man and a woman. He infuriated Hera by claiming that the woman had the greater pleasure, but that is another matter. What is of immediate interest to us is Sophocles's placement of Tiresias in this play as such a crucial figure, insofar as he represents not only bisexuality but bisexuality based upon the murder of the female element (snake) which can only be undone by another murder (of the male snake). The psychic density of the Tiresias myth only adds to the play's extraordinary complexity.

From the above mythical elements one could add many other features which become part of the psychic context.

1. That the return-of-the-exile story was a well-known pretext (or subsequently revisionist act) for invasion by a foreigner.
2. That children were sometimes abandoned and left to die, having been spiked in the foot, to stop the ghost of the child from coming back to haunt the parents.
3. That outside the cities were people in settlements not taking part in city life, people who were exiled for one reason or another—for example, younger sons who could not be included in the city space and so were abandoned to the fringes.

We could dwell on these different factors and deconstruct the play in a particular way following the logic of each element's contribution to Sophocles's argument. My aim, however, is only to establish that Sophocles's play operates on many planes of reference, and I shall now consider how this tells us something about the nature of the complex Freud associated with Oedipus.

The Evocation of Dense Psychic Texture

Sophocles constructs a drama that will evoke within the audience a dense texture of inner associations so subtle and complex that as they play upon the mind they invite the acute work of the ego to process them. But the ego will inevitably fail to grasp in consciousness the full meaning of the events—not simply as this is a cognitive impossibility but because the unconscious issues presented are so disturbing that the subject represses or splits off what is knowable. The drama invites the subject's psychic response to displace conscious frames of mind, which is partly achieved by subversive presentation of a myth which all presume to know in advance, thereby lulling the witnesses into a false and premature sense of the play's meaning.

Although the myth of Oedipus's life is not a complex tale, Sophocles dramatizes the story from so many interlaced dimensions (from Oedipus's view, from the leader's perspective, from Creon's place, from Jocasta's view) that its mythic integrity is subverted by multiple points of identification with its characters, challenging what we think we know.

For example, we know Oedipus discovers that he has in fact killed his real father; or rather, we know this will be true. But when, along with him, we hear that there were several men at the crossroads, like Oedipus, we have some momentary doubt. How could it have been he if there were several attackers? Indeed when the story of the murder is first put to Oedipus, his powerful conviction to root out the truth marries with Jocasta's later admonition to stop thinking and to forget. Creon's martial actions and Tiresias's befuddling riddles also bear the sense of powerful conviction and certainty that pervades the play. But this sense is continually undermined, as we know, by the course of events, which reveal more truth to challenge that sense.

If we were to review Oedipus's first response to Creon's

story of Laius's murder, we would, like some in the audience, note how Oedipus inserts psychic truth into the discourse. Speaking of the attendant who survived the murder of Laius, Creon says:

> He said thieves attacked them—a whole band, not single-handed, cut King Laius down. (135–40)

to which Oedipus replies:

> A thief, so daring, so wild, he'd kill a king? Impossible, unless conspirators paid him off in Thebes. (140–45)

Oedipus changes the story to murder by a single thief, and no one corrects his error. He repeats this error in conversation with the leader.

> LEADER: Laius was killed, they say, by certain travelers.
> OEDIPUS: I know, but no one can find the murderer. (330–35)

Note now how the leader responds:

> LEADER: If the man has a trace of fear in him he won't stay silent long, not with your curses ringing in his ears. (335–40)

Oedipus has transferred one truth into the prior taken, or objective version, so that now his truth usurps the former narrative account without any apparent conscious recognition of this.

How many people in the audience caught this? How many in Freud's Vienna recognized this, or how many today pick it up? We shall never know. But surely some will miss it. Perhaps they are feeling the sense of impending trauma as Oedipus echoes his own initial dispossession. He does not know that he is Theban and that he was abandoned by the king to die upon a mountain. We know this. And as he calls for the exile of the murderer and sets his people on a course of action, we know that he will re-create the original trauma to himself, now lived out in his mature years.

When he subsequently rails against Creon, who has in innocence gone to fetch Tiresias, who in the audience is not overcome with a sense—from the emotional unconscious— that Oedipus is correct to be suspicious and enraged? And if we are not, note how deftly Sophocles nudges us to recall something:

> CREON: . . . But this injury you say I've done you, what is it?
> OEDIPUS: Did you induce me, yes, or no, to send for that sanctimonious prophet?
> CREON: I did. And I'd do the same again.
> OEDIPUS: All right then, tell me, how long is it now since Laius . . .
> CREON: Laius—what did *he* do?
> OEDIPUS: Vanished, swept from sight, murdered in his tracks. (620–25)

Have we noticed that Creon breaks in on Oedipus to demand what Laius did, thereby calling attention to Laius's crimes? As Creon speaks, he unwittingly represents Laius in the heat of a moment, so when Oedipus expresses his sense that a deep injustice has been committed against him, we are reminded of his victimage. Do we recognize the expression of unconscious truth? Laius's crime? He "vanished"!

But perhaps this moment is lost upon the audience, some of whom are caught by Oedipus's suspicions that Tiresias is a "sanctimonious prophet." Caught up in thinking about something else, they do not hear Creon's question, thus failing to note its unconscious point.

The experience of being caught up in one's own particular train of thought is a feature of all human mental life, but one that especially fascinated Sophocles as he played upon the unconscious capacities of his audience by bringing them into the web of the play's complexity, displacing coherence with the fecund violence of emotional turbulence and wild associations.

We—or, I suggest, Sophocles—could argue that at any one moment in time the truth lies right before us. Certainly more than one critic has commented on Oedipus's extraordinary failure to see the truth before he set himself to suffer it. Why didn't he realize that, having killed the wealthy man at this crossroads, he had in fact killed a king? Why didn't he ask questions upon his arrival? Many more points along this track could be raised, but we know that human denial and the power of the wish are sufficient to blind.

And if Sophocles intends to set us an example of the extremes of mental process by putting Oedipus before our eyes, as certainly he does—when we learn that we should allow time to pass before moving to action and that we should listen to others—he does so only to signify a feature of our own personality: that we are a human complex.

Indeed, Sophocles lets us know—if we see it (and many have not)—the true riddle posed by the Sphinx, or perhaps I should say, the other riddle. We all know the manifest riddle and Oedipus solves it, to apparently rid the world of a scourge. But the Sphinx poses a hidden riddle, which Sophocles puts before his audience. In the streets of Athens, after the play was over, did one Athenian turn to his companion and ask, "Yes, but what was the true riddle?" I rather suspect so. Even as I think that, not having the text before them, they may have quarreled over what exactly was said.

What was the true riddle? Oedipus asks Creon why, after Laius was killed, the people of Thebes failed to investigate the crime and pursue the culprit. Creon replies:

The singing, riddling Sphinx. She . . . persuaded us to let the mystery go and concentrate on what lay at our feet.[1] (145–50)

Familiar? It should be. How like Jocasta, who urges Oedipus to forget: "From this day on, I wouldn't look right or left" (950). So the Sphinx who holds the city in its frightful female clutches is echoed by the near-wicked queen who urges denial. Look not to the left or right. But what if Oedipus looked below him, for example, at his feet, which name him? What if he did what the Sphinx said and concentrated on his feet? Perhaps by thinking of his affliction he would have connected it to the nature of child abandonment, as such children frequently had their feet punctured to prevent their ghosts from haunting the murderers. But what if Creon and his consort had in fact listened to this comment, which appears to evade the truth but which becomes the new riddle, that if recognized and solved would have prevented the horrors to come? For upon hearing of the stranger's name —Oedipus (swollen foot)—a particularly thoughtful Greek might have said, "Ah! This is the foot that lies at our feet: the swollen foot of your name." Focusing on Oedipus, then, as the clue to Laius's murder would have resulted in his arrest and prevented his marriage to Jocasta.

But perhaps this secret riddle has gone unnoticed by some. Certainly on my first readings of the play I "missed it," and, as with Oedipus, it is arguable that, having missed it, I was unaware of Creon's and Jocasta's complicity—among others, including Tiresias—in failing (refusing?) to stop the course of actions. Is this true? Am I right to see things this way? Or is it misguided? Is there something about my interpretation which is incorrect? Am I at the mercy of my own limitations, whatever they may be?

1. Fagle's translation is a literal rendering of the Greek text, thus remaining faithful to Sophocles's play on "feet," which renders the Sphinx's statement a new riddle.

Yet is that not part of the true riddle posed by the Sphinx? When Oedipus killed Laius, the people aimed to deliver themselves from this beast by answering her "old riddle," but now new events had usurped it and she added to it with a new one which no one saw (except perhaps Tiresias). The underlying realities that cause anguish change. They change, as Freud saw, because of the dynamic nature of internal mental life, where wishes, needs, defenses, and reparations change our feelings about ourself, others, and events. To have answered the secret riddle was not a matter of figuring it out. Had the Sphinx said, "I have a new riddle: the murderer of Laius will lie at your feet," some clever Greek would have thought, "Oedipus! Swollen foot," and the murderer would have been found. But the point I believe that Sophocles makes, and the reason Freud is drawn to this text, is that solving particular mental contents (i.e., riddles) requires an understanding of the psychic reality generating the changes of mental content, as any mind is always reformulating its contents, and to prevent the plague of rash action one must not become too set in one's ways.

So to heed this Sophoclean admonition I shall now set my chapter on a new, somewhat different course, which I shall weave into the question "Why Oedipus?" In what respects, then, does my argument bear on the Oedipal child's dilemma?

The Child's Discovery

Just as Athenian culture "knew" it had once, at least in legend, derived from a maternal deity, so too does each child. The infant lives within the complex laws and unconscious principles of being and relating that are primarily conveyed by the mother, even when she communicates the father's views, her culture, the social order, and above all her language: the symbolic.

The dawn of the Freudian Oedipal era in the child's life is between the ages of four and six, a time when contributions from many previously latent sources now impinge upon the child who must consider them. Prior to this, he or she was being protected and held by maternal provision of care so that disturbing mental contents were always seemingly processed by the mother's many acts of containment as she often functioned as an auxiliary to the infant's self.

During the infant phase of the subject's life, in what we might term the matrilinear order, psychic structure is being laid down as the infant builds inner models of the world—of himself and his objects—that find reliable statuses as continuous points of inner view. By virtue of early infantile defenses, different psychic structures can be established around various types of object set up around differing experiences of the mother, father, and parental couple.

In the good enough Oedipus Complex—so to speak—the infant has already slept with the mother and enjoyed the fruits of this triumph. This good position emerges from the intimacy of mother and infant who have killed the father, by temporarily holding off the outside world that he represents, and this killing off is a permissible pleasure, which the father supports as the not good enough mother. Then the father enters the scene as a new figure in his own right, but through the infant's, or now, I should say, child's body. It is the genital drive which puts the father and the child in a new place. A new psychic structure is being laid on, generated by libidinal development. It is at this stage in the boy's life that the mother is imaginatively specified as a different object of desire and the father is now seen as a different rival to the child's claim.

Anxiety about castration testifies to the specificity of this eros, as the zone determining the excitement is localized as a threat. But is it the fear of castration that drives the boy toward the increased identification with the father which eventually resolves his Oedipal dilemma? If this were so, if an anxiety became the source of an aim for identification, such an identification would itself be a psychopathy. One need only compare this to Klein's depressive position theory, for example, when the infant's realization of its harming the object of love inaugurates a new perspective in object relations. Fear of castration as the motive of identification would be a seriously retrograde act.

It is my view that the child resolves the Oedipal dilemma by a discovery that emerges out of his anxieties and desires. He or she has a claim upon the mother: no child is in any doubt about that. Smell of the mother is still inside the Oedipal child. But each child also realizes in quite a profound way that the father preceded the child's relation to the mother, and it is recognition of such precedents—on the part of both girl and boy—that is an identification: a correct identification of one's place, of one's position in time, that informs the child of the mother's prior desire.

The child may oppose this recognition and murderous fantasies may increase as he strives to deny the fact of lineage, something we know that Oedipus did by sleeping with his mother, to give symbolic birth to himself as well as to make his sons and daughters into brothers and sisters.

The child in the Oedipal dilemma discovers the patrilineal line along with the Name of the Father that breaks the illusions emerging from the infant's place in the matrilineal order. But it is the child's emergent genital primacy that drives him to this discovery, that in an odd paradoxical sense breaks the matrilineal mold as the erotic mother—now his or her object—displaces the infant from the child's place. So it is not the father whose frightful presence displaces the child in the first place, but the child's own erotic desire for the mother which creates in him a new object and a new self, as a new psychic structure arises out of this libidinal position.

It is at this age that the child philosopher emerges, asking about ontology, the origin of the universe, and the reason for death's existence. The child poses these questions because he is developing a sense of perspective that naturally derives from his continuous oscillation between being two children: the new child who sees the mother as erotic and the old child who is her infant. However, during this transitional period, in the course of "answering" questions about the origins of their body's genital urges, they discover with what sex they are identified, therefore with what parent they are identified, and they realize their lineage. As they are in conflict with themselves between the two child states, the father will be defined largely according to the child's inner state of private conflict. In the course of discovering his desire the child recognizes the desires of the mother and the father and becomes fascinated by the father's specificity—his difference.

My aim now is to come to the core of this chapter: I wish to discuss why and how the Oedipal dilemma (Freud favored this phrase) is displaced by the Oedipus Complex, or how the child's anguish in the triangle is resolved to the point of a form of liberation from it—a liberation from dilemma into complexity.

Psychic Complexity

As the child endures the Oedipal dilemma he recurrently splits in two: as child back to infant, returning to child. In the course of these movements he creates, destroys, and re-creates new sets of internal objects: the parents of infancy, the new parents of genital representation. We could say that the child is discovering the nature of internal representations, that fathers and mothers change within one according to internal self states. This is not so much a fully conscious recognition, except insofar as the child becomes interested in the nature of epistemology, which indicates preconscious recognition of the problems linked to knowing.

As Oedipus tells the Leader at Colonus that he is "born of the royal blood of Thebes," the Leader cries in horror: "You, you're *that* man—?" (235–40). All in Colonus know that man, who lives as a vividly disturbing internal object. But Oedipus stands before them as the actual other from whom all internal objects derive: "Your name, old stranger, echoes through the world" (330–35).

When Oedipus meets Theseus at his second crossroads ("And now, seeing you at this crossroads, beyond all doubt I know you in the flesh"), he meets a new father who recognizes the difference between an internal object and its actual otherness (620–25). Theseus promises to give Oedipus time to speak, telling him "I want to know," and this father who can delay his impulses, give himself time, and think about reality is the new father of the Oedipal child who though driven by desires is not so rash, so harsh, or so omnipotent: not, that is, so infantile (645–50). ". . . once a man regains his self-control, all threats are gone . . . Rest assured, no matter if I'm away, I know my name will shield you well" (750–55). If there is a father the absolute opposite of a Laius, it is present now in the person of Theseus.

Theseus is, however, simply a different paternal object. If Sophoclean tragedy tells us only one thing, it is that relations always change, nothing can be taken for granted; in other words, we are to be complex, indeed to live within the complex. The dream, for example, exemplifies to the child just how his objects change, leaving him bewildered by the shifting prophecies contained in these seemingly oracular moments. If the Western theatergoer finds it difficult to tolerate the Sophoclean hero's dispensation to the differing oracles, one perhaps only needs reminding that each night we dream we see and hear a strange other view of our life and our destiny.

This is a sobering discovery for the child as his infantile omnipotence would have all other minds and behaviors accord with his wishes, but now he begins to reflect on human difference and the inability to reach the other through omnipotence, a paradoxical occasion, as knowing now how unique the other is, he comes to realize the odd fact of his own peculiarity. In addition, he quietly recognizes that the place he has been living—formerly assumed to exist in order to further his needs—bears the name "family." He is in one. And there are other families which have altogether different characters, created by interacting subjectivities that transcend the individual contribution. The family is a group which dissolves the singularly powerful prior authorities of the mother and father.

The child whose Oedipal dilemma remains the organizing conflict of his life often sustains this personality conflict, in my view, because he cannot accept the labile and chaotic authority of the group. He remains attached to the father, or in combat with the authority of the parental couple, because such parental organizations are more comforting than the identity-defying features of the group where participants will find themselves continually displaced by ideas, feelings, and processes well beyond the influence of the individual.

Sophocles plays with that loss of definition that transpires through participation in the group as he alternately makes each of the figures in the play seem reasonable, empathic, searchingly wise, blind, vicious, stupid, and murderous. Who is Creon? Jocasta? Tiresias? . . . Oedipus? There seems a different figure for each shifting place in the group dynamic.

Furthermore, Sophocles was writing for a Greek audience that was somewhere between an oligarchy and a democracy. How was it to live in a democracy where one was a member of a group free to speak one's mind? What was the group that composed the democracy? We continue to pose this question today, not simply because governments are usually somewhere between democracies and dictatorships, but because these two states echo an inner problematic in man and woman: whether to stay inside a monarchical government or dictatorship, or whether to kill the king, revolt, and establish a group government.

There are anxieties in both directions. A monarchy can devolve into absolute rule. A leader can rule oppressively and compel the people to silence. This form of government seems a political analogue to the neurotic process, based as it is on the dominance of the ego, and its power to repress an unwanted view, when the only freedom of representation is by subtle derivative. In oppressed times allegory thrives as people read a hidden meaning beneath the manifest text presented to them.

A democracy can lead to a chaos in expression. Ideas are impossible to suppress, as no one has authority sufficient for such an action; but they can be split off and made bizarre in a deeply mad world that characterizes the psychotic process. In *Oedipus the King* the flux of mind of the chorus echoes the fickle movement of thought and feeling in the democratic process which permits any expression and invites cacophony.

Families live in what we term the household, and whether the "headship" tends toward the matriarchal or the patriarchal, above all else it is a group, an interpersonal place, arrived at from the many contributions of its members who can establish an atmosphere of place, even if their private representations of the persons there are inevitably idiomatic.

As I have suggested, this new object—the family group—echoes the divergent and coterminus internal contributions to the child's sense of his own complexity. This "spirit of . . . place" (75) that Oedipus finds at Colonus is a space sanctified by the founding father whose sense of fairness lives on in the hearts of the people. It is also a place combined with the maternal, as this sacred ground is the dwelling place of the Eumenides, who live under the mother earth.

At the point in the child's life when she or he can see the patrilineal and matrilineal lines, each becomes aware of who the father's parents are—particularly the father's father—and who the mother's mother is. This inauguration of a generational sense of personal place constitutes the emergence of a capacity to think about the links between grandparents (and their personalities) and parents (and their personalities). It is a line connected by a particularly mythic narrative as actual events, screen memories, embellishments, unconscious misreadings, and so on condense the grandparents' past—and what little history they know of their family—into the family's legend. (I shall discuss the nature of generational consciousness in the next chapter.)

However much the father's name may constitute a law, which among other things prohibits incest, it is not the father who establishes justice in the group. "Loose, ignorant talk started dark suspicions and a sense of injustice cut deeply too," the chorus tells Jocasta (775), implicitly recognizing the power of the group to usurp any single authority. "Strange response . . . unlawful," muses Oedipus upon hearing Tiresias refusing to speak the truth (368). How can criminal acts come to justice? An issue which we know strikes at the very heart of *Antigone.* In a child's conflict with the mother, or the father, or a brother, where is a just settlement to be found? In the magisterial entrance of the father, who upholds the law true to his name? But his decisions may not be just; a grievance may well continue long past his adjudication, based on the child's psychic reality, especially when a true injustice is committed by a family member. It is certainly at this age of complexity that the child realizes that his psychic claims—for justice among other things—not only compete with the equally intense psychic claims of other members of the group, but his own area of judicial consideration, his internal world, is often torn between opposing positions and, finally, his internal world is well beyond the knowing of even the most insightful and patient father. Psychic life itself puts one substantially out of the reaches of intersubjective knowing, even if it simultaneously enhances it.

This is one of the child's discoveries at this age: that one is only a part of necessarily competing subjectivities, that one's omnipotence is radically altered by this, and invocations of the name of the mother or the father do not conjure justice. Sophocles knew this well, as did all Greeks. For the household was that space created by each family, sponsoring its only shared inner reality but also the axis of many conflicts and injustices. To some extent the *polis* evolved out of a need to resolve conflicts between households. "You have to come to a city that practices justice," Theseus tells the transgressor Creon (1040). Creon earlier tries to invoke the civic sense in claiming Oedipus: "Years ago your city gave you birth" (860–65).

Beyond the psychic reality of the family in the civic place, men and women contribute to the body that supersedes and coordinates the authority of the household. For the child this new place will first be encountered at school, the place where I think child observers can clearly see whether or not the young have "resolved" the Oedipal dilemma. Many will cling to an internal loving mother as they refuse intercourse with their peers, while others will reflect the conflict either by assuming the law of the father or by hiding in terror. Equally, though all children will show traces of both prior authorities, those who have achieved the Oedipus Complex have discovered perspective and know something of the nature of psychic life that makes no one a natural power. To live in the group one must be able to appreciate and live with this sense of life's complexity.

In the adolescent.epoch there is a revival of the Oedipal child's discovery of the potential isolation suggested by the complexity of subjectivity. The adolescent feels the anguish of the shifting internal representations of self and other, just as he or she also lives inside a peer group that vividly announces the precarious nature of group dynamics. At a time of psychobiological growth, there is a re-emergence of transformed regressions, as the adolescent seeks deep first loves that provide sexual and emotional gratification, just as finding some way to be liked, to become one of the group, is an effort to overcome the anxiety generated by group life. By transforming the intrinsic nature of the group into a falsely organized peer culture, adolescent groups are like gangs congregated to fight the anxieties of groups themselves! As time passes, as anxieties diminish, as the fruits of complexity are appreciated—particularly the value of diverse perspectives—the need for group bonding wanes, as does the urge for intense symbiotic puppy loves.

"Time is the great healer, you will see," Creon tells Oedipus, and for once we can agree with him (1664). It is at this point that time seems to possess something naturally curative. Resolution of the Oedipus Complex leads to this curative sense of time, enabling internal and interpersonal conflicts to heal as the subject finds that with time comes increased perspective: that which has been split off or denied—in the interests of one's narcissistic economy, for example—comes back into the picture, rendering one and one's relations more complex.

Resolution of the Oedipal Dilemma

In his theory of the primal horde, Freud imagines the earliest stage of society, one dominated by a powerful father who kept the women to himself and banished his sons. Eventually these sons form a group which operates under different laws from those of the primal father because they enjoy a kind of parity with one another, a shared deprivation that was organizing, and one eventful day the gang of brothers killed and devoured the father, which Freud saw as a form of identification. In the second stage of social evolution, according to Freud in *Totem and Taboo*, "the patriarchal horde was replaced in the first instance by the fraternal clan," but in a third era of progression the family became the unit that returned to the fathers what had been taken by the primal horde (146).

In his theory of the clan's displacement of the father, Freud seems very close indeed to grasping that the group automatically displaces the authority of the father. And one may wonder if the totem meal that he believes stands in for the cannibalized father, theoretically to prevent further parricides, isn't more a commemorative mourning of the true end of the father: his displacement in the child's mind by a colony of new cathexes, libidinal interests, and idiomatic investments. In *Group Psychology and the Analysis of the Ego* I think Freud suggested a different model for the dissolution of the child's "father complex." "Each individual," he writes, "is a component part of numerous groups, he is bound by ties of identification in many directions, and he has built up his ego ideal upon the most various models" (129). It is the force of these "identifications in many directions" that breaks up the father complex, resulting in a series of *progressive disidentifications* as the child seeks to select objects that give more precise expression to his idiom.

Thus the Oedipal child learns that it is his fate to be born into a very specific family, and more importantly, to be a subject who holds or contains in his own mind an object world, a group of percepts, introjects, and identifications that deepens his sense of his own complexity and radically problematizes the authority of his narrative voice. But if the child's discovery of the complexity of the human being radicalizes perspective and in itself usurps the patriarchal structure, it sends him to a new place, inaugurating a new order which derives from this decentering of psychic structure. What is the child's sense of himself and of life at this moment in his evolution? Knox views Sophocles's play as a model for modern drama because it presents us with "our own terror of the unknown future which we fear we cannot control—our deep fear that every step we take forward on what we think is the road of progress may really be a step forward to a foreordained rendezvous with disaster" (133). I think this partly captures something of the Oedipal child's inner emotional reality, for the child is coming to know something, something really quite like Oedipus's discovery, that in a sense is quite tragic and certainly disturbing.

Oedipus's demand to know the cause of suffering results in discovery of his own unwitting fulfillment of a prophecy, and Sophocles permeates this play and *Oedipus at Colonus* with another peripeteia: the king gradually comes to encounter the force of his own personality and how it has also caused his undoing. As I have said, it is this discovery, the recognition that one is a psychic entity, possessed of a mind divided between interacting logics of consciousness and unconsciousness, that I think characterizes the Oedipal child's epiphany. It is not the fear of the castrating father who bars the child's erotic access to the mother; it is, as I have argued, the mind itself which holds the child in place. It is not an anxiety that stops the child from acting; it is mental consideration of the entire wish, one that inevitably involves a fear of the father, but as Freud also indicated, one that equally brings up the love of a father, identification with the father, and also a sense in the child—his own moral sense—that there's something wrong with the idea.

For this is the age, is it not, when the child comes to understand something about the oddity of possessing one's own mind? A little Odysseus, each child ventures into the world of daydreams, carried off by the mind's capacity to generate theaters for heroic action. The daydream in some respects is the first truly heroic place, where the child can objectify the self engaged in ideal action that brings acclamation and recognition by an implicit other. Oh, if the mind were so simple! How easy life would be. But this very same place also brings with it uncomfortable thoughts, disturbing emotions, and persecutory daydreams. The mind and its spontaneous conjurings displace the heroic self's envisioning of life, compelling the child to struggle with evil ideas and feelings. What, then, does the child do with his mind?

Until the child becomes an Oedipus Complex I think mental contents have been rather more easily "understood" as slightly external events, in which the child feels magically possessed by distressing mental contents, which may then be projected into the object world and, with luck, gracefully processed by loving parents. But with the breaking up of the patriarchal structure of the family by the social group and the patriarchal psychic structure by the group of competing internal objects, the child is invited by his own development to encounter the semi-independent "itness" of his own mind. This may be most vividly studied in that painful but gradual recognition in the child that the dream he dreams is not an event external to the self that awakening or parental soothing can dispel, but an internal event, entirely sponsored by the child's mind. To my way of thinking, this is the Oedipal child's moment of truth, when he discovers that it is his own mind that creates the nightmare dramas that match poor Oedipus's fate, a discovery for each child that in some ways matches the search that Oedipus inaugurates when he aims to get to the origin of a curse that dooms his civilization. That curse is the bittersweet fate one suffers in having a mind, one that is only ever partly known and therefore forever getting one into trouble, and one that in the extreme can be rather lost (as in the losing of a mind) and one whose discovery by the child is a most arresting moment.

In this respect, then, we may rightly speak of the universality of child abuse, if by this we mean that each human subject is anguished by some of the products of his or her own mind: from the passing murderous idea that shocks the self to envy of a friend's good fortune; from the turbulent and essential pain of guilt generated by inconsiderate actions to the persecutory anxieties derived from acting out. Our own subjectivity will abuse us all! However important it is to recognize the traumas derived from environmentally occasioned harm, such as sexual abuse, physical punishment, or severe emotional harm, it is always important to keep in mind Freud's discovery that in addition to such traumas, the mind in its own right would often be the agent of self traumatization.

But as the mind is often enough an anguishing phenomenon, so that over time a child recognizes that his own subjectivity fates him to episodic suffering, he also realizes through useful thinking that the same mind is also capable of helping him to contain and process disturbed thoughts. The mind is a problem-solving agency even if it stages the representations of self traumatizing ideas and feelings. Likewise, the group can function as a container of disturbed processes, even if its structure often invites distress.

The view that the superego is formed out of the relation to the father, and intrapsychically stands in his place, is too narrow a reading of this important psychic development. The arrival of the superego announces the presence of perspective, which is the psychically objective outcome of the Oedipal Complex, when the child discovers the multiplicity of points of view. The superego does indeed derive from identification, but by no means simply with the father, either in figure or in name, as its structure testifies to the achievement of perspective: the child can now look at himself and his objects through the many points of perspective offered by identifications.

As the child comes into the presence of his own mind, he is launched, in my view, on a most disturbing journey. This is a place where all of us live, moment to moment, in an area that I think Winnicott specified in his notion of essential aloneness, and certainly implied in his concept of the isolate that each of us is. As we develop, this mind becomes more complex, ironically enough in ratio to its sophistication. Psycho-development, then, is in part *devolutionary*, not evolutionary: a dismantling of both pre-Oedipal and Oedipal early childhood structures. Fathers and mothers, early wishes and urges, primary needs and satisfactions, fade into a kind of mnemic opacity as we move more deeply into quite unknowable realms. Some people, and perhaps they are among our artists and philosophers, sense this psycho-devolution as a fact of human life and aim to stay with it, to see if it can be accounted for or narrated, perhaps celebrated: but the risks to such adventurers are high. Most people, in my view, find consciousness of this aspect of the human condition—the complexity born of having a mind to oneself—simply too hard to bear.

Given the ordinary unbearableness of this complexity, I think that the human individual partly regresses in order to survive, but this retreat has been so essential to human life that it has become an unanalyzed convention, part of the religion of everyday life. We call this regression "marriage" or "partnership," in which the person becomes part of a mutually interdependent couple that evokes and sustains the bodies of the mother and the father, the warmth of the pre-Oedipal vision of life, before the solitary recognition of subjectivity grips the child. Ego development is thus a transformative regression: back to being in the family, this time through the vicarious rememberings generated through raising a family, absorbing oneself in cultivating a garden, and putting out of one's mind as best as one can quite what one has seen when leaving the garden in the first place. To go forward in life, we go back, back to the places of the mother and the father, where we can evoke these figures as inevitably comforting and practically as defensive alternatives to a madness always latent in groups: to the groups of social life, and more so to the group that is mental life.

As the child experiences the group's dissolution of the father complex, and as he strives to adapt to and become part of a social group, he gradually arrives at the exceptionally disquieting recognition that this cannot be done. How can one adapt to something that refuses to identify itself? Where is the core identity of the group to which one is called upon to adapt? Although the child is raised with a fictional entity in mind created out of parental and educational visions of the civic-minded collective to which the young child should affiliate, psychoanalytic studies of the group process have taught us what we already knew as children: not only that groups are not fair but that they often operate according to psychotic principles. It can be a form of madness to live in a group. Or the group as a reliable presence is a delusion, believed in because its labile reality would be a hard lesson to preach to the young even if they know it unconsciously and suffer the anguish of its reality.

But children do learn how to live in groups. Common tasks concentrate human collectivities and simplify matters wonderfully. There are festivals, manic moments, times of true accomplishment, inspiration, hope, and development; these are the occasions when it is wonderful to be in a group. But most children know that it is by transformative regression back to dyadic existence that the distresses of group life can be averted, so the finding of a close friend is a very particular aim of most children, although obviously some who will be loners find in their novels, or science projects, a reliable structure that serves the need to retreat from the madness that ego psychology terms reality. In the end, we all develop a false self (hopefully) that can assist our endurance of the madness of groups and we find passionate and narrowed interests (such as the form of work we choose or avocational interests) and most of all, we seek partners and a few close friends to be with us.

The Oedipal dilemma is replete with paradoxes and doubtless I have not helped matters by suggesting several others: in particular that the child's relatively simple psychic structures built around the dyadic and triadic relational situations are superseded by recognition of the mind's complexity. All along, of course, this mind has been developing and objects have been created as split-off fragments of the self, and from the dyadic and triadic structures; but the Sophoclean moment, if I may put it that way, is the self's recognition that a human life outlives the known relational structures. We are amidst two quite profound unconscious orders—our own mind and that of the group—which break the symbiotic and Oedipal cohesions. In time, a false self is evolved and engages the group, and false illusions of the self's unity are generated to assuage our anxieties about our personal complexity; these illusions and illusional engagements are absolutely essential to our life, and unsuitably named false if by that we mean not true of us—they are most certainly true of us all. And yet we do retreat, from my point of view, from the anguish of having a mind and living within a social order that outstrips our early childhood structures and wears thin our illusions of unity. We retreat very subtly back to transformed dyadic affiliations, back into triangular structures when we generate our own family, forward into passionate beliefs in the veracity of a single vision of reality (whether a psychoanalytic view, a political opinion, or a theological perspective), all unconsciously soothing—even when the occasions of mental pain themselves—because the mentally objectifiable dilemma is always preferable to the complex that is beyond its mental processing.

But if mental complexity ultimately defies the passing omnipotences of false organizations of content, and if the large groups of the human race—the groups we call nations, cities, institutions, and households—prove beyond the individual's successful organizational intentions, the diversity of such complexity allows each subject, as Winnicott said, to play with reality. One's unconscious use of objects, aimed to conjugate idiom into being, allows the subject to be disseminated through the complex events that constitute lived experience. We go with the flow. It is unconscious, not coherent, yet pleasurable. Though we cannot adapt to reality, as in some respects it does not exist, we play with it, bringing our subjectivity to the thingness of the object world and there—in an intermediate space—give reality to our life.

Why Oedipus then? Because when he picked this play to address the key problematic in human development, Freud selected a drama that represented that tension between our cohesions, whether relational (as in marital, family, or group) affiliations, or delusional (as in Oedipus's delusion of an organized persecution by Creon), and the psychic textures well beyond the possibility of mental organization, a dense complexity so intrinsic to the group process that it can only hold itself together through denials of its nature. Although Sophocles, like many Athenians, believed that it was the civic sense that could think through the madness of group life, I think he also constructed a play that defied anyone's psychic organization: a play that evoked a density of unconscious work in the audience that must have provoked an anxiety about the limits of comprehension. It is this tension between the limits of consciousness and the wayward destiny of unconsciousness, between the helpful internal objects of psychic life and the persecutory presences—which Klein brilliantly conceptualized as a constant tension between two positions, paranoid/schizoid and depressive—between the need for group life and the madness of such processes, that Sophocles brought to this play. Although *Oedipus at Colonus* would seem to celebrate the virtues of a well-governed *polis*, endowed with a spirit of place that is based on the integration of the matrilineal and the patrilineal lines, it is my view that our primary adult relations in life—marital, familial, ideo-logical, political—are necessary regressions from the logic of human development, in which transformed simplified struc-tures are found to comfort us against the harrowing com-plexity of life: be it the life of the mind or life in the strange mind of a social group. Complexity displaces the pre-Oedipal and Oedipal structures: the child discovers his own mind and the solitude of subjectivity. Knowing this, life becomes an effort to find inner sanctuary from the logic of psycho-development, and when this generative asylum is established it allows the subject to play with the samples of reality that pass by him during his lifetime.

11

Generational Consciousness

Looking back on the 1914–19 war, Vera Brittain wrote in the foreword to *Testament of Youth* that she felt "a growing sense of urgency, to write something which would show what the whole world . . . has meant to the men and women of [her] generation" (11). Perhaps she felt the need to capture her generation in a literary place because the new generation—she wrote her work in 1929–33—was so different. She did not think that "the bright young people of today, with their imperturbable realism, their casual, intimate knowledge of sexual facts, their familiarity with the accumulated experiences of us their foredoomed predecessors," had endured "one-tenth of the physical and psychological shock that the Great War caused to the modern girl of 1914" (45).

Brittain had grown up in an "unparalleled age of rich materialism and tranquil comfort," of private schools tucked away in rural retreats, a protected world that contained eros in the ritual of the school dance and appealed to the adolescent ideals as partnering links to the supportive society (50). Even if Brittain, like all adolescents, fashioned her ideals in opposition to the previous generations, she and her contemporaries were in fact aiming to renew the Victorian vision. "There, at the age of sixteen, I first began to dream how the men and women of my generation—with myself, of course, conspicuous among the galaxy of Leonardos— would inaugurate a new Renaissance on a colossal scale" (42). Little wonder, then, that when the young men went off to war they envisioned the conflict to be a sporting event that would field heroes and establish the ideal leaders of the future. "We were still in the trough of peace that had lasted a hundred years between two great conflicts," wrote Osbert Sitwell. "In it, such wars as arose were not general, but only a brief armed version of the Olympic Games. You won a round; the enemy won the next. There was no more talk of extermination, or of fights to the finish, than would occur in a boxing match" (in Fussell, 25). Convinced that their superior ideals and values would be sufficient to beat the Germans, as if virtue would quite naturally translate into physical prowess, the English of 1914 saw the war as a sport; they even likened it to cricket, and Lord Northcliffe's assertion that the Germans would lose because "football, which develops individuality, has only been introduced into Germany in comparatively recent times" was not seen as an extreme view (in Fussell, 26).

The lost generation of 1914–19, exterminated by the relentless thoughtlessness of an older generation ("if any question why we died, tell them, because our fathers lied," Kipling, 150), drastically altered Western consciousness. Writing after the Second World War, the critic Alfred Kazin said, "so many uncovered horrors, so many new wars on the horizon, such a continual general ominousness, that '*the* war' [that is, the Second] soon became war anywhere, any time —war that has never ended, war as the continued experience of twentieth-century man" (in Fussell, 74).

If the Great War transformed the consciousness of a generation within but two years (from 1914 to 1916) and if the "young men like flowers are cut and withered on a stem," something of that blind innocence that saw the battlefield as a football pitch is due to their impatience with the taciturn world of *fin de siècle* Europe (Read, 152). Though largely respectful of the generation of 1890, this generation was, according to Hughes, "looking for something more arresting and dogmatic than its seniors had provided . . . where the writers of the 1890s had restricted themselves to a questioning of the potentialities of reason, the young men of 1905 became frank irrationalists or even anti-rationalists . . . the younger men were no longer satisfied with the urbane development of their elders. Everywhere they were in search of an ideal and a faith" (339). The new generation was cultivating its own mood, which in that indescribable Babylon of historical dialectics no doubt figured into what Fussell terms the "insensate marches" of the Great War.

Across the Atlantic and in a different generational era, Arthur Miller came of age in the 1930s. Miller, in his autobiography, *Timebends*, usually writes of his generation by contrasting it with later ones. Standing on the stage of Hill Auditorium at the University of Michigan during a 1965 teach-in, as a fifty-year-old man he recalled his years at this same university in the mid-1930s. Both were radical times, idealistic epochs, full of fervor, but what was different? He found the atmosphere curiously festive, but when asked to speak he fretted out loud that the FBI was probably among them and that one day they would be held accountable for being there. "It was the wrong moment to be saying such a thing, here at the budding of a noble movement to end an unjust war, a moment when this generation had just begun to reach out and find its partners in protest" (100). But Miller had in mind his treatment during the 1950s when, before the House Un-American Activities Committee, he was held accountable for his political views of the 1930s, an act of generational violence that Miller captured in his play *The Crucible*, which largely characterizes one generation's attack on the other.

Looking at the generation forming in the 1960s, Miller realized "this was not the generation of the thirties" who engaged in a "symbolic ideological rhetoric" removed from the future threat of Hitler; the youth of the 1960s were less interested in putting pen to paper than in putting their bodies on the line: "they were personally up for grabs" due to conscription. Later Miller muses on the failure of the generation of the 1960s to "pass on their cataclysmic visions to an indifferent new generation," the generation that established itself in the 1970s (397).

Miller was born in 1915, fourteen at the time of the Crash, a teenager during the Depression years, at university during the New Deal. Barbara Raskin, the author of *Hot Flashes*, was born in the 1930s and is a figure of the 1950s. She identifies in almost anthropologic detail the traits of her generation. Indeed her main character, Diana Sargeant, is a forty-eight-year-old anthropologist who says, "I see the group in the individual, the common experiences of a generation in the idiosyncrasies of a particular person. The part embodies the whole" (2). And what are or were they like?

—We always looked good at airports.
—Back in the fifties, because we couldn't think of anything else to do, we carefully selected our china, glassware and silver patterns, registered at the nearest department stores, and married so that we could proceed with our lives.
—We have had numerous abortions.
—Few of us had many children. Three were usually plenty.
—Compulsive grievance collectors, we marred our marriages with melodrama.
—Unlike the next generation we had few lesbian encounters.
—We also liked Dexedrine. Ah, diet pills. We were never slim enough. We wanted there to be a space-to-see-through between our thighs when we stood up on sandy beaches.
—We were not, like the flappers, a happy-go-lucky crowd . . . Lots of us have had our heads shrunk and some of us

have already had our hearts, minds and faces lifted in a variety of ways.

Finally, turning to the next generation, she says:

—Our daughters worry about their eggs getting stale while they become lawyers and astronauts. Our sons are busy acquiring MBAs, BMWs and IBM PCs. They now spread sheets of flow charts, discuss condos or condoms, quote Dow Jones averages, do coke instead of drink it, and like bright lights and big cities. (2–14)

Raskin's fiction is a litany to her generation which she virtually sings in her prose. Kim Newman, a talented film critic, is young enough to be Raskin's son. Born in 1959, raised on the television screen and later the video, he had digested a phenomenal number of films before the age of twenty-five. In the introduction to his critique of horror films (*Nightmare Movies*) he finds his generational place by contrasting his contemporaries' taste in monster movies from the few films preferred by his parents to the movies he imagines the next generation will prefer. "Some kid out there has grown up with Freddy and Jason rather than Dracula and Frankenstein, and is graduating to the books and films of Stephen King and Clive Barker. He or she knows Empire and Trona better than Hammer and Corman" (xiii). Looking back to his generation's formation of taste, he writes: "In my early teens, I caught up with Universal films, the Hammer horrors, and Roger Corman's Edgar Allan Poe movies . . . I saw *The Exorcist* while doing my O levels. I saw *Suspiria* during my first week at the University of Sussex . . . I saw *Friday the 13th* while I was jobless and homeless in London in 1980" (xi).

Each of these writers—Vera Brittain, Arthur Miller, Barbara Raskin, and Kim Newman—has a keen sense of their own generation. They can define it clearly, differentiate it from older and younger generations, and in some respects analyze why their generation is the way it is. We might say that they have a *generational consciousness* which they can use to objectify their place in historical time and their particular contribution to social culture.

I shall take as my task the outline of a theory of generational consciousness. I must leave to the future the essential work of deeper consideration, but even a preliminary effort such as this has, it seems to me, a place within psychoanalytic theory, as the writers, filmmakers, and artists of our time are engaged in a most profound and intense transformation of the unconscious identity of a generation into consciousness.

What Is a Generation?

But what is a generation? This is not easily answered. In some respects it appears to be the interval between parents and children, so if we arbitrarily take the age of childbearing to be between twenty and twenty-five, then every twenty to twenty-five years a new generation is born. For many people there will be the presence of three generations in a lifetime: grandparents, themselves, and their children.

But, of course, we do not all go in heat every twenty to twenty-five years, creating a neat reproductive era to produce generational blocks of children who all mature at the quarter century to reproduce themselves. Indeed, there seems to be a new form of generational consciousness emerging about every ten years—or so the theorists of popular culture and historians believe, who define a meaningful difference in historical time by writing of the 1950s, the 1960s, the 1970s, and the 1980s.

However, though a couple who marry in 1948 and have children in 1950 will not see these children form their own generation until approximately 1970, there will obviously be an *intervening generation*. A couple who married ten years earlier, in 1938, and had children in 1940, will see these children form their generation in 1960. Looked at this way, no generation ever gives biological birth to the next generation. There is always an intervening generation, born of different parents, and bearing a different generational culture from the immediately preceding one.

Of course, this cannot be drawn in black and white. Just as we can find many features of the 1960s radicalism in the Beat movement of the 1950s, so too we can find elements of one generation inherited from another. I shall discuss the question of generational transmission later, but now I wish to create an arbitrary structure that I justify because it corresponds with our sense of cultural regeneration. Every ten years or so we redefine our culture, our values, tastes, artistic interests, political views, and social heroes. These change distinctly enough for such decades to be meaningfully identified. The decade seems to be about the smallest temporal unit available for objectification as a marker of collective culture. We all seem to know what is meant when we contrast the 1950s with the 1960s, or the 1940s with the 1980s, but we are unlikely to know quite what is meant when contrasting the early 1950s with the late 1950s, or the early 1980s with the late 1980s. And we would doubtless all arrive at a different sense of what is meant by contrasting between, say, 1953 and 1958, or 1962 and 1967.

Some would argue that a generation is not easily defined by decadal conception. "The notion of one generation," writes Marc Block, "is very elastic . . . it corresponds to realities which we feel to be very concrete . . . There are some generations which are long and some which are short. Only observation enables us to perceive the points at which the curve changes its direction" (in Hughes, 18). Hughes claims that although generations overlap and are arbitrarily defined, "at the same time they tend to shape their own definitions through common experiences. Around such experiences a 'clustering' again occurs" (18).

Perhaps it is more accurate to say that every ten years or so there is a potential for a new generation to emerge. A devastating war, such as that of 1914–18, may seem to eliminate an entire generation, so that the young men and women of the mid-1920s (latency-age children in the Great War) seem to found a contemporary generational culture blithely removed from the fate suffered by the immediately preceding generation. The generation of the 1960s seems etched in our mind, the youth of the 1970s less so, and here at the dawn of the 1990s the generation of the 1980s seems even less easily grasped.

But no doubt the passing of time and reflection will enable the group of three generations to reach an agreed definitional sense of each decade's generational signature: the first signs of that new generation's founding consciousness. Indeed, precisely because we are still a very superstitious people, still believe in deities, holy ghosts, knocking on wood, Friday the 13th, etc., we tend to psychically conceptualize decades as collective internal objects. Each of us contains a sense of the 1950s, 1960s, and 1970s, terms which evoke complex associations and memories.

So each decade is created by a new generation although other generations will also interpret this unit of time in their own way. And as there is always an intervening generation, there are always two sets of generational lines at any one time. If my grandparents were, say, born in 1900, married in 1918, conceived my parents in 1920, who met and married in 1938 and conceived me in 1940, and I bore my children, say, in 1960, we would compose a generational line that defines itself in terms of generational procreation through the following decades: 1920, 1940, 1960. At the same time, there is another generational line linking the set 1930, 1950, 1970. Each of these generational sets has its own decade as the occasion of its more or less precise use. Children born in the 1940s reached their sense of contemporaneity in the 1960s, and linked their parents and grandparents to the sixties. Their parents and grandparents contribute more, therefore, to that decade than the fallow generational set, which, not having children mature at that age, contributes less to the creation of culture at that time.

The Formation of a Generation

When a generation comes to "its decade," it does so having formed itself slowly in the course of its childhood. The parenting generation creates its own parental culture, which is that environment in which the children live and come to consciousness. I grew up in the 1950s; born in 1943, I was ten in 1953. The political objects presented to me and my contemporaries were Eisenhower, Stevenson, and Richard Nixon. I cannot recall Truman as President, although I do recall the first Stevenson-Eisenhower contest. My grandparents eschewed politics but presented me with memories of their youth at the turn of the century: an America of small towns, a California of citrus groves, avocado orchards, meandering Europeans, and hardworking émigrés from the Midwest. My parents were "in tune" with their generation. Toscanini, T. S. Eliot, Rachmaninoff, and Adlai Stevenson were good objects; Nixon, General Motors, the McGuire Sisters, and HUAC were bad objects. Each of us who was between ten and seventeen in 1950 could pick, I think, thousands of such cultural objects that we shared, which our parents and older generations presented to us (sometimes defining them as good or bad) and which we used differently.

I would like to define, as a subspecies of cultural objects, *generational objects* to identify those phenomena that we use to form a sense of generational identity. They may also have been used by preceding generations, but they do not serve as the formative matrix of a generation as they do for the children who, in experiencing them, unconsciously come together as a collective of youth through the sharing of objects.

If companions are those who break bread together, a generation is that mass of people who have broken generational objects together, who have been presented with objects, who have digested them, and who are slowly forming a vision of social reality as a result. And every act of digestion is a micro-destructive act. Parental objects are transformed by the children, who doubtless will always experience many presented objects as correlatives of those anxieties of being a child. The parental generation, recoiling from a fear of Stalinist Russia's aggression, presented the children of the 1950s with bomb drills. Several times a year we sat under our desks, a "sit-in" of the absurd. But who was to know that the next time we sat in, in Berkeley in 1964, we weren't indicating our generation's transformation of generational objects? In 1954 our parents asked us to sit under the desk to protect our heads and bodies from the bomb; in 1964 we reoccupied the schoolroom, shoved the desks aside, and announced ourselves as the exploded.

We know how each adolescence is a time of essential generational violence when the emerging generation must "trash" parents and their objects in order to fashion a vision of their own era. But I do not think the adolescent achieves generational consciousness, as the culture of childhood is still radically redefining itself and is not yet set.

We can note something of a pre-generational rooting around with objects if we consider our children's rooms. (Indeed a true anthropology of generational psychology would have a substantial museum of children's rooms, showing what selected average children did to their rooms during the course of their childhood, and *there*, by comparing the children of the 1930s, 1950s, and 1960s, we could see the rooting around among cultural objects that are part of the archaeology of generational consciousness.) A year ago, on the walls of my fifteen-year-old stepdaughter's room, one could see photos of James Dean, Sid Vicious, the Sex Pistols, Marilyn Monroe, and others. Now they are all gone. Up has come an Indian batik to decorate one wall, an Indian screen print, a Raoul Dufy poster, a Joan Collins Fan Club poster, and several collages. All these objects are her own choice. Next door my eleven-year-old son shows the more direct effect of his parents' creation of his space. He has put up a Beano poster, one or two kung fu posters, and a boomerang, while my wife and I have contributed a collection of American Indian tomahawks and gourds, a chart on the evolution of dinosaurs, and a few other things. In a year or two he will, quite rightly, fully own this space, and over the years this little gallery will show the evolution of his generation's culture before it is conscious of itself. A child's room is an intermediate space, between parental culture and the child's world, contributed to by both the emerging generation and the parents.

It is not until young people are "out" of the transformational years of adolescence, somewhere in their early twenties, that they fully sense themselves as a generational unit. Of course, this is partly to do with leaving home; indeed, each adolescent discovers that he is somewhere in between his family of origin and the small groups (spouses, children, colleagues, etc.) that will compose his future. The sense of isolation can be severe, but solace may be found through recognition that he or she is part of a mass: adolescent subculture. Adolescent mass culture is formed out of the abyss between generations when the adolescent is unconsciously involved in transforming himself from child to adult. The rock group may well be the trumpeting announcement of each new era, for musical ability is the first talent of which children are capable, and they can express their presence more expertly through music than any other representational form. What Richard Poirier says of the Beatles is somewhat true of other rock groups: individual identity is subsumed by a far more defining group identity. As such, a rock group mirrors adolescent group life, and although record companies may be in the hands of the previous generations, the adolescent consumer will exert the logic latent in the power of consumption to create out of the offerings a trend in musical fashion.

Generational violence is essential to generational identity. Indeed, only when an emerging generation clearly violates the previous generation's aesthetic can we identify the emergence of a new generation. So this substantially qualifies my ideal definition of generations sprouting up every ten years. For an examination of the nature of each generation would involve scrutinizing the nature of generational transition. How does a generation in formation situate itself in relation to the previous generations? How is an emerging generation interpreted, received, and facilitated by the older generation? An emerging generation that is sent off to war—and possible elimination—will differ in its intergenerational affiliations from a generation that is welcomed into a job market. In turn, an emerging generation may seriously shock the older generations—as happened to an extent in the 1960s when youth wore long hair, became accomplished civil disobedients, celebrated casual sex, and urged one another to drop out. The Beatles may have been so very popular because although they mocked the middle-class values of the older generations, they were also, as Poirier points out, reaching out a hand to all the generations. On the cover of the Beatles' 1967 LP *Sgt. Pepper's Lonely Hearts Club Band* were sixty-two faces, which included Oscar Wilde, H. G. Wells, Jung, and Johnny Weissmuller. They suggested, it seems to me, that the lonesomeness of youth in between their past and their future—a recollection not in tranquillity—speaks to a lonesomeness in all human beings, a band of humankind to be obscured by the warm fires of family life, yet inevitably to be felt throughout a lifetime.

Generational Objects

"Let the word go forth . . . that the torch has been passed to a new generation of Americans—born in this century, tempered by war, disciplined by a hard and bitter peace, proud of our ancient heritage." So spoke John Kennedy on that cold inaugural day in January 1960. A man who was to be more clearly seen as a generational figure than any other President in his century—who believed it was the new generation that would make the difference—Kennedy identifies the character of the new generation in his speech. In his brilliant work on the 1960s, Todd Gitlin contrasts Kennedy's speech with the New Left's manifesto, the Port Huron Statement, published only eighteen months later: "We are people of this generation, bred in at least modern comfort, housed now in universities, looking uncomfortably to the world we inherit." "The proud have come to power," writes Gitlin, referring to Kennedy's generation, "but the uncomfortable are beginning to gather" (66).

Each generation selects its generational objects, persons, events, things which have particular meaning to the identity of that generation. Any generation's objects are also potentially significant to another generation—take the Beatles, for example—but such generational objects will usually have a different meaning. Other objects, particularly historical ones, have a more precise definition. I have little recollection of the Second World War, and the generation born in 1953 has no memory of it: it was over. Yet this war is the single most significant generational object held in common by the youth who matured in their twenties during it.

When I hear popular songs of the early 1940s I can recall them fondly because they were among the treasured objects of my parents' generation, but the generation after 1953 would not have this relation to the songs of the 1940s.

When recalling the period in which we formed ourselves

into a generation, each of us can remember very precisely the songs, persons, and events that we associate with our era. A generational object is mnemic: it stores something of the experience we had of our time, but generational objects are not idiosyncratic: these are objects which yield our sense of our own generational time. As such, they are different from other mnemic objects, such as our recollections of the homes or cities in which we lived or the people in our family.

A generational object, then, is a person, place, thing, or event that the individual identifies as generationally defining and that upon recollection brings him a sense of his own generation.

Generational Identity

As I view it, a generation will have achieved its identity within ten years, roughly speaking between twenty and thirty—in the space between adolescent turbulence and the age of thirty when childhood, adolescence, and young adulthood can be viewed of a piece. The thirty-year-old will feel himself to be part of his generation, and he will, in the next few years, take note of a new generation defining itself in such a way that he can distinguish it from his own generation.

Although each generation passes through, interprets, and signifies the life span in its own way, its fundamental character is fashioned in the twenties. It will continue to experience and interpret new objects, but strictly speaking they are not generational ones, as they are not essential to the defining character of consciousness. Such objects are not so much mental representations as screen memories that express the nature of the generation's psychic life. Each generational object—for the 1960s the Beatles, Martin Luther King, Jr., the NASA program, etc.—gives rise to a complex character of experiences peculiar to that time. They sit inside us even when we aren't thinking of them, within our unconscious in an internal world where each object serves as a generating link to the people of our time.

Sometime in adolescence we become aware of our individual participation in a collective interpretive process. In our bedrooms, clothing, musical choices, linguistic inventions, and heroes we *fashion* our generation's interpretation of its moment in history. It does not take a plumped-up beaming middle-ager at a commencement address to tell adolescents that they occupy a particular collective moment in historical time: adolescents can feel it.

In the late teens we are aware of a participatory presence to existence: we are, each of us, part objects—or is it part subjects?—amidst a collective hermeneutic as our very large group touches objects, moments, people, events, things as signs of our interest. Even if, as is likely, we do not know what this all means, we become aware of our creation of meaning, which is somehow there for us, as objects to use during the course of our lifetime.

Generational Difference

Generations differ from one another, and this difference sharpens the sense one has of one's own time. Raskin speaking through her character Diana Sargeant: "The differences between our generation and our daughters' are extreme. While we carry 'notes from underground,' secret feminist samizdat, and Swiss army knives in our Gucci handbags, our daughters have to purchase and carry slippery packs of condoms and sickly rubber medical gloves in their purses" (343).

The emergence of a new generation helps us to see our own generation more closely, precisely because of the difference between generations and their choice of objects. If a generation is formed in our twenties, it is probably not until our thirties (and then for the rest of our life) that we become increasingly conscious of who we are and of who we will have been.

To what extent does a generation yield its cultural power to a new and culturally redefinitional generation? Gitlin argues that the generation formed in the Depression was bound to be at odds with the succeeding generations born in middle-class comfort and wealth. If this is so, then a generation can envy the succeeding generation's inheritance of a comfort created by the generation that had itself endured formative hardship. Indeed, envy may be an intrinsic feature of generational procreativity, an ironic envy equivalent, in some ways, to the mother's envy of the infant's feeding at her breast. To some extent the aspersion heaped upon the Yuppie generation may be born of an envy of this generation's remarkable capacity to process the American capitalist system. They are true children of America, and it may still be too early to judge whether—as is currently said—they have become greedy as a result of such early feeding, so greedy that nonnarcissistic ambitions, such as social care, are ignored.

When a new generation forms, it inevitably sends a shock through the prior generations. The passing of a time that moves oneself, one's friends, one's loved ones, and one's era to extinction arouses anxieties that thus far we have tended to conceptualize in terms of individual psychology—as in a mid-life crisis—rather than in social-psychological terms. For there are generational crises when one's cultural generativity is defined by succeeding generations that mold another vision of social reality. To be sure, a generation will pass on important objects that can be seen to directly affect subsequent culture. James Dean, Marilyn Monroe, and Elvis Presley personify complex visions of their time that have survived to be of interest to subsequent generations. Which figures survive their generation to be passed from one epoch to another? Only time will tell. Charlie Chaplin was a figure conveyed to other generations, but it is questionable whether he will survive the epochal transfer.

In the fate of one's generational objects we see the mortality of being; we watch our precious objects as they are discarded on the rubbish heap of history, and in this sense generational procreativity is cannibalistic: the new generation scraps the older ones and eats what it will of them, leaving the prior generations skeletonized.

Where are those beautiful cars with the tail fins? Where are the drive-in movies and hamburger joints? Where are the kids sitting on front porches? Where are these generational objects? They are gone except insofar as they exist in the collective memories of the millions of people who created and used them. Inevitably, therefore, nostalgia for one's youth involves a generational mourning: the objects one has created live a very short life as we move on through our time.

Generational Movement

Sometime in mid-life we become aware of how our generation moves through time. Each generation interprets and signifies the milestones. I am keenly aware, for example, that Erik Erikson's recent book *Vital Involvement in Old Age* typifies his generation's way of thinking through what it means to live through a lifetime. When I was an adolescent, my father gave me Simone de Beauvoir's *The Second Sex* to read to further my education, and when I now read Erikson, I feel myself in a generationally familiar place reading the works of members of an older generation who have a very special way of contemplating their lifetime.

At some point—I think it is in mid-life—one becomes aware that when the mothers and fathers disappear, then one is the last figure in a generational triangle, as the grandparents will ordinarily be long since dead. If one has seen how one's own culture is displaced by succeeding generations, now one sees how an entire triangle can face extinction unless one conveys this family history and the consciousness of previous generations to the new generations. Writing about the history of his family, Michael Ignatieff (born in 1947) says:

> My father is the very last of that generation, aged four in February 1917 . . . His memory just bestrides this abyss dividing everything before and everything after the revolution. I in turn am the last generation to know his generation, the last to be able to plumb their memory, to feel the presence of their past in the timbre of their voices and in the gaze they cast back across time. (5)

In 1977 Shirley Williams writes in the preface to *Testament of Youth*:

> It is an autobiography and also an elegy for a generation . . . I hope that a new generation, more distant from the First World War, will discover the anguish and pain in the lives of those young people sixty years ago; and in discovering will understand. (11)

My father, who reread *Testament of Youth* as part of his research for an autobiography specifically written for his children, gave the book to my wife and inscribed it as follows:

> Dear Suzanne, This will give you an idea of what your grandparents went through and how the England of 1914 evolved, for good or bad, into the England of today. If all those fine young men had not died in France, and all the women's emotions been savaged so harshly, what would it be

like now? One thing you'll be glad of: Oxford's attitude toward women's education changed radically!

Love, Sacha

One generation passes a book to a younger generation to convey the lives of the grandparents, many of whom have gone. But these eulogies also testify to a generation's consideration of what has now gone; it is a recollection in tranquillity of a generation removed from the face of the earth.

Generational transmission, then, occurs in discrete stages.

1. When parents present themselves and their objects to small children, they provide a culture of objects out of which the adolescents will fashion the consciousness of their own time.
2. When a generation is being usurped by a newly forming generation, it can give way generatively or meet the new age with hostility and destructive processes.
3. When the older generations disappear, the penultimate generation may or may not convey to the youth the spirit of the prior age, linking up the past with the present and with a future that will inevitably not include it.

Generational Potential Space

Each generation's consciousness is a potential space, to use Winnicott's concept, in which generational objects can be created and used to establish and in some ways think through the collective experiences and perspectives of the young adult population. Under favorable circumstances, a generation can "play" with objects in the effort to found its culture. If the generation of the 1960s could radicalize itself in very particular ways, it is because the immediately preceding generation had created the Beats, rebels without causes, rock and roll, *Mad* magazine, Arthur Miller, and C. Wright Mills. If the 1960s repudiated the generation of the 1950s, it also inherited its radicalism from the same era, and its right to play with generational objects was underwritten by probably the most permissive generational transmission in modern times. We may conceive of a generation that does not have space, time, or generational authority to play. The lost generation of 1914–18 had no such space.

Were we to study this psychology of generations closely, it would be of interest to contrast the nature of generational potential spaces, to note those objects selected as signatures of a generation's consciousness, and to analyze the field of such objects as unconscious ideas that may be generative or pathological. We know from the Hitler Youth that a generation is capable of collective pathology of consciousness. But we need to know more about the relation between the generations in Germany to know if generational processes played a significant part in the evolution of Hitler's power. For example, is there a structural responsibility to the generational triangle? What if the triangle collapses implosively, erasing the function of generational difference, where one generation serves to check and balance other generations, during times of social distress? Did a generational structure collapse in Hitler's Germany?

Generational objects, like screen memories, collect within an actual object (or event) the new generation's interpretation of its identity. It is a curious mix of the fashioned and the imposed, as the musical choices and lingual inventions rub shoulders with events beyond control: a war, an economic crisis, and so on. Yet generational objects are pop art objects, fashions, precisely because they weave into historic time. It is adolescence that is curiously true to the dialectic in human life between the personal and the social, the responsible and the irrational, the premeditated and the accidental. The reality of our world and the complexity of its events are not fathomable; their simple chaos is always somewhat beyond our organization. It is the adolescent who somehow most intensely lives this tension to its fullest, and who—upon recovery in the twenties—can form ideas of culture and society that identify the group's experience of life.

Generations form objects that signify the history of child-hoods, that speak to the collective march through time of a vast group expecting and expected to shape history but knowing that the cohesive organization of life's eventfulness is really beyond it.

Generational consciousness thus reflects a generation's interpretation of its place in historic time, a series of dreams derived from the day residues of the actual. In my view, crises in history—wars, economic collapses, assassinations, natural disasters—sponsor *generational work*, as the new generation weaves a conscious generational object into being out of unconscious interpretations of events that arise. Crisis sponsors consciousness.

As children, adolescents, and young adults we are played upon by reality as world leaders, world events, and world processes yoke us into generational sensitivity. We are called into history by the inevitably thoughtless solicitations of events and processes that force us to ponder our possible fates. Each generation seems to intensify generational objects (particularly in song and literature) during periods of crisis, which in turn more clearly identify the nature of the generation, differentiating it from preceding and succeeding ones, while generations coming into formation during times unmarked by consciousness-raising ordeals do not seem to possess such fine lines of generational demarcation. It is more difficult, therefore, to compare the generations of the 1970s and 1980s than those of the 1950s and 1960s, as the historical crises of the 1950s and 1960s sponsored increased generational work and therefore led to a heightened generational consciousness. In fact, we may wonder if the adoption by the generations of the 1970s and 1980s of the music, film idols, etc., of the 1950s and 1960s is partly due to the fact that these generations have less definition and find themselves very slightly identifying with another generation's consciousness. I tread on thin ice, as we are too close in time to form our own clear ideas of the generational identities of the 1970s and 1980s to "see them"; however, we may find that these generations' revival of musical styles and memories of the 1950s and 1960s reflects the extraordinary illumination of the 1960s which lures subsequent generations to partly create it as a generational object of their own, so that the *1960s* as a generational object of the 1980s is predominantly a musical object, or a collage of fashion, political style, and historic accident that collates the 1960s into a neat presence that might signify the "not us" object, even as the generation of the 1980s adopts the *1960s* as a generational object.

For those of us who "came of age" in the 1960s the present generation's cultivation of a 1960s object is somewhat bewildering, if instructive. We can see here more clearly how generational objects are formed as collective acts of unconscious nomination, dreamscapes that mythologize contemporary life by turning historical objects into screen memories. The generation of the 1980s creates a 1960s curiously devoid of struggle.

Each generation sees itself becoming history. As some of our generational objects (which signify the intensity of lived experience and hence of emotional reality) become historical objects, they change in their function. We, for whom Martin Luther King, Jr., or the Beatles were generational objects, watch our objects and ourselves being transformed before our very eyes into historic objects, simple notes of historical significance. So before our deaths we bear witness to succeeding generations' placement of ourselves in history, and as this natural process occurs we shall all be aware of an inevitable discrepancy between our generational objects and their new status as historical ones.

If the new generation (in a person's twenties) is allowed an illusion that it will single-handedly form and define contemporary culture, the mid-generations (those in their forties and fifties) will be left with "no illusions" of the capacity to definitively form culture. Indeed, they see themselves being replaced by a new vision of culture and social reality just as they are now placed *in history*. This fact of life should help us to consider the social-psychological facets of the mid-life crisis, as such a crisis is not only endogenously generated but also culturally sanctioned: we are converted from the generations of our time into unwitting national memorabilia, walking historical notes, old-timers.

Some time ago, while perhaps unfortunately staying in a hotel too close to the UCLA campus, I was somewhat distressed by the wave of youth culture. I noted a new and curious form of greeting in this new generation. You don't shake hands, you box each other gently with closed fists once, then grip hands—again gently—then link fingers, then grip again. I probably don't have the sequence of this greeting quite right, but it serves me here as a point of reference, as surely those of us in the 1960s recall our greeting rituals, perhaps the most notorious the V for victory sign, among others. So where are they now? What has happened to the art of greeting? To the signs of generational solidarity to be found in gripping one another?

By one's thirties these greeting rituals dissipate so that by the forties and fifties one gives way to the conventional handshake, just as linguistic peculiarities ("I'm hip" or "Far out, man") give way to conventional expressions of recognition ("I understand" or "How surprising"). One becomes conventionalized as one loses the authorial rights of generational idiosyncrasy licensed to the incoming generation.

There in that place of generational emergence are signs aplenty of the collective experience of the subjectifying of reality, as a generation is composed of "brothers" or "sisters" who are linked together in their time. But as time passes, as the frames of time are defined by the emergence of a new generation, the greeting signs of the brothers and sisters— that secret friendship—give way to a social convention as one joins the preceding generations.

So each new generation is a period of intense subjective life, a time for the simple self who feels himself to be part of a collective process carrying him along inside it. Music, fashion, lingual expressions, social idioms, seem to give immediate expression to the parts of the self which take their place in the plenitude of generational objects. This period of the immersion of self in the culture gives way in and through time to the complex self who collects these selves into one more or less objectifiable location, when one reflects on those selves as objects. In the course of generational progression one is less immersed in social culture, less idiosyncratic and more conventional, and increasingly inclined to see the self and its objects more clearly. This is in part what is meant by wisdom: that knowledge accrued out of reflected-upon experiences.

For those of the mid-generations, now less immersed as simple selves in the process of culture and more as objectified objects in historic time, this is a time of transformation— from the simple self inside a process that seems to carry the parts of the self, to the complex self who sees the self inside historical time. I think of this evolution as similar to the progression from the world of sleep and dream, when one is a simple self inside the process, to the awakened and conscious complex self who reflects upon the experiences as an object. But the dreaming experience can never be assembled through consciousness, and with this in mind one must conclude that the experience of being part of the formation of a generation is beyond conscious narrative yet remains inside its participants in the course of time as an increasingly dear internal object.

There are stages, then, in the evolution of a generation which we may identify.

1. In childhood an emerging generation plays with the objects provided by the parental generation and some of these objects will reflect the adults' generational preoccupation in their time, a type of unconscious transmission of collective identity through the provision of objects.
2. At the same time historical crises (or significant events and persons) offer themselves to the children, whose peer culture transforms these episodes and persons into collectively shared events. These would be the earliest generational objects.
3. In adolescence the new generation begins to sense its collective identity and does so in some opposition to parental culture.
4. In the early twenties a person is caught up in generational narcissism, participating in an illusion of vision formation as it transforms culture into the generation's image. This is a time of the generational simple self immersed in process.
5. In our thirties there is increasing recognition of the boundaries of one's generation created by the new generation's incremental occupation of generational space.
6. In the forties and fifties we recognize that one's generational objects—dear to the formation and sense of our generational identity—are timebound. The individual sees his generation now transformed into a historical object, a movement from deep par-

ticipatory subjectivity (the simple self) to the objectified.

7. In one's sixties and seventies we sense our passing from lived experience of our generation into history's time as we become a historical object that will succeed us.

We travel together, then, as a unit in time, a time unit, collecting itself into meaning just as it lives amidst the circumstantial that evades hermeneutic integrity. As world events move in a kind of familiar chaos, we choose objects to collect ourselves in a meaningful group, even if what we mean by what we signify is not clear to us. Like it or not, it is the destiny of each generation to signify itself, to choose its signifiers: we use those forms (music, books, fashion) to objectify generational identity. Generational consciousness is thus a collective identification; the individual subject "lives within" a field of generational objects that unconsciously interpret these persons' view of their experience of place and of time. I am part of my generation, and the generational objects of my time put me in touch with the peer group's processing of its formation. I may not particularly like my generation's objects, but, as I have said, the choice of objects—those sanctioned as articles of generational identity—does not emerge from desire but results from unconscious interpretation of collectively lived experience.

So aren't all historical events inevitably generational objects? I do not think so. Some "events" evoke or capture the imagination of an era. The Western invasion of Suez and the launching of Sputnik happened about the same time. They are events in history, but the Soviet launch of Sputnik evoked something within my generation that was not equaled by the Suez invasion or even the Hungarian revolution.

I was at a party in my early adolescence, lost in embrace with my girlfriend, when someone mentioned the Soviets' launch of Sputnik. The party stopped. No one knew what to make of it. We became another generation in historical time to look at the skies with a new eye: it could and did contain small artificial-looking stars that moved around our earth signifying a race of arms. The heavens would never be the same.

Sputnik was an event. But it had a high evocative register at the time. It sponsored intense peer-group work for my generation, just forming itself in mid-adolescence. We talked and talked and talked about it. At the party one of the girls burst into tears: the world was ruined. An aspirant football player said it didn't matter, we would be putting something up in space soon.

Nonetheless, we all felt conscripted by the event, pressed into time, knowing something was expected of us; and in the newspapers and journals and on television, an America that felt it was behind spoke in a hurried voice about how it was in the hands of a new generation that would catch up.

But on the day of the party I simply remember how literally this event—announced as it was—cooled me off. The passion of my girlfriend's and my—I cannot call it lovemaking: perhaps undifferentiated kinesthetic reciprocity with increasing genitalized urgency—anyway, our private erotic universe was intersected by the externally eventful. Not the eventful arrival of a parent who barged in wanting to know what the hell was going on, but the strange arrival of something new and unusual: history itself and our future came into the room and broke us up.

At times culture is a form of psychic work, a representation of social issues and historical events. In 1957 Leonard Bernstein's *West Side Story* opened on Broadway to considerable acclaim: a cultural object that partly processed social conflict in New York and America. Perhaps the song "Purple People Eater," top of the pops in 1958, expressed a white fear, not of being eaten by a purple creature, but of being devoured by the angry black whose discontent was increasingly evident. Is it possible that another hit song of 1958,

"Catch a Falling Star," was so popular because this cultural object *screened* the Sputnik experience of the year before? Can we say that certain cultural objects are screen objects that work the actual with the internal, or that rework the actual into the fantastical, which then signifies the collective effort of thought brought to bear on collective existence? The arts, then, are sometimes screen areas which produce screen objects that reflect the work of culture upon the actual.

So among the many cultural objects of 1958, we may find one or two songs that screen the actual into a special object, and we may also note the ever more specific cultural objects—"Catch a Falling Star"—which for a newly forming generation will bind that group into its specific identity in time: a generational object.

Participation in a generation occupies only a portion of our cultural life. Just as we all need, to varying extent, to be part of our time, so too we need to participate in metagenerational culture, by which I mean that we seek out cultural objects—hundreds, even thousands of years old—precisely because they seem to speak our participation in a *universal order*. When we gaze about the rooms of the Uffizi or the Louvre, when we walk the streets of Rome, when we listen to Beethoven, or when we read Sophocles, we are inhabiting a metagenerational space that serves our need to be in a universal order.

So if there is a potential generational space with generational objects which bind us in our own time, there is also a potential universal order with universal objects that free us to participate in a timeless space.

Each of us chooses the balance of our participatory investments. Some of us are exceptionally reluctant to take part in generational consciousness. Some will refuse popular songs, contemporary literature, the politics of one's time, etc. Certain schizoid personalities, for example, appear oblivious to their own era; they seem curiously disembodied from their time, moving only in the universal order. One of my patients, who was a classics scholar, had never read any contemporary literature, did not read newspapers, had no knowledge of contemporary culture, and possessed no generational affinity. Or at least he appeared not to. In his own earnest manner he had found contemporary culture offensive; since childhood he had rejected peer culture and walked the school grounds with leather briefcase and early signs of the universal order, such as poetry books, classical texts, and afigurational clothing that held him in limbo from his own era. This is not the occasion to discuss him further, but only to point him out; I am sure we all know such persons.

So there are many different relations one may have to one's generation and one's place in generational time—from those who embrace and represent their generational location to those who take complete refuge in the universal order.

Each social class, race, and gender will also situate itself differently in its relation to the consciousness of its time, factors which both further problematize the sense of one's generation and yet enrich this form of consciousness with the complexity of the positions involved.

Intergenerational dialectics involves each of us in acts of violence, reception, and generation. We oppose our elders; they oppose us. They do or do not find a way to receive us, to leave a space for our generational birth, as we take their generational objects, historicize some, and make them available for a universal order that may place one generation into a metagenerational place.

Such intergenerational dialectics, painful and ruthless though it may be, can also be a true pleasure. Some months ago I was thinking out loud about a dinner party I was looking forward to. "So *who* is coming?" asked my fifteen-year-old stepdaughter, Nisha. I named a few people. "Oh no! Not more crusties," she said. "What is a crusty?" I asked, feeling the force of her rejection. "You are a crusty," she said. "What is that?" "Oh, you know, you people," she laughed, and I replied, "You mean, us middle-aged people?" and she nodded. "So what else is there?" I asked. "Wrinklies," she replied, and I discovered that wrinklies were true elders. "And you, what are you?" I countered. "We don't have a name," she said. "Oh yes, you do. You are a softie," which lit her up into the intergenerational dialectic, now named along with the crusties and the wrinklies.

References

Anzieu, Didier. *The Skin Ego*. New Haven: Yale, 1989.———.
    Psychic Envelopes. London: Karnac, 1990.
Arendt, Hannah. *The Origins of Totalitarianism*. London: Deutsch,
    1986.
Baldwin, James. *Giovanni's Room*. 1957. London: Black Swan, 1984.
Beetham, David. *Marxists in Face of Fascism*. Manchester: Man-
    chester, 1983.
Bergson, Henri. *Creative Evolution*. 1911. Lanham: University Press
    of America, Inc., 1983.
Bettelheim, Bruno. *The Informed Heart*. 1960. London: Penguin,
    1987.
Bion, Wilfred. "Learning from Experience." 1962. In *Seven Ser-
    vants*. New York: Aronson, 1977. 1–111.
———. "Transformations." 1965. In *Seven Servants*, 1–183.
Bloom, Harold. *The Anxiety of Influence*. New York: Oxford, 1973.
Bollas, Christopher. *The Shadow of the Object*. London: Free Asso-
    ciations, 1987.
———. *Forces of Destiny*. London: Free Associations, 1989.
Brenman, Eric. "Cruelty and Narrow-mindedness." In Spillius,
    Vol. 1, 256–70.
Brittain, Vera. *Testament of Youth*. 1933. New York: Wideview,
    1980.

Burn, Andrew Robert. *The Pelican History of Greece*. London: Penguin, 1966.

Calder, Alexander. "What Abstract Art Means to Me." In *Theories of Modern Art*. Ed. Herschel B. Chipp. Berkeley: California, 1968. 561–62.

Casement, Patrick. *On Learning from the Patient*. London: Tavistock, 1985.

Chasseguet-Smirgel, Janine. *Creativity and Perversion*. London: Free Associations, 1985.

Coltart, Nina. " 'Slouching Towards Bethlehem' . . . or Thinking the Unthinkable in Psychoanalysis." 1986. In Kohon, 185–99.

Cotta, Sergio. *Why Violence?* 1978. Gainesville: Florida, 1985.

Cowan, James. *Mysteries of the Dream-Time*. Bridport: Prism, 1989.

Crane, Hart. "General Aims and Theories." In Gibbons, 179–83.

Derrida, Jacques. *Of Spirit*. Chicago: Chicago, 1987.

Duncan, Dennis. "The Feel of the Session." *Psy. & Contemp. Thought*. 13:3–22.

———. "The Flow of Interpretation." *Int. J. Psycho-Anal*. 70:693–70.

Ehrenzweig, Anton. *The Hidden Order of Art*. 1967. Berkeley: California, 1971.

Einstein, Alfred. "Letter to Jacques Hadamard." In Ghiselin, 43–44.

Erikson, Erik, Joan Erikson, and Hannah Kivnick. *Vital Involvement in Old Age*. New York: Norton, 1986.

Fairbairn, Ronald. *Psychoanalytic Studies of the Personality*. London: Tavistock, 1952.

Federn, Ernst. "Some Clinical Remarks on the Psychopathology of Genocide." 1960. In *Witnessing Psychoanalysis*. By Ernst Federn. London: Karnac, 1990.

Foucault, Michel. "Sexual Choice, Sexual Act: An Interview with Michel Foucault." 1982. In *Salmagundi*. No. 58–59 (Fall 1982–Winter 1983), 10–24.

Freud, Sigmund. *Studies on Hysteria*. 1893–95. Standard Edition. London: Hogarth, 1957. 2, 1–323.

———. *The Interpretation of Dreams*. 1900. SE. 4, Vol. 1, 1–338.

————. "Analysis of a Phobia in a Five-year-old Boy." 1909. SE. 10, 3–149.

————. "Recommendations to Physicians Practising Psycho-Analysis." 1912. SE. 12, 111–20.

————. *Totem and Taboo*. 1913. SE. 13, 1–162.

————. "Group Psychology and the Analysis of the Ego." 1921. SE. 18, 67–143.

————. "Some Neurotic Mechanisms in Jealousy, Paranoia, and Homosexuality." 1922. SE. 18, 223–59.

————. *The Ego and the Id*. 1923. SE. 19, 1–66.

————. *The Future of an Illusion*. 1927. SE. 21, 3–56.

Fussell, Paul. *The Great War and Modern Memory*. Oxford: Oxford, 1975.

Gardner, Brian. *Up the Line to Death*. London: Methuen, 1986.

Gardner, Howard. *Frames of Mind*. London: Paladin, 1984.

Ghiselin, Brewster. *The Creative Process*. New York: Mentor, 1952.

Gibbons, Reginald. *The Poet's Work*. Chicago: Chicago, 1979.

Gitlin, Todd. *The Sixties*. New York: Bantam, 1987.

Gramsci, Antonio. "On Fascism." In Beetham, 82–87.

Graves, Robert. *The Greek Myths*: Vol. 1. London: Penguin, 1977.

Green, André. *On Private Madness*. London: Hogarth, 1986.

Greimas, Algirdas Julien. *On Meaning*. Minneapolis: Minnesota, 1987.

Hampshire, Stuart. *Innocence and Experience*. London: Allen Lane, 1989.

Hartman, Heinz. *Ego Psychology and the Problem of Adaptation*. 1939. New York: IUP, 1958.

Heaney, Seamus. *Preoccupations*. London: Faber, 1980.

Hedges, Lawrence. *Listening Perspectives in Psychotherapy*. New York: Aronson, 1983.

Hepworth, Barbara. "Some Statements by Barbara Hepworth." Pamphlet. Barbara Hepworth Museum, St. Ives.

Hinshelwood, Robert D. *A Dictionary of Kleinian Thought*. London: Free Associations, 1989.

Holland, Norman. *5 Readers Reading*. New Haven: Yale, 1975.

Holleran, Andrew. *Dancer from the Dance*. 1978. New York: Bantam, 1983.

Hollinghurst, Alan. *The Swimming Pool Library*. London: Chatto, 1988.

Hughes, H. Stuart. *Consciousness and Society*. New York: Vintage, 1958.

Ignatieff, Michael. *The Russian Album*. 1987. London: Penguin, 1988.

John-Steiner, Vera. *Notebooks of the Mind*. New York: Perennial, 1985.

Khan, Masud. *Alienation in Perversions*. London: Hogarth, 1979.

Kipling, Rudyard. "Common Form." In B. Gardner, 150.

Knox, Bernard. "Greece and the Theatre." 1982. Introduction. *The Three Theban Plays*. By Sophocles. London: Penguin, 1984. 13–30.

Kohon, Gregorio. *The British School of Psychoanalysis: The Independent Tradition*. London: Free Associations, 1986.

Kovel, Joel. *White Racism*. 1970. London: Free Associations, 1988.

Kuper, Leo. *Genocide*. London: Penguin, 1981.

Lacan, Jacques. *The Four Fundamental Concepts of Psycho-Analysis*. 1973. London: Hogarth, 1977.

Lakoff, George. *Women, Fire, and Dangerous Things*. Chicago: Chicago, 1987.

Lifton, Robert J. *The Nazi Doctors*. New York: Basic, 1986.

Lowell, Amy. "The Process of Making Poetry." In Ghiselin, 109–12.

Lukács, Georg. *Soul and Form*. London: Merlin, 1974.

Lyotard, Jean-François. "The Dream Work Does Not Think." *The Lyotard Reader*. Ed. Andrew Benjamin. Oxford: Blackwell, 1989. 19–55.

Matte-Blanco, Ignacio. *The Unconscious as Infinite Sets*. London: Butterworth, 1975.

———. *Thinking, Feeling, and Being*. London: Routledge, 1988.

McDougall, Joyce. *Plea for a Measure of Abnormality*. New York: IUP, 1980.

———. *Theatres of the Mind*. 1982. New York: Basic, 1985.

Meltzer, Donald. *Dream-Life*. Strath Tay: Clunie, 1983.

——— and Meg Harris Williams. *The Apprehension of Beauty*. Strath Tay: Clunie, 1988.

Merrick, Gordon. *One for the Gods.* 1971. New York: Avon, 1972.

Miller, Arthur. *The Crucible.* 1953. London: Penguin, 1968.

———. *Timebends.* London: Methuen, 1987.

Miller, John William. *The Midworld of Symbols and Functioning Objects.* New York: Norton, 1982.

Milner, Marion. *The Suppressed Madness of Sane Men.* London: Tavistock, 1987.

Milosz, Czeslaw. *Ars Poetica.* In Gibbons, 3–4.

Moore, Henry. "Notes on Sculpture." In Ghiselin, 73–78.

Mussolini, Benito. "Dottrina del Fascismo." *Encyclopaedia Britannica.* Chicago: Chicago, 1983. 7, 182–88.

Newman, Kim. *Nightmare Movies.* 1984. London: Bloomsbury, 1988.

Nietzsche, Friedrich. *Ecce Homo.* 1908. London: Penguin, 1980.

Ong, Walter J. *Interfaces of the Word.* Ithaca: Cornell, 1977.

O'Sullivan, Noel. *Fascism.* London: Dent, 1983.

Pessôa, Fernando. "Toward Explaining Heteronymy." In Gibbons, 5–15.

Picasso, Pablo. "Conversation with Picasso." In Ghiselin, 55–60.

Pine, Fred. *Drive, Ego, Object and Self.* New York: Basic, 1990.

Poincaré, Henri. "Mathematical Creation." In Ghiselin, 33–42.

Poirier, Richard. "Learning from the Beatles." 1967. In *The Performing Self.* By Richard Poirier. New York: Oxford, 1971. 86–111.

Pontalis, J.-B. *Frontiers in Psychoanalysis.* London: Hogarth, 1981.

Raskin, Barbara. *Hot Flashes.* New York: St. Martin's, 1987.

Read, Herbert. "A Short Poem for Armistice Day." In B. Gardner, 151–52.

Rechy, John. *Numbers.* 1967. New York: Grove, 1981.

Robinson, Paul. "Dear Paul." In *Salmagundi.* No. 58–59 (Fall 1982–Winter 1983), 22–41.

Rosenfeld, Herbert. *Impasse and Interpretation.* London: Tavistock, 1987.

Searles, Harold. *Collected Papers on Schizophrenia and Related Subjects.* New York: IUP, 1965.

Snyder, Gary. "The Real Work" (excerpts from an interview). In Gibbons, 283–94.

Sontag, Susan. *Illness as Metaphor*. New York: Farrar, Straus, 1976.

Sophocles. *Oedipus the King*. In *The Three Theban Plays*. By Sophocles. London: Penguin, 1984.

———. *Oedipus at Colonus*. In Sophocles, 159–251.

Spender, Stephen. "The Making of a Poem." In Ghiselin, 112–25.

Spillius, Elizabeth. *Melanie Klein Today*: Vol. 1. London: Routledge, 1988.

Stern, Fritz. *The Politics of Cultural Despair*. 1961. Berkeley: California, 1974.

Stokes, Adrian. *A Game That Must Be Lost*. Cheadle Hulme: Caranet, 1973.

Stoller, Robert. *Perversion: The Erotic Form of Hatred*. 1976. London: Quartet, 1977.

Symington, Neville. "The Analyst's Act of Freedom as Agent of Therapeutic Change." In Kohon, 253–70.

Thomson, Peter G. "On the Receptive Function of the Analyst." *Int. Rev. Psycho-Anal.* 7:183–205.

Valéry, Paul. "The Course in Poetics: First Lesson." In Ghiselin, 92–106.

Vendler, Helen. *The Music of What Happens*. Cambridge: Harvard, 1988.

Winnicott, D. W. *Playing & Reality*. London: Tavistock, 1971.

Wordsworth, William. "The Two-Part Prelude." In *The Pedlar, Tinturn Abbey, The Two-Part Prelude*. By William Wordsworth. 1799. Ed. Jonathan Wordsworth. Cambridge: Cambridge, 1990. 41–76.

Zibordi, Giovanni. "Towards a Definition of Fascism." 1922. In Beetham, 88–96.

Index